Patterns of French

SECOND EDITION

SECOND EDITION

Patterns

# of French

Rodney K. Ketcham

HARPUR COLLEGE

Jean Collignon

DOUGLASS COLLEGE

Harcourt, Brace & World, Inc. *New York · Burlingame*

ILLUSTRATOR: FRANKLYN WEBBER

Contents

Foreword

The new *Patterns of French* will be found to represent a marked change in emphasis from the first edition. While the authors are still convinced that basic grammar must be the essence of a beginning language text and therefore have retained its presentation virtually unaltered except for an occasional clarification or a slight change in order, the manner of drilling on patterns has been substantially up-dated to reflect the latest thinking in language-teaching method. Increased stress has been laid on the manipulation of model constructions through extensive substitution and transformation drills; and to enhance the effectiveness of these drills, they have been recorded on tapes for use in the language laboratory. Thus the new text better answers the demands of the growing body of American teachers who are coming to feel that the shortest and most effective route to language competence lies in the mastery of patterns rather than in mere reliance on the application of rules.

The recordings, which proved so successful in the original edition, have been increased from four sides to eight, making it possible to include more material, double repetition of the pattern sentences of Units 1 to 4, longer pauses for student repetition, and pauses following all sentences in all units. The records and tapes have been prepared under the direction of Jack L. Ulsh of the Foreign Service Institute, Department of State. The speakers on the records are Suzanne Cohen, Juliette Chapat, and Robert Salazar, all of the Foreign Service Institute; Mme Cohen and M. Salazar recorded the tapes.

In order to make the book fit more realistically into the limited hours of a beginning college course, the long unit vocabularies of the earlier edition have been drastically cut. The drills emphasize a more thorough mastery of a hard core of high-frequency items, and words of lesser frequency appearing in the *Lectures* but not elsewhere in the text are given in footnotes instead of in the vocabularies, to be learned only if the instructor so wishes. As before, cognates have been omitted from the unit vocabularies but included in the final French-English vocabulary. Since the pattern sentences are to be memorized until they can be given unhesitatingly in response to the English, it has not seemed necessary to repeat in the unit vocabularies the words which first appear there.

The use of phonetic symbols in the general French-English vocabulary has been retained. Full tables of verbs will be found in the Appendix as before. Other features retained which proved useful to many teachers are the everyday French expressions used in English, the list of common *faux amis*, the résumé of English grammar terms, and the selection of poems for memorization.

The authors wish to reaffirm their indebtedness to the persons who assisted in the preparation of the first edition, and to express appreciation to the many French teachers who kindly offered suggestions for improvements on the older book, including particularly Dr. Willi Uschald and Mr. C. D. McIntyre of Harpur College; Professor Nelson Brooks of Yale University; Professor Joseph A. Palermo of the University of Connecticut; Mme Nicolette Pernot Ringgold, formerly of Wellesley College; Professor Norman B. Spector of the University of Chicago; Professor C. Beaumont Wicks of the University of Alabama; and, above all, to Professor Cortland Eyer of the Pennsylvania State University, whose wide experience and clear judgment served as a constant guide in the preparation of drill material, and whose critical reading of the text helped in clarifying many a point.

R.K.K.

J.C.

December 1960

Introduction

French may be termed a direct descendant of Latin. As in the case of Italian, Spanish, Catalan, Provençal, Portuguese, and Roumanian, what was once the "Romans' language" has become a "Romance language" of today.[1] A knowledge of Latin may therefore be of considerable help in learning the vocabulary of these languages, although it is by no means indispensable. The English language is full of Latin and French derivatives, the latter dating chiefly from the Norman conquest, which made French the official language of England for a time. Hence the English-speaking student of French has a great advantage from the outset, being able to guess intelligently at many French terms.

While it is true that French and English have many words of common origin, some of them even alike in meaning and spelling, the sounds of the two languages are so different that it is impossible for a native speaker of the one to understand a native speaker of the other without special training. For the professional linguist, no sound in French is completely identical to any sound in English. For this reason, by far the best assurance of a good pronunciation is a competent instructor who can be heard and imitated. In addition, the recordings provided with each copy of this book and the drill tapes available for it will be of great help to the student in acquiring a good pronunciation. As a further aid, the general French-English vocabulary at the back of the book contains a phonetic transcription of each entry. A brief description of the international phonetic alphabet as used in this book follows.

---

[1] The term "Romance language" is modern English for the medieval *langue romane*, a widespread vernacular tongue used for many popular poems and nonlearned works, as opposed to the more classic and rigid Latin of scholarly writings.

The international phonetic alphabet

Vowels [1]   SYMBOL   APPROXIMATE DESCRIPTION

[ɑ]   **a** in *palm;* mouth fairly wide open

[a]   between **a** in *palm* and **a** in *cat;* avoid **a** in *cat;* mouth not so wide open as for [ɑ] above

[ɛ]   **e** in *pest*

[e]   **a** in *maple*

[i]   **i** in *machine* or *police*

[ɔ]   **o** in *morning*

[o]   **o** in *open* or *poker*

[u]   **oo** in *moon* or *loop*

[ø]   **a** in *maple* with lips perfectly round and pursed fairly small; lips should protrude noticeably

[œ]   **e** in *pest* with lips rounded to about size of end of finger; lips should protrude as for [ø] above, but be wider open

[y]   **i** in *police* with lips rounded *very* small and protruding, opening no more than pencil size

[ɥ]   similar to [y], but shorter, sliding into the following vowel with consonantal force; try saying [y] followed quickly by [i] or [e]

[ə]   the first **a** in *parade,* or the **e** in *the* (as in *the man*)

[ã]   **on** in *honk,* but be sure to keep tongue down behind lower teeth. In all combinations with **n,** do not let tip of tongue rise to roof of mouth

[ɛ̃]   **an** in *sank,* but keep tongue down behind lower teeth; mouth is slightly more open than for *sank*

[ɔ̃]   **on** in *bone,* but keep tongue down behind lower teeth; do not pronounce the **n**

[œ̃]   nasal form of [œ] above; keep tongue down, touching back of lower teeth

Consonants   SYMBOL   APPROXIMATE DESCRIPTION

[b]   **b** in *bet*

[d]   **d** in *deft,* but tongue should hit tip of upper teeth instead of roof of mouth

---

[1] English speakers and most Americans tend to spread vowels out, so that they begin with one sound and end with another. E.g., *pay* becomes *pay-ee, poor* becomes *poo-er,* and *few* becomes *fee-oo.* This "off-glide" must be strictly avoided in French, as it is completely foreign to it. There is a kind of tenseness and purity to French vowels which will require a good deal of attention and practice on the part of the average student. Proper French pronunciation is achieved only by more vigorous articulation and much greater use of the lip muscles than for American English.

SYMBOL	APPROXIMATE DESCRIPTION
[f]	**f** in *fast*
[g]	**g** in *go*
[j]	**y** in *yes*
[k]	**k** in *king*
[l]	**l** in *low*, but with tongue on upper teeth instead of roof of mouth
[m]	**m** in *mat*
[n]	**n** in *now*, but with tongue on upper teeth instead of roof of mouth
[p]	**p** in *peep;* less release of air than in English
[r]	rolled either with the tongue or with the soft palate (uvula). The latter **r** is the so-called "Parisian **r**," best done by imitation
[s]	**s** in *sing*
[t]	**t** in *team;* tongue should touch upper teeth instead of roof of mouth
[v]	**v** in *valley*
[w]	**w** in *west*
[z]	**z** in *zebra*
[ʃ]	**sh** in *shine*
[ʒ]	**s** in *measure* or **si** in *fusion*
[ɲ]	**ni** in *onion*, but keep tongue down behind lower teeth. Do not let tongue rise to roof of mouth

French spelling combinations with their usual pronunciations

Oral Vowels and Diphthongs

SPELLING	SYMBOL	EXAMPLES
â; a before silent consonant or double **s**; **a** before [z]	[ɑ]	mât [mɑ] pas [pɑ] classe [klɑːs] [1] raser [rɑze]
à; a before one or more pronounced consonants other than double **s** or [z]	[a]	là [la] lac [lak] nappe [nap]
è; ê; e before two consonants; final **et** (but some speakers tend to sound final **et** as [e])	[ɛ]	lève [lɛːv] être [ɛːtr] leste [lɛst] chalet [ʃalɛ]

---

[1] The symbol [ː] means that the vowel is drawn out.

SPELLING	SYMBOL	EXAMPLES
é; e before silent consonant other than final t; the word et (*and*)	[e]	bébé [bebe] nez [ne] et [e]
e when final, or before a single consonant other than a final consonant	[ə] (or silent)	me [mə] lorsque [lɔrskə] chaque [ʃak] pelure [pəlyɪr]
î; i except when nasal; y	[i]	île [iːl] Nice [nis] Ypres [iːpr]
û; u except when nasal or before a vowel	[y]	flûte [flyt] lune [lyn]
o before a pronounced consonant other than [z]	[ɔ]	porte [pɔrt] molle [mɔl]
ô; o before a silent consonant; o before [z]	[o]	hôte [ot] pot [po] chose [ʃoːz]
ai except as final letters of verb ending	[ɛ]	mai [mɛ] mais [mɛ]
ai as final letters of verb ending (also, for some speakers, monosyllables like vais and sais)	[e]	ai [e] serai [səre] allai [ale]
au before r and in a few special cases	[ɔ]	Maure [mɔːr] taureau [tɔro] Paul [pɔl]
au except before r	[o]	Pau [po] cause [koːz] Gaule [goːl]
eau in all cases	[o]	beau [bo] château [ʃɑto] Sceaux [so]
ei in all cases except nasal	[ɛ]	neige [nɛʒ] pleine [plɛn]
eu or œu before pronounced consonant except [z]	[œ]	peur [pœːr] cœur [kœːr]
eu or œu when final, or before silent consonant or [z]	[ø]	peu [pø] creux [krø] vœu [vø] nœud [nø] creuse [krøːz]
oi except when nasal	[wa] or [wɑ]	moi [mwa] mois [mwɑ] poids [pwɑ]

SPELLING	SYMBOL	EXAMPLES
ou, où, oû (all cases)	[u]	trou [tru] où [u] voûte [vut]

Nasal Vowels and Diphthongs

RULE: Any vowel will be nasal (resonant or bell-like, as in [ɑ̃, ɛ̃, ɔ̃, œ̃]) when followed by a single **m** or **n** which is not itself followed by a vowel. To produce a nasal, the **m** or **n** must be either final or followed by a consonant other than itself. If the **m** or **n** is double, or both occur together, or if they are followed by a vowel, no nasal is produced.[1]

EXAMPLES

NASAL	NOT NASAL
plan [plɑ̃]	planer [plane]
fin [fɛ̃]	fine [fin]
un [œ̃]	une [yn]
mien [mjɛ̃]	mienne [mjɛn]
ombre [ɔ̃br]	omelette [ɔmlɛt]
semble [sɑ̃:bl]	semer [səme]
plomb [plɔ̃]	automne [otɔn]
	homme [ɔm]

SPELLING	SYMBOL	EXAMPLES
an, am, en, em	[ɑ̃]	pan [pɑ̃] chambre [ʃɑ̃:br] rente [rɑ̃:t] membre [mɑ̃:br]
in, im, ein, ain, aim	[ɛ̃]	vin [vɛ̃] timbre [tɛ̃:br] plein [plɛ̃] plain [plɛ̃] faim [fɛ̃]
ien	[jɛ̃]	rien [rjɛ̃] vient [vjɛ̃]
on, om	[ɔ̃]	long [lɔ̃] bombe [bɔ̃:b]
oin	[wɛ̃]	coin [kwɛ̃] point [pwɛ̃]
un, um	[œ̃]	brun [brœ̃] humble [œ̃:bl]

---

[1] Initial **em–** or **en–** is a frequent exception: **emmener** [ɑ̃mne], **ennui** [ɑ̃nyi].

Nonfinal Consonants

SPELLING	SYMBOL	EXAMPLES
b	[b]	bas [bɑ] bébé [bebe]
c before **e, i,** or **y**; **ç**	[s]	farce [fars] ici [isi] Nancy [nɑ̃si] garçon [garsɔ̃]
c before **a, o,** or **u**; **c** before a consonant	[k]	car [kar] corps [kɔɪr] cure [kyɪr] crier [krie] clique [klik]
d	[d]	dans [dɑ̃] fardeau [fardo]
f	[f]	force [fɔrs] agrafe [agraf] offrir [ɔfriɪr]
g before **e, i,** or **y**	[ʒ]	large [laɪrʒ] région [reʒɔ̃] gymnase [ʒimnaɪz]
g before **a, o,** or **u**	[g]	gamme [gam] Argonne [argɔn] aigu [ɛgy]
h is normally silent		heure [œɪr] homme [ɔm] rhume [rym] Berthe [bɛrt]
j	[ʒ]	Jacques [ʒak] Jules [ʒyl] déjà [deʒa]
k (rare in French)	[k]	kiosque [kjɔsk]
l (see also below)	[l]	loi [lwa] Celte [sɛlt]
ll after all vowels except **i**; also in **mille, millier, million, milliard, ville, village, tranquille;** and in certain proper names	[l]	balle [bal] celle [sɛl] colle [kɔl] tulle [tyl] ville [vil] Millet [milɛ]

SPELLING	SYMBOL	EXAMPLES
ll after **i** (with above exceptions); in these combinations do not pronounce the **i** unless it is the only vowel	[j]	fille [fiːj] aille [aːj] veille [vɛːj] bouillon [bujɔ̃]
m when not forming a nasal vowel	[m]	mer [mɛːr] lame [lam] femme [fam]
n when not forming a nasal vowel	[n]	nul [nyl] lune [lyn] bonne [bɔn]
p	[p]	police [pɔlis] nappe [nap]
qu usually [k], occasionally [kw]	[k] or [kw]	plaque [plak] qui [ki] équateur [ekwatœːr]
r	[r]	rue [ry] brave [brav] carré [kare]
s when initial or double; **s** beginning a syllable (i.e., after a consonant); **s** before a consonant	[s]	sale [sal] passer [pɑse] penser [pɑ̃se] sport [spɔːr]
s when single between vowels	[z]	cause [koːz] oser [oze]
t except in **tion** or other combinations where English has [ʃ] (e.g., *initiate, spatial*)	[t]	tel [tɛl] bateau [bato] cette [sɛt]
t in **tion** and combinations where English has [ʃ]	[s]	nation [nasjɔ̃] initier [inisje] essentiel [ɛsɑ̃sjɛl]
v	[v]	vallée [vale] rive [riːv]
w (rare in French)	[v] or [w]	wagon [vagɔ̃] tramway [tramwɛ]
x (no fixed pronunciation; best learned in individual words)		
z	[z]	seize [sɛːz] zéro [zero]

SPELLING	SYMBOL	EXAMPLES
ch in almost all cases (rarely [k])	[ʃ]	fraîche [frɛʃ] chose [ʃoːz] (Michel-Ange [mikɛlãːʒ], archéologie [arkeɔlɔʒi])
ph	[f]	phare [faːr] téléphone [telefɔn]
th	[t]	Berthe [bɛrt] Thomas [tɔmɑ]
gn	[ɲ]	Champagne [ʃãpaːɲ] mignon [miɲõ] cygne [siːɲ]

Final Consonants

RULE: Final consonants are normally silent except **c, r, f, l** (remember the word "CaReFuL"), and even these four are sometimes silent. There are occasional exceptions to this general rule, but they are best learned in individual words. Final **q** is pronounced, but is relatively rare.

EXAMPLES

SILENT		PRONOUNCED	
nid [ni]	gras [grɑ]	parc [park]	bal [bal]
long [lõ]	bout [bu]	car [kar]	coq [kɔk]
coup [ku]	noix [nwɑ]	nef [nɛf]	
corps [kɔːr]	chez [ʃe]		

Final **l** is normally silent in the endings **ail, eil, ouil,** which are pronounced as though written **aille, eille, ouille.**

EXAMPLES   travail [travaːj]   vermeil [vɛrmɛːj]   fenouil [fənuːj]

Pronunciation Drill

[a]	patte [pat]	matte [mat]	la [la]	battre [batr]	chatte [ʃat]	balle [bal]	lame [lam]
[ɑ]	pâte [pɑːt]	mât [mɑ]	las [lɑ]	basse [bɑs]	chat [ʃɑ]	Bâle [bɑːl]	l'âme [lɑːm]

[ɛ]	net [nɛt]	mettons [mɛtɔ̃]	donnait [dɔnɛ]	avais [avɛ]	cède [sɛd]	est [ɛ]	blette [blɛt]
[e]	nez [ne]	métal [metal]	donnai [dɔne]	avez [ave]	céder [sede]	et [e]	blé [ble]
[i]	lit [li]	si [si]	pli [pli]	ligne [liːɲ]	gui [gi]	figue [fig]	Yves [iːv]	issue [isy]
[y]	lut [ly]	su [sy]	plu [ply]	lune [lyn]	aigu [ɛgy]	fugue [fyg]	uvule [yvyl]	utile [ytil]
[o]	sot [so]	flot [flo]	mot [mo]	eau [o]	haut [o]	dos [do]	vôtre [votr]
[ɔ]	sotte [sɔt]	flotte [flɔt]	mort [mɔːr]	or [ɔːr]	hotte [ɔt]	dossier [dɔsje]	votre [vɔtr]
[ø]	jeu [ʒø]	nœud [nø]	œufs [ø]	bœufs [bø]	eux [ø]	peu [pø]	pleut [plø]
[œ]	jeune [ʒœn]	neuf [nœf]	œuf [œf]	bœuf [bœf]	heure [œːr]	peur [pœːr]	pleure [plœːr]
[w]	oui [wi]	Louis [lwi]	soin [swɛ̃]	loueur [lwœːr]	fouet [fwɛ]	ouest [wɛst]	joint [ʒwɛ̃]
[ɥ]	huis [ɥi]	lui [lɥi]	suinte [sɥɛ̃ːt]	lueur [lɥœːr]	fuit [fɥi]	huette [ɥɛt]	juin [ʒɥɛ̃]
[u]	bout [bu]	fou [fu]	vous [vu]	noue [nu]	Poitou [pwatu]	outil [uti]	boudin [budɛ̃]
[y]	but [by]	fut [fy]	vu [vy]	nue [ny]	pointu [pwɛ̃ty]	utile [ytil]	butin [bytɛ̃]
[ɔ̃]	bon [bɔ̃]	on [ɔ̃]	donjon [dɔ̃ʒɔ̃]	ton [tɔ̃]	ombre [ɔ̃ːbr]	tombeau [tɔ̃bo]	tromper [trɔ̃pe]
[ɑ̃]	ban [bɑ̃]	en [ɑ̃]	dansant [dɑ̃sɑ̃]	tant [tɑ̃]	ambre [ɑ̃ːbr]	flambeau [flɑ̃bo]	tremper [trɑ̃pe]
[ɛ̃]	lin [lɛ̃]	brin [brɛ̃]	des fins [de fɛ̃]	maint [mɛ̃]	timbre [tɛ̃ːbr]	malin [malɛ̃]	plein [plɛ̃]
[œ̃]	l'un [lœ̃]	brun [brœ̃]	défunt [defœ̃]	Meung [mœ̃]	humble [œ̃ːbl]	Melun [məlœ̃]	Lauzun [lozœ̃]
[wɛ̃]	loin [lwɛ̃]	joins [ʒwɛ̃]	point [pwɛ̃]	lointain [lwɛ̃tɛ̃]	moins [mwɛ̃]	soins [swɛ̃]	rejoins [rəʒwɛ̃]
[jɛ̃]	lien [ljɛ̃]	chien [ʃjɛ̃]	bien [bjɛ̃]	maintien [mɛ̃tjɛ̃]	mien [mjɛ̃]	siens [sjɛ̃]	retiens [rətjɛ̃]
[ʃ]	chatte [ʃat]	chaque [ʃak]	manche [mɑ̃ːʃ]	chemin [ʃmɛ̃]	sache [saʃ]	cache [kaʃ]	plancher [plɑ̃ʃe]
[ʒ]	jatte [ʒat]	Jacques [ʒak]	mange [mɑ̃ːʒ]	jamais [ʒamɛ]	sage [saːʒ]	cage [kaːʒ]	danger [dɑ̃ʒe]

[j]	fille	fillette	aille	pareil	chandail	Corneille
	[fiːj]	[fijɛt]	[aɪj]	[parɛij]	[ʃɑ̃daɪj]	[kɔrnɛij]
[ɲ]	vigne	vignette	agneau	peigne	Champagne	Compiègne
	[viːɲ]	[viɲɛt]	[aɲo]	[pɛɲ]	[ʃɑ̃paɲ]	[kɔ̃pjɛɲ]

Linking (*liaison*)

Final consonants, even those normally silent, are often linked to the following word if it begins with a vowel or mute **h,** so that the second word appears to the ear to begin with a consonant: un‿arbre [œ̃ naɪrbr], ces‿habitants [se zabitɑ̃]. Linking occurs most frequently between the following:

ARTICLE (OR ADJECTIVE) AND NOUN	les‿enfants [le zɑ̃fɑ̃] nos‿amis [no zami] de beaux‿hommes [də bo zɔm]
PREPOSITION AND OBJECT	chez‿eux [ʃe zø] en‿hiver [ɑ̃ nivɛir]
PRONOUN SUBJECT AND VERB (OR VERB AND PRONOUN SUBJECT IN A QUESTION)	nous‿avons [nu zavɔ̃] ils‿ont [il zɔ̃] Ont-ils? [ɔ̃ til] Est-elle? [ɛ tɛl]

Except for these general rules, linking is better learned by imitation than by precept. It should be noted that linking never occurs after **et** (*and*): **lui et elle** [lɥi e ɛl].

Intonation and Stress

Not only words, but phrases and sentences, are articulated differently in French and English. A marked distinction is the rising inflection at the end of each breath group of words in French, with a final drop in pitch at the end of a sentence. The student will do well to practice saying whole phrases as soon as he is able, with the aid of the recordings and his instructor. In individual words, a good rule for the beginning student is to stress all syllables equally except the last, which receives slightly more emphasis than the others. Words ending in unaccented **e** will stress the preceding vowel if there is one.

Final unaccented *e*

The letter **e,** if it has no written accent, is normally silent when final, unless it is the only vowel in the word: **table** [tabl], **lune** [lyn]. It is also silent in the verb endings **es** and **ent**: **manges** [mãːʒ], **aiment** [ɛm]; and in the plural endings **es** of nouns and adjectives where this **e** is not the only vowel: **femmes** [fam], **bonnes** [bɔn]. In poetry and song, normally silent **e** becomes [ə] to give an extra syllable under certain circumstances: **Il pleure dans mon cœur** [il plœrə dã mɔ̃ kœːr].

Written French

French differs from English not only orally but in writing as well, though to a smaller degree.   Perhaps the three most noticeable distinctions are:

1. The use of accents and the cedilla.
2. The much more sparing use of capital letters (e.g., names of days and months are not capitalized in French, nor are adjectives of nationality).
3. The tendency to separate what appear to be two complete sentences by a comma rather than a period.

Accents and cedilla

French has three written accents: *circonflexe* [^], *grave* [`], and *aigu* [´].   The *circonflexe* may occur over any vowel except **y**: **â, ê, î, ô, û.**   The *grave* may occur over three vowels: **à, è, ù** (in the combination **où** only).   The *aigu* is limited to one vowel: **é.**   The accents are not stress marks, but bear a limited relation to pronunciation, as indicated in the phonetic treatment of vowel sounds given earlier.   While the French themselves are often lax in the writing of accents, the latter are really a part of the spelling of words, and any omission or wrong use should be considered an orthographical error.

The cedilla [¸] indicates that a **c** is pronounced soft, like an **s**: **garçon** [garsɔ̃], **reçu** [rəsy].   It is necessary only to indicate softness before **a, o,** or **u**, as **c** is regularly soft without the cedilla before **e, i,** or **y**: **race** [ras], **ici** [isi], **Nancy** [nãsi].

Syllabification

In general, syllables in French tend to begin with consonant sounds and end with vowel sounds: **a·mé·ri·ca·ni·sa·tion** [a·me·ri·ka·ni·za·sjɔ̃].   When two consonants come together, they will normally be separated unless the second of the two is **l** or **r**:

pas-ser [pɑ-se]   res-ter [rɛs-te]
BUT
cri-bler [kri-ble]   cou-vrir [ku-vrir]

When three consonants come together, usually the syllable will divide between the first and second:

ar-bre [ar-br]   sem-bler [sã-ble]

1

Nouns and Articles

Voici and *Voilà*

Être and *Avoir*

Possession

PATTERN SENTENCES

1. Bonjour, monsieur.[1] Vous êtes étudiant ici?

2. Oui, mademoiselle.[1] Je suis un étudiant de français.[2]

3. Vous êtes dans la classe de M. Lasalle?

4. Non, j'ai le [3] professeur Dupont. Il est Français.[2]

5. Voilà le professeur Lasalle. Il a un livre à la main.[4]

6. Les étudiants du professeur ont aussi des livres.

1. Good morning. You're a student here?

2. Yes. I'm a French student (i.e., a student of French).

3. You're in Mr. Lasalle's class?

4. No, I have Professor Dupont. He's a Frenchman.

5. There's Professor Lasalle. He has a book in his hand.

6. The professor's students also have books.

---

[1] The French use polite forms of address, such as **monsieur, madame,** and **mademoiselle** (abbr. **M., Mme, Mlle**), more frequently than we do, though in a conversation between students they might well be omitted.

[2] Note that **Français** is capitalized when it refers to a person ("he's French," "he's a Frenchman"), but not when it refers to the French language. The same is true for **Anglais** (*English*), **Allemand** (*German*), etc.

[3] French commonly retains an article with a title other than **monsieur, madame,** or **mademoiselle,** unless the person is being addressed directly.

[4] French says simply "in the hand" when ownership is clear.

I

7. Vous avez là une revue. Elle est au professeur?
8. Oui, mais les journaux sont aux étudiants.
9. Nous sommes neuf dans la classe. Et vous?
10. Nous sommes dix. Nous avons déjà une leçon pour demain.
11. Nous aussi. Mais voici l'heure de la classe. Au revoir.
12. Et voilà des amis. A bientôt.

7. You've got a magazine there. Does it belong to the teacher?
8. Yes, but the newspapers are the students'.
9. There are nine of us in the class. And you?
10. There are ten of us. We already have a lesson for tomorrow.
11. So do we. But here it is class time. So long.
12. And there are some friends. I'll be seeing you.

1. Nouns and articles

In French all nouns, even for inanimate objects, are either masculine or feminine. The singular definite articles are **le** (masculine) and **la** (feminine).

le professeur the teacher	**la femme** the woman, wife
le crayon the pencil	**la famille** the family
le bureau the desk	**la porte** the door
le stylo the pen	**la fenêtre** the window
le pays the country	**la carte** the map

Before a vowel or mute **h**,[1] the vowel of the article is replaced by an apostrophe, and the noun and article are pronounced as one word.

l'an (*m.*) the year	**l'âme** (*f.*) the soul
l'homme the man	**l'herbe** (*f.*) the grass

The plural of the definite article is in all cases **les.**[2]

les crayons   les hommes   les femmes   les âmes   les ans

Since **l'** gives no clue to gender, nouns beginning with a vowel or mute **h** are best learned with the indefinite article (*m.*, **un**; *f.*, **une**).

un an a year   **un homme** a man   **une âme** a soul

The indefinite article has no plural as such, but when one seems called for, **des** is used. It may be translated **some** or **any,** or left untranslated.

des âmes souls   **des hommes** men, some men, any men

---

[1] Mute **h** is the common **h**. Aspirate **h**, also silent, does not permit the dropping of the preceding vowel. The latter **h**, found chiefly in nouns of non-Latin origin, will be written thus: *haut, *haine in the vocabularies, indicating that article and noun are to be written and pronounced as two words: **le haut, la haine.**

[2] The **s** of **les** is silent before a pronounced consonant, but before mute **h** or a vowel it is pronounced like **z,** and gives the effect of belonging with the noun rather than with the article: **les hommes, les âmes.**

The article is generally repeated with each noun in French.

> **un homme et une femme** a man and woman
> **la table et la chaise** the table and chair

2. Plural of nouns

Nouns usually form their plural in **s,** as in English, but most nouns ending in **al** and **au** form their plural in **aux;** and those in **eu,** in **eux.**[1]

le cheval the horse	**les chevaux** the horses
un château a castle	**des châteaux** castles
le feu the fire	**les feux** the fires

Nouns already ending in **s** or **x** (or **z**) do not change in the plural, nor do family names, whatever the ending.

le bois the wood(s)	**les bois** the woods
une voix a voice	**des voix** voices
un nez a nose	**des nez** noses
Brun Brown	**les Brun** the Browns

The plural forms of **monsieur, madame,** and **mademoiselle** are **messieurs, mesdames,** and **mesdemoiselles.**

A. Read each sentence aloud, then reread substituting the words in parentheses for the italicized words in the sentence.

1. Vous avez *un livre.* (*un journal, une classe, un professeur, une leçon*)
2. Voici *le professeur.* (*l'étudiant, la femme, l'homme, le Français*)
3. Voilà *la carte.* (*le bureau, la fenêtre, le pays, la porte*)
4. J'ai *un stylo.* (*une chaise, une table, une revue, un crayon*)
5. Voilà *les étudiants.* (*les professeurs, les hommes, les femmes, les journaux*)

B. Read each sentence aloud, then reread substituting the words in parentheses for the italicized word in the sentence. If necessary, change the article to agree with the noun.

1. Voici une *chaise.* (*crayon, bureau, femme, étudiant*)
2. Il a le *journal.* (*revue, stylo, livre, crayon*)
3. Vous avez une *leçon.* (*stylo, chaise, bureau, journal*)
4. Voilà la *porte.* (*chaise, crayon, homme, fenêtre*)
5. J'ai des *revues.* (*stylos, classes, livres, journaux*)

---

[1] Since the final **s** or **x** is normally silent, orally the plural can often be identified only by the form of the article, which therefore takes on a greater significance than in English.

3. *Voici* and *voilà*

Voici (*here is, here are*) and **voilà** (*there is, there are*) point out location and are in effect answers to a spoken or an unspoken question: **"Où . . . ?"** (*"Where . . . ?"*) The words used with **voici** and **voilà** are direct objects, not subjects.

> **Où est le livre?** Where is the book?
> **Voilà le livre.** *There is* the book.
> **Où est le professeur?** Where is the professor?
> **Voici le professeur devant la fenêtre.** *Here is* the professor in front of the window.
> **Où sont les journaux?** Where are the newspapers?
> **Voici les journaux sur la table.** *Here are* the newspapers on the table.
> **Où est le livre?** Where is the book?
> **Voilà le livre sous le bureau.** *There is* the book under the desk

NOTE: **Voici** and **voilà**, in spite of their English translation, have no connection whatsoever with the verb **être** (*to be*), but are contractions of old imperatives (**vois ici . . .**, *see here . . .*; and **vois là . . .**, *see there . . .*), which explains why they have no subject, take direct objects, and thus may be used with both singular and plural nouns without change.

C. Read each sentence aloud, then reread, making the nouns plural.

Voilà l'Anglais.	Voilà un homme.
Voici la porte.	Voilà une femme.
Voilà le monsieur.	Voilà une fenêtre.
Voici le journal.	Voilà un livre.
Voilà l'étudiante.[1]	Voilà une carte.
Voilà la Française.	Voici un crayon.
Voilà le pays.	Voilà une chaise.
Voilà le bois.	Voilà un cheval.
Voici le bureau.	Voici un stylo.

4. Irregular present tense of *être* and *avoir*

être *to be*	**avoir** *to have*
je suis *I am*	j'ai *I have*
tu es *you are*	tu as *you have*
il (elle) est *he (she, it) is*	il (elle) a *he (she, it) has*
nous sommes *we are*	nous avons *we have*
vous êtes *you are*	vous avez *you have*
ils (elles) sont *they are*	ils (elles) ont *they have*

---

[1] Many nouns have a masculine and a feminine form. **Étudiant** and **Français** are examples of nouns which add an **e** in the feminine form.

NOTE: The second person singular is used only to a member of the family, a friend of long acquaintance, a child, or a pet. **Vous** is the general term for *you*, taking a plural verb whether referring to one person or to more than one. *It* and *they* take the gender of the noun they replace, either masculine or feminine. When *they* includes both masculine and feminine subjects, **ils** is used.

IMPORTANT: Students accustomed to Latin or Spanish, in which subjects may be omitted, must remember that in French it is essential at all times (except in commands) to express the subject.

5. Omission of article after *être*

After the verb **être,** unmodified nouns of title, status, trade, profession, or nationality generally occur without an article.

> **M. Dupont est professeur.**   Mr. Dupont is a teacher.
> **Jeanne est secrétaire.**   Jean is a secretary.
> **Il est Français.**   He is a Frenchman.
> **Nous sommes amis.**   We are friends.
> BUT
> **Je suis un étudiant de français.**   I am a student of French.

D. Read each sentence aloud, then reread substituting the words in parentheses for the italicized word. Make any changes that are necessary.

    a. 1. *Vous* êtes dans la classe. (*Il, Ils, Tu, Nous*)
       2. *M. Lasalle* est professeur. (*Vous, Tu, Je, Elle*)
       3. Nous *sommes* devant la fenêtre. (*suis, êtes, est, sont*)
       4. *Ils* sont amis. (*Nous, Les étudiants, Vous, Jean et Robert*)
       5. Il *est* derrière le bureau. (*sommes, es, suis, sont*)

    b. 1. *Vous* avez une revue. (*Il, Je, Tu, Nous*)
       2. *J'*ai un livre à la main. (*Vous, Tu, Elle, Le professeur*)
       3. Elles *ont* des journaux. (*avons, avez, ai, a*)
       4. *Il* a le professeur Dupont. (*Ils, Tu, Nous, Je*)
       5. Elle *a* des livres de français. (*ont, as, avons, avez*)

E. Express in French.

    1. Good morning, madam. Good morning, ladies. Good morning, gentlemen. Good morning, young ladies. 2. I am here. Here is the desk. I am behind the desk. There is the pencil. It is under the desk. 3. You have a book. The book is on the desk. The desk is in front of

the door. It is here. 4. John is a student. Jean is a student too.[1] She is a French girl. We are friends. 5. She has a desk. I have a desk also. The students have desks. We are students. We have books. 6. The teacher is an Englishman. He has a book in his hand. You have books in your hand too. You are students.

6. Contractions of *de* and *à*

The prepositions **de** (*of*, *from*) and **à** (*in, at, to*) combine with the articles **le** and **les,** but not with **la** or **l'**.

de + le becomes *du*	à + le becomes *au*
de + les becomes *des*	à + les becomes *aux*

EXAMPLES

du livre   of the book   **au professeur**   to the teacher
des femmes   of the women   **aux messieurs**   to the gentlemen
BUT   BUT
de l'Anglais   of the Englishman   **à l'homme**   to the man
de la femme   of the woman   **à la famille**   to the family

Note that certain French prepositions include **de,** such as **près de** (*near*), which becomes **du, de l',** or **des** as required. Compare English *back of, on top of.*

7. Possession

Possession, when nouns are involved, is not expressed by an apostrophe, as in English, but by a phrase with **de** (*of*).

> **le livre du professeur**   the teacher's book (the book of the teacher)
> **le cahier de Louise**   Louise's notebook

Similar expressions not indicating ownership, but merely kind or type, are done in the same way, but always omit the article.

> **une voix d'homme**   a man's voice, i.e., a masculine voice
> **des revues de femmes**   women's magazines

The expression *belong to* and its equivalents are best rendered in French by **être à.**

> **Le cahier est à Robert.**   The notebook { belongs to Robert. / is Robert's.
> **Les revues sont au professeur.**   The magazines belong to the teacher.

---

[1] See Pattern Sentences for position of adverb.

F. Read aloud, then reread substituting the words in parentheses for the italicized word, making any necessary changes in the sentence.

1. Le livre est au *professeur*. (*l'étudiant, l'homme, Jean, l'ami de Robert*)
2. Les journaux sont aux *étudiants*. (*la femme, le professeur, l'Anglais, les hommes*)
3. Voilà les amis du *professeur*. (*Jean, les étudiants, la famille, le monsieur*)
4. Le stylo de *Robert* est sur la table. (*le professeur, l'étudiant, M. Dupont, la femme*)

LECTURE[1]

Nous sommes maintenant dans la salle de classe. La salle a une porte et quatre fenêtres. Sur le mur nous avons une carte de France.

Le professeur est devant la classe, derrière le bureau. Il a sur le bureau des livres, un dictionnaire et des revues. Les livres sont des livres de français.

Nous avons aujourd'hui une leçon de français. Le français, un des descendants du latin, est aujourd'hui la langue de plusieurs millions de personnes dans des pays d'Europe (la France, la Belgique, la Suisse), et de plusieurs millions de personnes dans des pays hors d'Europe. Comme l'anglais, le français a des différences de prononciation et d'usage entre les régions du pays.

La France et les États-Unis sont amis. Aujourd'hui les deux pays sont des républiques. L'histoire des deux pays a des choses en commun dans le passé et dans le présent. Voilà[2] pourquoi la France et le français ont de l'intérêt[3] pour nous.

G. Complete the following sentences, basing your response on the *Lecture*. Practice each until you can give the complete sentence unhesitatingly without referring to the *Lecture*.

1. Nous sommes maintenant ____. 2. La salle de classe a ____ porte et ____ fenêtres. 3. Sur le mur nous avons ____. 4. Le professeur a sur le bureau ____, ____ et ____. 5. Les livres sont ____. 6. Nous avons aujourd'hui ____. 7. Le français est aujourd'hui la langue ____ de personnes. 8. La France, la Belgique et la Suisse sont des pays ____. 9. La France et les États-Unis sont ____. 10. Aujourd'hui les deux pays sont ____. 11. L'histoire des deux pays a des choses en commun ____ et ____. 12. Voilà pourquoi le français a ____ pour nous.

---

[1] See Unit vocabulary. This word is a good example of a false cognate. A generous list of words of this type, under the heading *Faux Amis*, will be found in the Appendix.

[2] **Voilà** occasionally signifies "that is" rather than "there is."

[3] The use of **de** with the article indicates "a certain amount of...." A thorough explanation of this construction will be given later.

VOCABULARY[1]

NOTE: Nouns should be learned with the definite article or, for words beginning with a vowel or mute **h,** the indefinite article if appropriate. Idioms will be found at the head of the vocabulary.

en commun in common

un **Anglais** Englishman
    aujourd'hui today
la **Belgique** Belgium
le **bois** wood
le **bureau** desk, office
la **carte** map, card, menu
la **chaise** chair
le **cheval** horse
la **chose** thing
    comme like, as
le **crayon** pencil
    derrière behind
    deux two
    devant in front of
le **dictionnaire** dictionary
    entre between, among
les **États-Unis** United States
la **famille** family
la **femme** woman, wife
la **fenêtre** window
une **histoire** history, story

hors de outside, outside of

un **homme** man
un **intérêt** interest
la **langue** tongue, language
la **lecture** reading
    maintenant now
le **mur** wall
le **passé** past
le **pays** country
la **personne** person
    plusieurs several
la **porte** door
    pourquoi why
    quatre four
la **salle** room, hall; **salle de classe** classroom
    sous under
le **stylo** pen
la **Suisse** Switzerland
    sur on, upon
    un, une a, an, one

PATTERN SENTENCE DRILL

Read each sentence aloud, then reread, making progressive changes by substituting each new word in its proper position. Make whatever changes are necessary for agreement.

Example:	J'ai un crayon.	J'ai un crayon.
	_____ stylo.	J'ai un stylo.
	Il _____.	Il a un stylo.
	___ des ___.	Il a des stylos.
	_ avons ___.	Nous avons des stylos.

---

[1] The Vocabulary is for the exercises and *Lecture*. Expressions used in the Pattern Sentences will not normally be repeated here unless an extension of meaning requires it. True cognates, and words whose meaning can readily be inferred by appearance or context, will likewise be omitted. Words which the student will need in order to understand the *Lecture* but which he will not be required to know in subsequent lessons will be given in footnotes.

1. Vous êtes étudiant ici?
   Il _____?
   _____ étudiante _?
   _____ sont _____?
   Ils _____?

2. Je suis un étudiant de français.
   _____ étudiante _____.
   Elle _____.
   __ êtes _____.
   _____ étudiantes _____.

3. Vous êtes dans la classe de M. Lasalle?
   _____ professeur Dupont?
   Ils _____?
   _____ sommes _____?
   Elles _____?

4. Il est Français.
   Elle _____.
   _____ Anglaise.
   Il _____.
   _ sont_____.

5. Voilà le professeur Lasalle.
   _____ un ami.
   _____ amie.
   Voici _____.
   _____ des _____.

6. Il a un livre à la main.
   _____ revue _____.
   ___ des _____.
   _ ont _____.
   Vous _____.

7. Les étudiants du professeur Dupont ont des livres.
   _____ leçon.
   _____ M. Lasalle _____.
   L'étudiant _____.
   _____ des _____.

8. Vous avez une revue.
   _____ journal.
   ____ avons _____.
   _____ des _____.
   Elles _____.

9. Elle est au professeur?
   Ils_____?
   _____ aux _____?
   _____ homme?
   ___ est _____?

10. Les journaux sont aux étudiants.
    _____ femme.
    La revue _____.
    _____ sont _____.
    _____ hommes.

11. Nous sommes neuf dans la classe.
    Vous _____.
    ____ sont _____.
    _____ dix _____.
    _____ salle.

12. Nous avons déjà une leçon pour demain.
    Ils _____.
    ____ as _____.
    _____ aujourd'hui.
    _____ leçons _____.

2

Aller and *Faire*

Word Order

Negation

Time Expressions

PATTERN SENTENCES

1. Bonjour, monsieur. Comment allez-vous aujourd'hui?
2. Je vais très bien, merci. Et vous?
3. Pas mal. Il fait beau ce matin, n'est-ce pas?
4. Très beau. Va-t-il faire du soleil demain?
5. Je ne sais pas. Allez-vous en ville s'il fait mauvais?
6. Non, je vais rester à la maison.
7. Que faites-vous dimanche?
8. Nous faisons toujours une promenade le dimanche.
9. Est-ce qu'il fait froid ici en hiver?
10. En hiver il fait bien froid, et il neige de temps en temps.
11. En automne quel temps fait-il?
12. En automne, et aussi au printemps, il fait frais.

1. Good morning. How are you today?
2. I'm very well, thanks. And you?
3. Not bad. Fine weather this morning, isn't it?
4. Very beautiful. Is it going to be sunny tomorrow?
5. I don't know. Are you going downtown if the weather is bad?
6. No, I am going to stay home.
7. What are you doing Sunday?
8. We always go for a walk (ride) on Sundays.
9. Is it cold here in the winter?
10. In the winter it is quite cold, and it snows from time to time.
11. In the fall what's the weather like?
12. In the fall, and also in the spring, it is cool.

II

8. Irregular present tense of *aller* and *faire*

aller *to go*	**faire** *to make, do*
je vais *I go (am going, do go)*	je fais *I make, I do*
tu vas *you go*	tu fais *you make*
il va *he goes*	il fait *he makes*
nous allons *we go*	nous faisons *we make*
vous allez *you go*	vous faites *you make*
ils vont *they go*	ils font *they make*

Note that French verbs have but one form for each person of each tense, where English often has two or three equivalents.

Elle *va* à l'école. She { *goes* / *does go* to school. / *is going* }

Va-t-elle à l'école? *Is* she *going* } / *Does* she *go* } to school?

The progressive forms (*is going, are going,* and the like) and the emphatic forms (*does go, do go,* and the like) do not exist in French.

A. Read aloud, then reread substituting words in parentheses for italicized words and making any necessary changes.

  a. 1. *Je* vais en ville. (*Vous, Elle, Nous, Jean*)
     2. Il *va* à la classe de français. (*vont, vas, allons, vais*)
     3. *Les garçons* vont à l'école à pied. (*Vous, Je, Il, Jean et Marie*)
     4. *Nous* allons à la campagne. (*Elles, Jean, Vous, Tu*)
     5. Elle *va* au cinéma. (*allez, allons, vont, vais*)

  b. 1. *Il* fait des voyages en été. (*Vous, Elles, Tu, Les professeurs*)
     2. *Les étudiants* font le devoir. (*Jules, Nous, Elle, Elles*)
     3. Nous *faisons* une promenade. (*faites, fait, font, fais*)
     4. *Vous* faites cela très bien. (*Nous, Jean, Elle, Jean et Marie*)
     5. Tu *fais* souvent ce voyage. (*font, faites, faisons, fait*)

9. Word order: subject and verb

In French, the declarative order of subject and verb is generally identical with English.

Jean *est* un garçon. *John is* a boy.
Il *a* le papier et l'encre. *He has* the paper and the ink.

In interrogative order, simple inversion of subject and verb is common, if the subject is a pronoun. When a pronoun follows a verb, it is always connected to it by a hyphen.

> **Est-il ici?** *Is he* here?
> **Vont-ils en ville?** *Are they going* downtown?
> **Pleut-il?** *Is it raining?*

In the third person singular of a question, if the verb ends in a vowel, the sound of a **t** is always heard between verb and subject, probably because most verbs in older French ended in **t** in the third person singular. It is customary to write in this **t** in the interrogative, separated by hyphens.

DECLARATIVE	INTERROGATIVE
Il a. He has.	**A-t-il?** Does he have?
Elle va. She is going.	**Va-t-elle?** Is she going?
Il neige. It is snowing.	**Neige-t-il?** Is it snowing?

Inversion may also be used with a noun subject, if there is an interrogative expression such as **Où?** (*Where?*), **Comment?** (*How?*), **A qui?** (*Whose?*), or unmodified **Combien?** (*How much?*).

> **Où *est la chaise?*** Where *is the chair?*
> **Comment *va la famille?*** How *is the family?*
> **A qui *est l'auto?*** Whose *car is it?*
> **Combien *coûte cette robe?*** How much *does this dress cost?*

When a noun subject appears without an interrogative expression, and usually when it appears with modified **Combien?** (*How much? How many?*), **Pourquoi?** (*Why?*), and **Quand?** (*When?*), the subject is first stated separately, after which the pronoun and verb are inverted in the usual way.

> **Pierre et Marie sont-ils dans la salle de classe?** *Are Peter and Mary* in the classroom?
> **Combien d'enfants *les Dupont ont-ils?*** How many children *do the Duponts have?*
> **Pourquoi *Jean est-il* ici?** Why *is John* here?
> **Quand Jean et Marie *vont-ils* à la campagne?** When *are John and Mary going* to the country?

A second way of stating a question is to prefix **est-ce que** (*is it that*) to the declarative without other change. Questions in the first person singular are often done in this way.

> **Jean va à Paris.** John is going to Paris.
> **Est-ce que Jean va à Paris?** Is John going to Paris?
> **J'ai le cahier de Marie.** I have Mary's notebook.
> **Est-ce que j'ai le cahier de Marie?** Do I have Mary's notebook?

When an affirmative answer is expected, still a third method is used. The statement is made in the declarative, and **n'est-ce pas** (*isn't it*) is added. Although the English equivalent may vary with the original statement, as "didn't he?" "aren't you?" or the like, the expression **n'est-ce pas?** remains invariable.

> **Vous avez un fils, n'est-ce pas?** You have a son, haven't you?
> **Ils sont dans la maison, n'est-ce pas?** They are in the house, aren't they?

B. Read each sentence, then restate it as a question, following the pattern given.

a. *Pattern:* Vont-ils en ville?
   1. Il neige.
   2. Il fait mauvais.
   3. Elle est ici.
   4. Vous avez un livre de français.
   5. Il a un crayon.

b. *Pattern:* A qui est le crayon?
   1. Les bureaux sont aux étudiants.
   2. Le cahier est au professeur.
   3. Les revues sont à la femme.
   4. La carte est au garçon.
   5. Le crayon et le stylo sont à Marie.

c. *Pattern:* Jean va-t-il à Paris?
   1. Marie est à la campagne.
   2. Les étudiants vont en ville.
   3. Jacques a les journaux.
   4. Les enfants sont dans la maison.
   5. Le livre est sur la table.

d. *Pattern:* Est-ce que j'ai un bureau?
   1. Il fait beau ce matin.
   2. Je suis dans la salle de classe.
   3. Vous allez à la campagne.
   4. Je vais en ville demain.
   5. Jean fait le devoir pour demain.

10. Simple negation

A verb is made negative by placing **ne** before it and **pas** after it. **Pas** is really the word for *step*, and the use of two words to express the negative may have grown out of some such expression as "I shall *not* go a *step*," as we often say. At any rate, in French the double negative is not only correct but generally "de rigueur" if a verb is present. If no verb is present, **ne** is omitted.

> **Suzanne va à l'école.** Susan is going to school.
> **Guillaume ne va pas à l'école.** William is not going to school.
> **Nous sommes dans la maison.** We are in the house.
> **Vous n'êtes pas dans la maison.** You are not in the house.
> BUT
> **Pas aujourd'hui, merci.** Not today, thank you. (no verb, hence no **ne**)

In the interrogative, hyphenated forms are treated as one word, so that the **pas** must wait until after the subject.

> **Ne va-t-elle pas à l'école?** Isn't she going to school?
> **Ne sont-ils pas dans la classe?** Aren't they in the class?

11. Elision

Any monosyllable ending in **e** will normally drop this **e** before a vowel or mute **h.** So also will certain longer words ending in **que,** such as **puisque** and **lorsque. La** will similarly drop its **a. Si** drops its **i** before **il** or **ils.** An apostrophe marks this elision.

> **Marie n'est pas l'amie d'Henri.** Mary is not Henry's (girl) friend.
> **puisqu'elle est ici** since she is here
> **lorsqu'ils vont à l'école** when they go to school
> **s'il va** if he goes
> **s'ils vont** if they go
> BUT
> **si elle va** if she goes

The vowels **o, u,** and **y** are never dropped.

C. Read each sentence aloud, then restate it in the negative.

1. Je vais au cinéma maintenant.
2. Elle est à la maison ce matin.
3. Nous sommes souvent en ville.
4. Il neige beaucoup en hiver.
5. Jeanne fait le devoir pour demain.
6. Allez-vous quelquefois en ville?
7. Jean et Marie vont-ils à l'école en auto?
8. Vas-tu à la campagne quand il pleut?
9. Les deux messieurs sont professeurs.
10. Le garçon va-t-il à Paris?

D. Express in French.

1. Are the children in the country? 2. Aren't the children in the country? 3. Is the family going downtown? 4. No, they are not going downtown. 5. Does Jean have a pen? 6. Does she have a notebook? 7. Doesn't she have a pencil? 8. Why aren't you going to school today? 9. We don't always do the assignment. 10. Why don't the boys do the assignment?

12. Special uses of *aller* and *faire*

Besides indicating motion, **aller** is commonly used to form a practical future, just as we use the progressive forms of *go* in English.

> **Je *vais rester* ici.** I *am going to stay* here.
> **Elle *va visiter* le château.** She *is going to visit* the castle.
> ***Allez*-vous *rester* ici demain?** *Are* you *going to stay* here tomorrow?

Aller occurs in many expressions of health or physical condition.

> **Comment allez-vous?** How are you?
> **Je vais bien, merci.** I am well, thanks.
> **Elle ne va pas bien aujourd'hui.** She is not well today.

The third person singular is used with **ça** in a colloquial expression commoner among friends than the more formal **Comment allez-vous?**

> **Comment ça va?** How are you? How goes it?
> **Ça va bien?** Are you well? Everything O.K. with you?

The third person singular of **faire** is regularly used in certain weather expressions. Learn the following common expressions:

Il fait beau (temps). The weather is fine.
Il fait mauvais. The weather is bad.
Quel temps fait-il? What's the weather?
Il fait très chaud. It is very warm.
Il fait du vent. It is windy.

Il fait bien froid. It is quite cold.
Il fait sombre. It is dark.
Il fait frais. It is cool.
Il fait du soleil. It is sunny.
Il fait du brouillard. It is foggy.

E. Read each question aloud, then answer in a complete sentence, first in the affirmative and then in the negative.

1. Allez-vous rester ici ce matin?
2. Jean va-t-il visiter le monument?
3. Est-ce que les garçons vont faire cela?
4. Allons-nous faire une promenade?
5. Tu vas rester avec nous, n'est-ce pas?
6. Ça va bien?

F. Read aloud, then state the contrary or approximate contrary without using a negative.

1. Il fait beau. 2. Il fait chaud. 3. Il fait très chaud. 4. Il fait du soleil. 5. Il fait bien froid.

13. Time expressions

Days of the week are not capitalized in French. All are masculine.

lundi	Monday	**vendredi**	Friday
mardi	Tuesday	**samedi**	Saturday
mercredi	Wednesday	**dimanche**	Sunday
jeudi	Thursday		

Without an article a day of the week means, as in English, the nearest day named; with the definite article, customary time is indicated.

> **Je vais à la campagne dimanche.**   I'm going to the country Sunday.
> **Je ne vais pas à l'école le dimanche.**   I don't go to school Sundays.
> **Il pleut tous les samedis.**   It rains every Saturday.

Learn the following time expressions:

> **le matin**   in the morning
> **l'après-midi**   in the afternoon
> **le soir**   in the evening
> **ce matin**   this morning
> **cet après-midi**   this afternoon
> **ce soir**   this evening, tonight
> **demain soir**   tomorrow night
> **mardi soir**   Tuesday night
> **tous les jours**   every day
> **tous les soirs**   every night

G. a. Agree, then disagree by changing only the time expression, as in the example.

> *Q.* Vous allez à la campagne dimanche, n'est-ce pas?
> *A.* Oui, je vais à la campagne dimanche.
>   Non, je vais à la campagne jeudi.

1. Vous allez à l'école le matin, n'est-ce pas?
2. Jean va au cinéma l'après-midi, n'est-ce pas?
3. Les garçons vont à la campagne mardi, n'est-ce pas?
4. Tu fais une promenade tous les jours, n'est-ce pas?
5. Les étudiants font les devoirs ce soir, n'est-ce pas?

b. Agree, then disagree in any suitable manner, as in the example.

> *Q.* Vous faites les devoirs, n'est-ce pas?
> *A.* Oui, je fais les devoirs (*or* nous faisons les devoirs).
>   Non, je ne fais pas les devoirs (*or* je vais en ville)

1. Jeanne fait une promenade, n'est-ce pas?
2. Elle va bien, n'est-ce pas?
3. Il va faire mauvais demain, n'est-ce pas?
4. Les étudiants vont à la campagne, n'est-ce pas?
5. Il fait chaud au printemps, n'est-ce pas?

LECTURE

— Bonjour, Jacques. Comment ça va?

— Pas très bien. J'ai mal à la tête ce matin.

— Quel dommage ! N'allez-vous pas en classe, alors?

— Pas aujourd'hui. Je vais rester à la maison.

— Qu'avez-vous là?

— J'ai ici un livre avec des descriptions de la vie en France.

— Mais la vie en France n'est-elle pas comme la vie ici?

— Pas tout à fait. Par exemple, voici une page avec un calendrier.[1] Lundi est au commencement de la semaine, et non pas [2] dimanche.

— Vraiment? Mais pendant la semaine on [3] fait comme ici, n'est-ce pas?

— Au contraire. Les enfants vont à l'école le samedi, et ne vont pas à l'école le jeudi.

— Sans blague ! Voilà une différence, certainement.

— Encore une différence. Au milieu de la journée on a souvent deux heures pour le déjeuner. Chic, n'est-ce pas?

— D'accord. Et est-ce qu'on a des distractions [4] comme aux États-Unis?

— On va quelquefois au cinéma et au théâtre. Mais très souvent, on va au café vers la fin de l'après-midi. Là, on a un apéritif.[5]

— Mais quand a-t-on le dîner?

— Assez tard le soir. Le dimanche, les Français font souvent une promenade à la campagne, comme ici. Mais pas toujours en auto. Plus souvent on va à pied. Ou de temps en temps on va au cinéma.

— La vie en France a certainement l'air très agréable. Quand allons-nous faire le voyage?

H. 1. Jacques a ____ ce matin. 2. Il ne va pas ____. 3. Il va rester ____. 4. La vie en France n'est pas tout à fait comme ____. 5. Lundi est au commencement ____. 6. Les enfants vont à l'école ____. 7. On a souvent deux heures pour ____. 8. On va quelquefois ____ et ____. 9. Très souvent, on va au café ____. 10. On a le dîner ____. 11. Le dimanche, les Français ____. 12. La vie en France a certainement ____.

---

[1] **le calendrier** *calendar*

[2] **Non pas** frequently occurs instead of the simple **pas.**

[3] **On** is a personal pronoun used when no specific individual or individuals are intended. It is variously translated "they," "you," "people," etc. For fuller explanation, see Unit 7, Section 38.

[4] **les distractions** *amusements, recreation*

[5] **Un apéritif** is an alcoholic drink intended to whet the appetite for dinner.

VOCABULARY

à la campagne in (to) the country
à pied on foot
à qui? whose?
au contraire on the contrary
avoir l'air to seem
avoir mal à la tête to have a headache
Comment ça va? How are you? How are things?

agréable pleasant
alors then
assez enough, rather, quite
avec with
beaucoup much, many
le **café** coffee, café
le **cahier** notebook
cela (ça) that
certainement certainly
chic nice, swell
le **cinéma** movies
le **commencement** beginning
le **déjeuner** lunch
le **devoir** assignment, homework
le **dîner** dinner
une **école** school; **à l'école** at (to, in) school
encore yet, still, again; **encore un(e)** another

D'accord Right! Agreed!
en auto by car
en été in the summer
il pleut it rains, it is raining
par exemple for example
Quel dommage! Too bad!
Sans blague! No kidding!
tout à fait entirely, absolutely

l'**enfant** (*m. or f.*) child
la **fin** end
le **garçon** boy
la **journée** day (duration stressed)
le **milieu** middle, midst
ou or
pendant during
plus more
quand when
quelquefois sometimes, once in a while
la **semaine** week
souvent often
tard late
le **théâtre** theater
vers toward
la **vie** life
le **voyage** trip
vraiment really

PATTERN SENTENCE DRILL

1. Comment allez-vous aujourd'hui?
   _____-tu _____?
   _____ ce soir?
   _____ la famille _?
   _____ ça va _____?
2. Je vais très bien.
   Elle _____.
   _ allons _____.
   _____ mal.
   Ça _____.

3. Il fait beau ce matin.
   _____ sombre _____.
   _____ après-midi.
   _____ du vent _____.
   _____ soir.

4. Va-t-il faire mauvais demain?
   _____ du soleil _____?
   _____ dimanche?
   _____ frais _____?
   _____ ce soir?

5. Allez-vous en ville s'il fait mauvais?
   _____ du soleil?
   _____ à la campagne _____?
   _____ pleut?
   _____-il _____?

6. Je vais rester à la maison.
   Nous _____.
   _____ ville.
   _____ faire une promenade.
   __ allez _____.

7. Que faites-vous dimanche?
   _____ -nous _____?
   _____ aujourd'hui?
   ____ font _____?
   _____ à la campagne?

8. Nous faisons toujours une promenade le dimanche.
   _____ souvent _____.
   Il _____.
   _____ soir.
   _____ faites _____.

9. Est-ce qu'il fait froid ici en hiver?
   _____ printemps?
   _____ frais _____?
   _____ pleut _____?
   _____ en France_____?

10. En hiver il fait bien froid.
    _____ frais.
    __ printemps _____.
    _____ chaud.
    __ été _____.

11. Il neige de temps en temps.
    _____ très souvent.
    _ pleut _____.
    _____ quelquefois.
    _ fait du brouillard __.

12. En automne, et aussi au printemps, il fait frais.
    _____ vent.
    __ hiver _____.
    _____ souvent _____.
    ___ _____ neige.

3

Regular Verbs

Meanings of Certain Verbs

Cardinal Numerals

Hour and Date

PATTERN SENTENCES

1. Quelle heure est-il maintenant?	1. What time is it now?
2. Il est près de dix heures.	2. It's nearly ten o'clock.
3. Déjà dix heures? Alors, nous commençons bientôt.	3. Ten o'clock already? Then we begin shortly.
4. Pas avant dix heures dix. Le professeur est toujours en retard.	4. Not until ten ten. The teacher is always late.
5. Les étudiants entrent dans la classe à l'heure.	5. The students go into class on time.
6. Mais quelquefois nous attendons M. Lasalle plusieurs minutes.	6. But sometimes we wait several minutes for Mr. Lasalle.
7. Lorsqu'il arrive, il commence la leçon tout de suite.	7. When he comes, he begins the lesson right away.
8. Il essuie le tableau noir et cherche un morceau de craie.	8. He erases the blackboard and looks for a piece of chalk.
9. Nous corrigeons d'abord les fautes dans le devoir.	9. First we correct the mistakes in the assignment.
10. Nous finissons la leçon à onze heures précises.	10. We finish the lesson at eleven o'clock sharp.

11. Écoutez-vous le professeur quand il parle?

12. Pas toujours, mais je regarde bien la pendule.

11. Do you listen to the teacher when he is talking?

12. Not always, but I watch the clock carefully.

14. Regular verbs

Like most languages, French has a certain number of irregular verbs, such as the four already studied. The vast majority of verbs, however, fall into three "regular" conjugations:

CONJUGATION	INFINITIVE ENDING	EXAMPLE
I	er	**donner** (*to give*)
II	ir	**finir** (*to finish*)
III	re	**perdre** (*to lose*)

NOTE: The infinitive is the *to* form listed in the dictionary as the basic form of a verb.

CONJUGATION I The present tense of CONJUGATION I is formed by dropping the **er** of the infinitive and adding to this stem these endings:

e	ons
es	ez
e	ent

All these endings are silent except **ons** and **ez**.

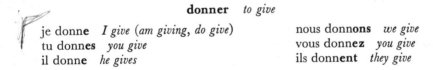

donner   *to give*

je donne	*I give (am giving, do give)*	nous donn**ons**	*we give*
tu donn**es**	*you give*	vous donn**ez**	*you give*
il donne	*he gives*	ils donn**ent**	*they give*

Peculiarities of spelling   Verbs of CONJUGATION I whose stem ends in **c** which is soft (like *s* in *sing*) in the infinitive need a cedilla under the **c** in the first person plural to keep it soft before the **o**.

nous commençons   we begin   **nous plaçons**   we place

Similarly, verbs whose stem ends in soft **g** (like *s* in *treasure*) need an **e** after the **g** to keep it soft in the first person plural.

nous mangeons   we are eating   **nous nageons**   we are swimming

NOTE: For conditions under which **c** and **g** are soft or hard, see Introduction, page xvi. Verbs ending in **yer** normally change **y** to **i** before the silent endings (**e, es, e, ent**), although this is optional with verbs in **ayer**.

> **essuyer: il essuie** *he wipes*
> **employer: ils emploient** *they use*
> BUT
> **payer: il paie** *or* **il paye** *he pays*

CONJUGATIONS II AND III   To form the present tense of CONJUGATION II, the **r** is dropped from the infinitive, and the following endings are added:

s	ssons
s	ssez
t	ssent

The singular endings, and the **ent** of the third person plural, are silent.

finir *to finish*

je fini**s**	*I finish*	nous fini**ssons**	*we finish*
tu fini**s**	*you finish*	vous fini**ssez**	*you finish*
il fini**t**	*he finishes*	ils fini**ssent**	*they finish*

The present tense of CONJUGATION III is formed by dropping the **re** of the infinitive and adding the endings **s, s, —, ons, ez, ent**. These endings are all silent except **ons** and **ez**.

perdre *to lose*

je perd**s**	*I lose*	nous perd**ons**	*we lose*
tu perd**s**	*you lose*	vous perd**ez**	*you lose*
il perd	*he loses*	ils perd**ent**	*they lose*

NOTE: Verbs of CONJUGATION III whose stems do not end in **c** or **d** add a **t** in the third person singular: romp**re** **il rompt**.

A. Combine the three elements in each line to form a sentence, making the verb agree with the subject and supplying an article for the object, as in the example. Then see how many other combinations of these subjects, verbs, and objects you can make into *natural* sentences.

> *Example:*   Il   trouver   livre
>   Il trouve le livre   *or*   Il trouve un livre.

1. Je	trouver	stylo
2. Nous	finir	devoirs
3. Jacques	employer	craie
4. Les femmes	choisir	livres
5. Vous	perdre	crayon

B. Read aloud, then reread substituting the words in parentheses for the italicized word and making any necessary changes.

1. *Vous* mangez beaucoup.   (*Nous, Jean, Tu, Elles*)
2. *Nous* essuyons le tableau noir.   (*Marie, Je, Vous, Ils*)
3. *Le professeur* commence la leçon.   (*Vous, Nous, Je, Elles*)
4. *Vous* essayez le chapeau.   (*Elle, Nous, Je, Jean*)
5. *Il* corrige les fautes.   (*Vous, Nous, Les professeurs, L'étudiante*)
6. *Nous* employons des crayons.   (*Je, Vous, Jean et Marie, Tu*)

15. Meanings of certain verbs

Certain verbs include the idea expressed in English by the verb plus a preposition. For instance, **regarder** means not only *to look* but *to look at*, **écouter** not only *to listen* but *to listen to*, **chercher** both *to look* and *to look for*, **demander** both *to ask* and *to ask for*, **payer** *to pay* and *to pay for*, **attendre** *to wait* and *to wait for*. When translating into French, the student must be careful not to express *at*, *to*, and *for* when using these verbs.

Je regarde le tableau noir.   I look at the blackboard.
Nous écoutons le monsieur.   We listen to the gentleman.
Elle cherche la craie.   She is looking for the chalk.
Ils demandent l'heure.   They are asking for the time.
Allez-vous payer les livres?   Are you going to pay for the books?
Elle attend la fin du mois.   She is waiting for the end of the month.

On the other hand, **entrer** requires a preposition in French, where English *to enter* does not.

Les messieurs entrent dans le salon.   The gentlemen enter the living room.

C. Read each sentence aloud, then reread substituting words in parentheses for italicized words and making any necessary changes.

1. Je regarde le *monsieur*.   (*étudiante, phrase, phrases, tableau noir*)
2. *Nous* cherchons les livres.   (*Je, Elle, Les étudiants, Vous*)
3. Je demande un *dictionnaire*.   (*revue, journaux, crayons, morceau de craie*)
4. Il paie le *chapeau*.   (*livres, déjeuner, revue, stylos*)
5. Attendez-*vous* le garçon?   (*il, nous, ils, elle*)
6. Nous entrons dans la *salle de classe*.   (*maison, hôtel, école, café*)

D. Express in French.

1. He listens to the children.   2. We are going to listen to the teacher.
3. We look at the blackboard.   4. They are looking for the mistakes.

5. I am looking for a dictionary.   6. We do not look at the clock.   7. Are you waiting for the teacher?   8. She is asking for the time.   9. George pays for the dinner.   10. Are the students entering the classroom?   11. Are they entering the school?   12. She tries on the hat.

16. Cardinal numerals

The cardinal numbers from *one* to *fifty* are:

1	un	16	seize
2	deux	17	dix-sept
3	trois	18	dix-huit
4	quatre	19	dix-neuf
5	cinq	20	vingt
6	six	21	vingt et un
7	sept	22	vingt-deux
8	huit	23	vingt-trois
9	neuf	30	trente
10	dix	31	trente et un
11	onze	32	trente-deux
12	douze	40	quarante
13	treize	41	quarante et un
14	quatorze	42	quarante-deux
15	quinze	50	cinquante

Et is used only with **un,** other compounds having hyphens.   All the cardinal numbers are invariable except **un,** which adds **e** before a feminine noun.

> **un homme**   one man
> **une femme**   one woman
> **vingt et une phrases**   twenty-one sentences

NOTE: The **q** of **cinq** is pronounced (like *k*), unless the following word begins with a consonant or aspirate **h: cinq arbres** [sɛ̃ karbr].   In dates, the **q** is always pronounced: **le cinq décembre** [lə sɛk desã:br], but **cinq chevaux** [sɛ̃ ʃəvo].   The **x** of **six** and **dix** is pronounced like *s* when counting, like *z* before mute **h** and vowels, but is silent before pronounced consonants.   The **f** of **neuf** is pronounced like *v* in the expression **neuf heures** (*nine o'clock*).   No *liaison* and no elision occur before **huit** and **onze: le huit octobre** [lə ɥi tɔktɔbr], **le onze novembre** [lə ɔ̃:z nɔvã:br], **les huit filles** [le ɥi fi:j], **les onze garçons** [le ɔ̃:z garsɔ̃].

quel = what before
quelle = what

17. Time of day

To ask the time of day, we say: **Quelle heure est-il?**   Possible answers are:

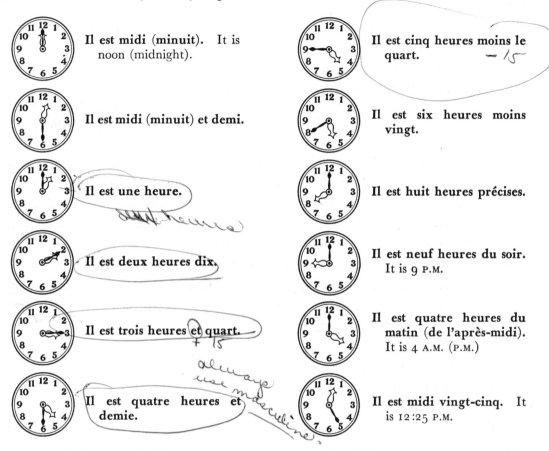

Il est midi (minuit).   It is noon (midnight).

Il est cinq heures moins le quart.   *– 15*

Il est midi (minuit) et demi.

Il est six heures moins vingt.

Il est une heure.

Il est huit heures précises.

Il est deux heures dix.

Il est neuf heures du soir.   It is 9 P.M.

Il est trois heures et quart.   *+ 15*

Il est quatre heures du matin (de l'après-midi).   It is 4 A.M. (P.M.)

Il est quatre heures et demie.   *always use masculine*

Il est midi vingt-cinq.   It is 12:25 P.M.

NOTE: *Half-past* is **demi** (masculine to agree with **midi** and **minuit**) or **demie** (feminine to agree with **heure**).

18. Dates: day and month

To ask the date, one says: **Quel jour sommes-nous?** or **Quel jour du mois est-ce?** or **Le combien sommes-nous?**   Answers may be:

> **Nous sommes samedi le treize août.**   Today is Saturday, August 13.
> **C'est aujourd'hui le vingt-huit septembre.**   Today is September 28.
> **C'est aujourd'hui lundi le premier avril.**   Today is Monday, April 1.

The months are: **janvier, février, mars** [mars], **avril, mai, juin, juillet, août** [u], **septembre, octobre, novembre, décembre.** Traditionally the names of months are not capitalized.

NOTE: In giving the date, except for "the first" (**le premier**), the numbers used are cardinals.

E. Answer in a complete sentence.

a. Quelle heure est-il?

1. *4:55* 2. *6:05* 3. *9 o'clock sharp*
4. *11:45* A.M. 5. *2:10* P.M. 6. *7:00* P.M.

b. A quelle heure commençons-nous?

1. at *5:20* 2. at *12:30* P.M. 3. at exactly *10:15*
4. at midnight 5. at *8:00* A.M. 6. at *3:25* P.M.

F. Using the formula **Un et deux font trois,** solve the following orally.

1. *4+6* 2. *2+19* 3. *7+8* 4. *10+16* 5. *24+5* 6. *12+13*
7. *41+7* 8. *18+27* 9. *35+15* 10. *20+11*

G. Quel jour sommes-nous? (Answer in a complete sentence.)

1. Saturday, July 1 2. Wednesday, September 3 3. Friday, April 7
4. Sunday, February 12 5. Tuesday, August 31 6. Monday, December 29 7. Thursday, March 13

LECTURE

Il est maintenant onze heures du matin. La classe de français ne commence pas avant onze heures dix. Le professeur arrive à l'heure aujourd'hui, et nous commençons la leçon tout de suite. A midi moins vingt M. Lasalle va au tableau noir. D'abord il donne quelques exemples de verbes à la classe. Nous écoutons bien le professeur quand il parle.

Lorsqu'il finit les verbes, le professeur commence à parler de la France. Il explique que la journée des élèves à l'école secondaire (le lycée ou le collège [1]) n'est pas exactement comme ici. Les classes commencent de bonne heure, à huit heures du matin, et continuent jusqu'à onze heures ou midi. Puis les élèves rentrent à la maison pour le déjeuner. Papa rentre aussi du bureau, et les membres de la famille

[1] The **lycée,** formerly a private school, and the **collège,** a municipal school, are now both public institutions carrying secondary education to a level roughly equivalent to our sophomore year in college.

déjeunent ensemble. Les élèves ne retournent pas à l'école avant deux heures, et les classes finissent à cinq heures du soir. Souvent, quand un élève désire poser des questions sur le devoir du lendemain, il reste plus tard.

De retour à la maison, on continue les préparations pour les classes du lendemain, ou l'on [1] a un peu de repos avant le dîner. On dîne vers huit heures du soir, et après, on essaie de finir les devoirs.

Lorsque j'entends la description de la journée des élèves, je décide que la vie en France n'a pas l'air si agréable après tout. Ici, on dîne vers six heures et demie ou sept heures, mais j'ai déjà faim à cinq heures. Comment est-il possible d'attendre si longtemps?

H. 1. Il est maintenant _____. 2. La classe de français commence à _____. 3. Nous commençons la leçon _____. 4. Le professeur donne _____ à la classe. 5. Quand il finit les verbes, le professeur commence _____. 6. En France, les classes commencent à _____. 7. Elles continuent jusqu'à _____ ou _____. 8. Les élèves _____ pour le déjeuner. 9. Les classes finissent _____. 10. Après le dîner, on essaie _____. 11. Je décide que la vie en France _____. 12. J'ai déjà faim à _____.

VOCABULARY

après tout after all
avoir faim to be hungry
de bonne heure early

de retour back
plus tard later

après after, afterward
avant before; (*with neg.*) until, before
le **chapeau** hat
choisir to choose
continuer to continue
déjeuner to have lunch
demander to ask for, ask
désirer to wish, desire
dîner to have dinner, dine
l'**élève** (*m. or f.*) pupil, student
employer to use
ensemble together
entendre to hear

essayer to try, try on; **essayer de** to try to
exactement exactly
expliquer to explain
le **jour** day
jusqu'à up to, until
le **lendemain** next day
longtemps a long time; **si longtemps** such a long time
manger to eat
le **mois** month
payer to pay for, pay
peu little, few; **un peu de** a little

---

[1] **l'** serves merely to separate the vowel sounds and has no meaning.

la **phrase** sentence
  poser to put, ask
  puis then, next
  que that, which
  quelque some; (*pl.*) a few, some

rentrer to go back, come back
le **repos** rest
  retourner to go back
  si so
  trouver to find

PATTERN SENTENCE DRILL

1. Il est près de dix heures.
  _____ deux _____.
  ____ maintenant _____.
  _____ précises.
  ____ déjà _____.

2. Nous commençons bientôt.
  Vous _____.
  ____ finissez _____.
  _____ tout de suite.
  Je _____.

3. Pas avant dix heures dix.
  ___ après _____.
  _____ trois _____.
  _____ et demie.
  _____ moins le quart.

4. Le professeur est toujours en retard.
  L'étudiant _____.
  _____ souvent _____.
  _____ de bonne heure.
  Les étudiants _____.

5. Les étudiants entrent dans la classe à l'heure.
  Le garçon _____.
  _____ la salle _____.
  _____ en retard.
  _____ de bonne heure.

6. Quelquefois nous attendons M. Lasalle plusieurs minutes.
Souvent_____.
_____ ils _____.
_____ les étudiants _____.
_____ quelques _____.

7. Il commence la leçon tout de suite.
_____ les devoirs _____.
Ils _____.
_ finissent _____.
_____ à l'heure.

8. Il essuie le tableau noir.
Nous _____.
_ regardons _____.
_____ le professeur Lasalle.
Vous _____.

9. Nous corrigeons d'abord les fautes dans le devoir.
Vous _____.
____ regardez _____.
_____ sur le tableau noir.
_____ la phrase _____.

10. Nous finissons la leçon à onze heures précises.
Il _____.
_____ lecture _____.
_____ une heure _____.
_____ et quart.

11. Écoutez-vous le professeur quand il parle?
Regardez _____?
_____ l'élève _____?
_____ les élèves _____?
_____ lorsque _____?

12. Je regarde bien la pendule.
_____ maison.
_____ longtemps ___.
_ cherche _____.
Nous _____.

4

Pronoun Objects

Imperatives

Reflexives

*Mettre, Se battre,
S'asseoir*

PATTERN SENTENCES

1. Regarde[1] la robe dans la vitrine, Alice.
2. Je la regarde, Jeanne.
3. Entrons dans la boutique l'examiner de près.
4. Bonjour, mesdemoiselles. Vous désirez . . .?
5. Montrez-nous la robe dans la vitrine, s'il vous plaît.
6. Je vous la montre volontiers, mesdemoiselles. La voici.
7. Mettez-vous près de la lumière, et regardez-la bien.
8. Elle vous plaît? Désirez-vous l'essayer?

1. Look at the dress in the shop window, Alice.
2. I am looking at it, Jean.
3. Let's go in the shop and look at it closely.
4. Good afternoon, young ladies. You wish . . .?
5. Show us the dress in the window, please.
6. I'll show it to you gladly, ladies. Here it is.
7. Stand near the light, and take a good look at it.
8. You like it?[2] Do you want to try it on?

---

[1] Since Alice and Jean are assumed to be old friends, the familiar form is used when they are addressing each other.

[2] Literally, *it pleases you?*

9. Montre-la-moi un moment, Alice, je te prie.
10. Moi,[1] je ne l'aime pas du tout.
11. Elle ne te va pas bien.
12. Eh bien, allons-nous-en! Au revoir, monsieur, et merci.

9. Let me see it a minute, Alice, please.
10. *I* don't like it at all.
11. It doesn't suit you.
12. Well, let's go. Good-bye, sir, and thank you.

19. Pronoun objects

Pronoun objects in the first and second persons are:

me	me, to me	**nous**	us, to us
te	you, to you	**vous**	you, to you

These may be direct or indirect and, except in affirmative commands, always precede the verb. In this respect they differ from noun objects which follow the verb as in English.

Le monsieur *me* regarde. The gentleman is looking at *me*.
Il *me* donne un exemplaire de *Gil Blas*. He gives (*to*) *me* a copy of *Gil Blas*.
Le professeur *vous* cherche. The teacher is looking for *you*.
Il désire *nous* montrer une carte de France. He wants to show *us* a map of France.

While the first and second person pronoun objects may be direct or indirect without change of form, the third person objects have two forms.

DIRECT		INDIRECT [2]	
le	him, it	**lui**	him, to him, her, to her, it, to it
la	her, it		
les	them	**leur**	them, to them

EXAMPLES

Je *le* trouve. I find *him (it)*.
Je *lui* donne un crayon. I give (*to*) *him (her)* a pencil.
Nous *les* regardons. We watch *them*.
Nous *leur* envoyons une lettre. We send *them* a letter.
Il *leur* parle. He talks *to them*.
Voici le crayon. *Le* désirez-vous? Here is the pencil. Do you want *it?*
Où est le stylo? *Le* voilà. Where is the pen? There *it* is.

Le and **la** elide with a vowel or mute **h** like the articles.

Où est le livre? *L'*avez-vous? Where is the book? Do you have *it?*
J'aime la maison. *L'*habitez-vous maintenant? I like the house. Are you living in *it* now?

---

[1] **Moi** is used here for emphasis.
[2] *To* is expressed or understood.

On the other hand, the pronouns **le** and **les** do not combine with **de** and **à** as the articles do.

>**Il décide *de le* faire.** He decides to do *it*.[1]
>**J'essaie *de les* trouver.** I am trying to find *them*.
>**Nous continuons *à le* faire.** We continue to do *it*.[1]

Besides the pronoun objects already listed, there is a reflexive third person **se** (referring to the subject) which may be either masculine or feminine, singular or plural, direct or indirect.

>**Il *se* corrige.** He corrects *himself*.
>**Elle *se* regarde dans la glace.** She looks at *herself* in the mirror.
>**Ils *se* parlent.** They are talking to *each* other *or* They are talking to *themselves*.

A. Respond by substituting a pronoun object for the noun, as shown in the pattern.

    a. *Pattern:* Voici les garçons; les voici.

        1. Voici la boutique; _____.
        2. Voici les robes; _____.
        3. Voici la vitrine; _____.
        4. Voilà la maison; _____.
        5. Voilà le chapeau; _____.

    b. *Pattern:* Je trouve le garçon; je le trouve.

        1. Je cherche le chapeau; _____.
        2. Il corrige la phrase; _____.
        3. J'essaie la robe; _____.
        4. Elle aime la maison; _____.
        5. Ils envoient les lettres; _____.

    c. *Pattern:* Elle donne le livre à Jacques; elle lui donne le livre.

        1. Nous donnons le crayon à l'étudiant; _____.
        2. Il prête le dictionnaire aux garçons; _____.
        3. Je parle au monsieur; _____.
        4. Nous parlons aux messieurs; _____.
        5. Parlez-vous à Louise? _____?
        6. Est-ce que tu prêtes les revues aux étudiantes? _____?

B. Answer affirmatively, using pronouns for objects, as in the examples.

>*Q.* Trouvez-vous le garçon?
>*A.* Oui, je le trouve.
>*Q.* Commence-t-elle à étudier la leçon?
>*A.* Oui, elle commence à l'étudier.

---

[1] Note that some verbs require **de**, others **à**, before a following infinitive.

1. Regardez-vous le tableau noir?
2. Est-ce que vous étudiez la le-çon?
3. Casse-t-il la craie?
4. Est-ce qu'elle décide de faire le devoir?
5. A-t-elle les crayons?
6. Est-ce qu'elles continuent à examiner le livre?
7. Regarde-t-il le professeur?
8. Est-ce qu'ils changent les phrases?
9. Parlent-ils aux messieurs?
10. Est-ce qu'ils essaient de finir la leçon?

20. Order of pronoun objects

If a direct pronoun object and an indirect pronoun object occur in the same sentence, their order before the verb is governed by the following table:

$$\left.\begin{matrix} \textbf{me} \\ \textbf{te} \\ \textbf{se} \\ \textbf{nous} \\ \textbf{vous} \end{matrix}\right\} \text{ before } \left\{\begin{matrix} \textbf{le} \\ \textbf{la} \\ \textbf{les} \end{matrix}\right\} \text{ before } \left\{\begin{matrix} \textbf{lui} \\ \textbf{leur} \end{matrix}\right.$$

EXAMPLES

Je *le lui* donne.   I give *it* to *him.*
Il *me le* donne.   He gives *it* to *me.*
Elle *nous les* donne.   She gives *them* to *us.*

Negative **ne** precedes all pronoun objects.

Elle ne *nous les* donne pas.   She does not give *them* to *us.*

21. Imperatives

Most imperatives (commands) are simply indicative forms with the subject omitted.[1]
The commonest are the second persons without **tu** and **vous.**

Finis les devoirs! Finish the assignments.
Allez vite! Go quickly!
Attendez! Wait!

CONJUGATION I omits the **s** in the singular.

Regarde! Look!
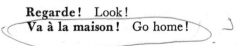
Va à la maison! Go home!

---

[1] For the few exceptions, see Unit 15, Section 86.

French also uses the first person plural as a command, where English would use the expression "Let us" or "Let's."

> **Finissons la leçon!** Let's finish the lesson!
> **N'oublions pas les cartes.** Let's not forget the maps.

If the command is affirmative, pronoun objects follow the verb like noun objects, but are connected to it by a hyphen.

> **Oublions-le!** Let's forget it.   **Parlez-lui!** Speak to him!

But if the command is negative, the objects are in their usual place before the verb.

> **Ne l'oublions pas!** Let's not forget it.
> **Ne lui parlez pas!** Don't speak to him!

Moi and **toi** replace **me** and **te** after an affirmative imperative.

> **Regardez-moi!** Look at me.
> BUT
> **Ne me regardez pas!** Don't look at me.

If more than one pronoun object follows the affirmative imperative, **le, la,** and **les** precede other objects.

> **Donnez-le-moi!** Give it to me. (BUT **Ne me le donnez pas!**)
> **Rendez-la-nous!** Give it back to us.
> **Envoyez-les-lui!** Send them to him (her).

C. Read aloud, then reread substituting pronouns for the expressions in italics.

1. Je trouve *le livre.*
2. Nous parlons *aux enfants.*
3. Vendez-vous *la maison?*
4. Regardez *le tableau!*
5. Finissons *les devoirs!*
6. Corrige *la faute.*
7. Ne cassez pas *la vitrine!*
8. Donnez-moi *la lettre!*
9. N'oublions pas *les crayons.*
10. Je vais vous envoyer *le journal.*[1]
11. Il donne *le livre au monsieur.*
12. Ne montrez pas *la lettre à la dame!*

22. Reflexives

A reflexive verb is one whose subject and object are one and the same, as "She *hit herself* in the eye," or "The children *saw themselves* reflected in the water." In French are found not only such obvious and literal examples but also many which have no equivalent in English usage. For instance, *to go to bed* in French is **se coucher** and *to sit down* is **s'asseoir.** Once such constructions were common in English, as in "now I

---

[1] The object pronoun precedes the infinitive but not the main verb, unless it is the object of the main verb.

lay me down to sleep," "*get thee* gone," and the like, but today reflexives are much less common than in French. Following are some examples illustrating the meanings of nonreflexive and reflexive forms (it is customary to list reflexive infinitives with the third person singular reflexive pronoun **se**). These common verbs should be committed to memory.

aller to go	**s'en aller** to go away
asseoir to seat	**s'asseoir** to sit down
battre to beat	**se battre** to fight
coucher to put to bed	**se coucher** to go to bed, lie down
dépêcher to dispatch, dismiss	**se dépêcher** to hurry, hasten
habiller to clothe, dress	**s'habiller** to get dressed
mettre to put, put on (clothes)	**se mettre** to place oneself, stand
	se mettre à to start to, set about
	se mettre en route to start out
trouver to find	**se trouver** to be, be located, be found

begin *always followed by inf*

23. Present tense of *mettre* and the reflexives *se battre* and *s'asseoir*

mettre	**se battre**	**s'asseoir**
to put	*to fight*	*to sit down*
je mets	je me bats	je m'assieds [1]
tu mets	tu te bats	tu t'assieds
il met	il se bat	il s'assied
nous mettons	nous nous battons	nous nous asseyons
vous mettez	vous vous battez	vous vous asseyez
ils mettent	ils se battent	ils s'asseyent

In the imperative, reflexive objects obey the general rule for pronoun objects, following the verb in the affirmative, preceding it in the negative.

> **Dépêchez-vous!**   Hurry up!
> **Ne vous dépêchez pas!**   Don't hurry.
> **Couche-toi tout de suite!**   Go to bed immediately.
> **Ne te couche pas trop tard.**   Don't go to bed too late.
> **Mettons-nous en route!**   Let's get started.
> **Ne nous mettons pas en route si tôt.**   Let's not start so soon.

When a reflexive infinitive occurs, its reflexive object changes to agree with its logical subject.

> **Je vais *me* coucher.**   I am going to go to bed.
> **Les garçons vont *se* coucher.**   The boys are going to go to bed.

---

[1] For alternative forms of this highly irregular verb, see Appendix, page 220.

D. Substitution Drill.

1. *Je* m'habille vite. (*Tu, Nous, Elle, Vous*)
2. *Nous* nous en allons bientôt. (*Je, Il, Ils, Tu*)
3. *Il* se met en route tout de suite. (*Ils, Vous, Je, Elle*)
4. *Je* me bats avec les garçons. (*Nous, Elle, Elles, Vous*)
5. Se dépêche-t-*elle* de finir les phrases? (*Elles, Vous, Il, Tu*)
6. *Je* ne me couche pas de bonne heure. (*Il, Nous, Ils, Elle*)
7. *Nous* nous asseyons près de la fenêtre. (*Tu, Il, Vous, Ils*)

E. Read aloud, then reread substituting the verb in parentheses for the verb in the sentence.

1. Mettez-vous ici, s'il vous plaît. (s'asseoir)
2. Alors, va-t'en ! [1] (se dépêcher)
3. Habillons-nous de bonne heure. (se mettre en route)
4. Ne vous battez pas, messieurs ! (se dépêcher)
5. Ne nous couchons pas. (s'asseoir)

F. Express in French.

1. Is he going to give us the dictionary? 2. Is he going to give it to us? 3. He is looking for them. 4. She is going to try them on. 5. Go to school ! [2] 6. Let's go look for them ! 7. Go away ! 8. I am going to show her the mistakes. 9. Don't speak to them ! 10. He always goes to bed on time. 11. We start out at six o'clock in the morning. 12. Do John and Julius fight often? 13. She puts on the hat. 14. I'm going to look at it up close. 15. Don't stand near the door. 16. The dress suits her very well ! [3]

LECTURE

Lorsque le professeur entre dans la classe ce matin, il indique la carte de France au mur, et se met à nous parler ainsi:

« Regardez la carte ! [4] Voici la France, et voilà la Manche au nord. »

Alors il nous explique que la France, autrefois un assemblage [5] de provinces, se

---

[1] **En** always follows other pronoun objects. In the familiar command form of **s'en aller, toi** is replaced by **t'**.
[2] Give both **tu** and **vous** forms for imperatives.
[3] "Her" will be indirect object.
[4] See map on page 82.
[5] **un assemblage** *collection*

divise actuellement en départements. D'ordinaire la géographie du pays détermine le nom du département, par exemple, au nord-ouest, « la Manche, » et au sud-est, « les Bouches du Rhône. »

Puis le professeur nous parle des fleuves, et il nous les indique sur la carte.

« Mettez-vous ici un moment, s'il vous plaît! » continue-t-il.

Nous nous mettons devant la carte.

« Avez-vous un crayon? » me demande-t-il.

Je lui réponds: « Oui, monsieur.

— Prêtez-le-moi un moment, je vous prie. Voici la Loire. Regardez-la bien, et remarquez que la source se trouve dans le Massif Central. Le fleuve passe par un pays riche en histoire, et puis se jette [1] dans l'Atlantique près de la ville de Nantes. Les villes de Paris et de Rouen se trouvent sur la Seine, qui coule [2] vers la Manche. Remarquez combien la Seine serpente, [3] surtout en Normandie. »

Le professeur continue à parler un peu, mais enfin il s'arrête et nous nous asseyons. Quand l'heure sonne, tout le monde s'en va. Je me mets en route pour la ville avec un ami, et je lui demande: « Jacques, est-ce que tu t'intéresses à l'histoire de France?

— Oui, je m'intéresse surtout à la Révolution, me répond-il.

— Allons donc au cinéma cet après-midi. Dans le film il s'agit de la vie de Marie-Antoinette.

— Vraiment? Mais n'est-il pas trop tard? Il est presque quatre heures.

— Non, on ne commence pas avant quatre heures et quart le vendredi. Alors, dépêche-toi ! » [4]

G. 1. Le professeur entre ＿＿ et se met ＿＿. 2. Autrefois la France était un assemblage de ＿＿. 3. Actuellement la France se divise en ＿＿. 4. D'ordinaire la géographie du pays détermine ＿＿. 5. Le professeur indique ＿＿ sur la carte. 6. Il me demande: « Avez-vous ＿＿? » 7. Je ＿＿ réponds: « Oui, monsieur. » 8. Alors il me dit: « Prêtez-＿＿. » 9. La Seine passe par les villes de ＿＿. 10. Quand le professeur s'arrête, nous ＿＿. 11. Après la classe, tout le monde ＿＿. 12. Jacques s'intéresse surtout à ＿＿.

---

[1] **se jette** *empties*
[2] **coule** *flows*
[3] **serpente** *winds, twists*
[4] Written conversations in French generally begin and close with quotation marks, but change of speaker throughout the body of the conversation is indicated simply by a dash.

VOCABULARY

d'ordinaire usually
s'agir de to be about, be concerned with

  actuellement now, today
  ainsi thus, in this way
  s'arrêter to stop (**de** *before following infinitive*)
  l'Atlantique Atlantic Ocean
  autrefois formerly, once
  casser to break
  changer to change
  combien how much
la **dame** lady
  décider to decide
  diviser to divide; **se diviser** to be divided
  donc then, therefore
  enfin finally, at last
  envoyer to send
  l'est (*m.*) east
  étudier to study
le **fleuve** river
  indiquer to indicate
  s'intéresser (à) to be interested (in)

tout le monde everybody

la **lettre** letter
la **Manche** English Channel
le **nom** name
le **nord** north
la **Normandie** Normandy
  oublier to forget
  l'ouest (*m.*) west
  par by, through
  presque nearly, almost
  prêter to lend
  qui who, which
  remarquer to notice, note
  répondre (à) to reply (to), answer
  riche rich
  sans without
  sonner to strike, sound, ring
le **sud** south
  surtout especially
  trop too, too much, too many
  vendre to sell
  vite quickly, fast

PATTERN SENTENCE DRILL

1. Regarde la robe dans la vitrine.
  _____ livre _____.
  Regardez _____.
  _____ sur le bureau.
  Mets _____.

2. Je la regarde.
  _ les _____.
  ____ cherche.
  Vous _____.
  ____ cherchons.

3. Entrons dans la boutique l'examiner de près.
   _____ maison _____.
   _____ les _____.
   Entrez _____.
   _____ regarder _____.

4. Montrez-nous la robe dans la vitrine.
   Donnez _____.
   _____ -lui _____.
   _____ chapeau _____.
   _____ -moi _____.

5. Je vous la montre volontiers.
   Elle _____.
   __ nous _____.
   _____ les _____.
   _____ tout de suite.

6. Mettez-vous près de la lumière.
   _____ -toi _____.
   _____ table.
   _____ derrière _____.
   Mettons _____.

7. Regardez-la bien.
   Examinez _____.
   _____ -les _____.
   Examinons _____.
   _____ de près.

8. Elle vous plaît?
   _____ te _____?
   _____ lui _____?
   _____ répond?
   Il _____?

9. Désirez-vous l'essayer?
   _____ -il _____?
   _____ les _____?
   _____ vendre?
   _____ -ils _____?

10. Montre-la-moi un moment !
    Donne _____ !
    _____ -les _____ !
    _____ -nous _____ !
    _____ tout de suite !

11. Je ne l'aime pas du tout.
    ____ les _____.
    ____ désire _____.
    Il _____.
    ____ désirons _____.

12. Elle ne te va pas bien.
    _____ vous _____.
    _____ lui _____.
    Elles _____.
    _____ me _____.

5

Adjectives

Adjectives as Nouns

Il y a vs. *Voilà*

Dire, Lire, Écrire, Vivre

PATTERN SENTENCES

1. Y a-t-il un bon restaurant dans ce quartier?
2. Oui, il y a un bon restaurant tout près d'ici.
3. Est-ce que les repas sont chers dans cet établissement?
4. Pas trop chers, et la cuisine est excellente.
5. Les propriétaires sont un Parisien et une Parisienne.
6. Je suis content d'apprendre cela, car j'aime la cuisine française.
7. Eh bien, où se trouve ce restaurant?
8. Le voilà de l'autre côté de la rue, numéro quarante-cinq.
9. Voici la carte. Voyons, qu'est-ce qu'il y a de bon?
10. Je lis: « Bifteck aux pommes frites, avec haricots verts. »

1. Is there a good restaurant in this section?
2. Yes, there is a good restaurant very near here.
3. Are the meals expensive in this place?
4. Not too expensive, and the cooking is excellent.
5. The proprietors are a Parisian man and woman.
6. I am glad to learn that, for I love French cooking.
7. Well, where is this restaurant?
8. There it is on the other side of the street, number 45.
9. Here is the menu. Let's see, what is there that's good?
10. I read: "Steak and French fried potatoes, with string beans."

11. Fameux! C'est un plat délicieux.
Dites! Avez-vous faim?

12. Si j'ai faim? Mon ami, je ne mange
pas pour vivre — je vis pour manger!

11. Wonderful! It's a delicious dish.
Say! Are you hungry?

12. Am I hungry? My friend, I don't
eat to live — I live to eat!

24. Adjectives: position and agreement

Adjectives in French differ in two important respects from those in English.

1. Descriptive adjectives generally follow the noun.

> **un chien blanc**   a white dog
> **une ville anglaise**   an English city
> **un livre intéressant**   an interesting book
> **des animaux sauvages**   wild animals
> **une boîte carrée**   a square box
> **un étudiant américain**   an American student

2. While in English only the limiting adjectives *this* and *that* show agreement (by becoming *these* and *those* in the plural), in French all adjectives, regardless of position in the sentence, agree with the noun they modify in both gender and number.

> *ce* **garçon**   *this* boy
> *cette* **femme**   *this* woman
>
> **la maison** *verte*   the *green* house
> **les maisons** *vertes*   the *green* houses
>
> **Le devoir est** *difficile*.   The assignment is *hard*.
> **Les devoirs sont** *difficiles*.   The assignments are *hard*.
>
> **Le professeur est** *fatigué*.   The teacher is *tired*.
> **La famille est** *fatiguée*.   The family is *tired*.

The following common adjectives usually precede the noun, as in English.

beau	beautiful, handsome	**joli**	pretty
bon	good, kind	**long**	long
court	short	**mauvais**	bad, wrong
gentil	nice	**méchant**	naughty, wicked
gros	big, bulky, fat	**nouveau**	new
haut	tall, high	**petit**	small
jeune	young	**vieux**	old

The limiting (nondescriptive) adjectives also precede the noun.

ce	this, that	**plusieurs**	several
tel	such	**nul**	no, not any
autre	other	**aucun**	no, not any
quelque	some	**premier**	first
quelques	some, a few	**chaque**	each

Certain adjectives have different meanings when preceding or following a noun.

un pauvre homme   a poor (unfortunate) man
un homme pauvre   a poor (impoverished) man
un brave homme   a worthy man, a good fellow
un homme brave   a brave man
un cher ami   a dear friend
un livre cher   a dear (expensive) book
un grand homme   a great man
un homme grand   a tall man
la dernière semaine   the last week (of a given period of time)
la semaine dernière   last week (the week before the present one)
un seul homme   only one man
un homme seul   a man alone, a lonely man

25. Forms of adjectives

Most adjectives are made feminine by simply adding **e** to the masculine. Those ending already in an unaccented (silent) **e** remain unchanged.

grand, grande tall   **bleu, bleue** blue   **carré, carrée** square
sage, sage wise   **rose, rose** pink   **sale, sale** dirty

Some adjectives double the consonant before adding the **e**.

bon, bonne good   **pareil, pareille** similar   **net, nette** neat
tel, telle such   **gros, grosse** fat   **bas, basse** low

Adjectives ending in **er** take a grave accent on the **e** before the feminine ending.

dernier, dernière last   **cher, chère** dear   **premier, première** first

NOTE: The linking of the final consonant of some adjectives to the initial vowel or mute **h** of a following word causes phonetic changes which appear to make a masculine sound like a feminine. E.g. **bon** [bɔ̃], but **bon enfant** [bɔnɑ̃fɑ̃]; **premier** [prəmje], but **premier homme** [prəmjɛrɔm]; etc.

Adjectives in **eux** usually change to **euse** for the feminine.

heureux, heureuse happy   **joyeux, joyeuse** merry   **creux, creuse** hollow

A few adjectives have irregular feminines:

ce, cette this, that   **faux, fausse** false
blanc, blanche white   **public, publique** public
sec, sèche dry   **vieux, vieille** old
frais, fraîche cool, fresh   **beau, belle** beautiful
doux, douce sweet, mild   **nouveau, nouvelle** new
long, longue long   **fou, folle** mad, crazy

Four of these adjectives have special masculine singular forms before a vowel or mute **h**:

ce monsieur   *cet* homme   le vieux château   un *vieil* ami
un beau jour   un *bel* enfant   un nouveau livre   un *nouvel* hôtel

Adjectives form their plurals like nouns by adding **s** or **x**, remaining unchanged if they already end in **s** or **x**.

bon, bons
bonne, bonnes } good

heureux, heureux
heureuse, heureuses } happy

beau (bel), beaux
belle, belles } beautiful

gris, gris
grise, grises } gray

The plural of both **ce** and **cette** is **ces**. The masculine plural of **tout** (*all*) is **tous**.

NOTE: **Ce (cet), cette** may mean either *this* or *that*, and **ces** may mean either *these* or *those*. To make a distinction between *this* (*these*) and *that* (*those*), **-ci** or **-là** may be added to the noun: **ce livre-ci,** *this book;* **ce livre-là**, *that book;* **ces livres-ci,** *these books;* **ces livres-là,** *those books.* However, **-ci** and **-là** are used only when the distinction is indispensable, or when emphasis is intended.

A. Complete the following sentences, using the pattern as a model.

a. *Pattern:* Ce restaurant est bon; c'est un bon restaurant.
  1. Ce chapeau est nouveau; _____.
  2. Ce chien est petit; _____.
  3. Ce garçon est jeune; _____.
  4. Ce livre est gros; _____.
  5. Cet enfant est méchant; _____.
  6. Cette rue est longue; _____.
  7. Cette histoire est courte; _____.
  8. Cette maison est vieille; _____.
  9. Cette dame est belle; _____.
  10. Cette robe est jolie; _____.

b. *Pattern:* Ce repas est cher; c'est un repas cher.
  1. Ce livre est intéressant; _____.
  2. Ce devoir est difficile; _____.
  3. Ce chapeau est sale; _____.
  4. Ce chien est blanc; _____.
  5. Cet animal est sauvage; _____.
  6. Cet enfant est sage; _____.
  7. Cet étudiant est fatigué; _____.
  8. Cette robe est bleue; _____.

9. Cette boîte est carrée; _____.
10. Cette femme est heureuse; _____.

B. Complete each sentence in **A** by making it plural, following the pattern below.

Pattern: Ce stylo est bleu; ces stylos sont bleus.

C. Substitution Drill.

1. Ce *bifteck* est très sec. (*viande, vins*)
2. Les *repas* sont très chers. (*boutique, livres*)
3. *Jean* est bien gentil. (*Jeanne, Les enfants*)
4. C'est un beau *garçon*, n'est-ce pas? (*enfant, étudiante*)
5. Cette *dame*-là est canadienne. (*monsieur, professeurs*)
6. Ce jeune *homme* est heureux. (*femme, hommes*)
7. Le premier *devoir* n'est pas long. (*leçon, phrases*)
8. Un tel *ami* est rare. (*amie, amis* [1])
9. J'ai un nouveau *chapeau* gris. (*robe, cahiers*)
10. Est-ce que l'*eau* est fraîche? (*pain, haricots verts*)

26. Adjectives used as nouns

Adjectives are frequently used as nouns. If the nouns are abstract, the gender is masculine singular.

le vrai   the true   **le beau**   the beautiful

If they refer to people or things, they have the gender and number of the noun replaced or understood.

la belle   the beauty (i.e., the beautiful woman)
le grand   the tall (fellow)
les riches   the rich
Voici les bonnes pommes, et voilà les mauvaises.   Here are the good apples, and there are the bad (ones).
Il y a un grand paquet et un petit.   There is a big package and a small (one).

27. Nouns like adjectives

Many personal nouns have two forms, as though they were adjectives.

un ami   a (male) friend   **une amie**   a (girl) friend
un étudiant   a student   **une étudiante**   a co-ed

---

[1] Plural of **un tel** is **de tels**. **Des** becomes **de** when an adjective precedes the noun. See Unit 8, Section 43.

un **Français** a Frenchman	une **Française** a Frenchwoman
un **Parisien** a Parisian	une **Parisienne** a Parisian woman
un **acteur** an actor	une **actrice** an actress
un **masseur** a masseur	une **masseuse** a masseuse
un **danseur** a dancer	une **danseuse** a dancer

28. Infinitives with adjectives

Adjectives governing an infinitive do so by means of a preposition, some adjectives using **de,** some **à.**

> **Je suis content *de* le faire.** I am glad to do it.
> **Nous sommes heureux *d'*accepter le cadeau.** We are happy to accept the gift.
> **Il est prêt *à* commencer.** He is ready to begin.
> **Cette leçon est difficile *à* étudier.** This lesson is hard to study.

In the case of **difficile,** if the subject is impersonal **il,** the preposition is **de.** This is true of any adjective used with impersonal **il.** E.g., **Il est difficile de faire le devoir. Il est impossible de fermer la porte. Il est intéressant de visiter les cathédrales.**

29. *Il y a* vs. *voilà*

Il y a and **voilà** are both translated *there is* or *there are.* **Il y a,** however, merely states existence, while **voilà** points out. Both may mention location, but only **voilà** actually points to it. **Il y a** in effect answers such questions as "Is there any?" "Are there any?" "How many are there?" or "How much is there?" whereas **voilà** answers the question "Where?" Finally, **il y a** has an interrogative form (**y a-t-il?**), while **voilà** does not.

> **Y a-t-il des paquets ici?** Are there some packages here?
> **Oui, il y a des paquets ici.** Yes, there are some packages here.
> **Où sont les paquets?** Where are the packages?
> **Les voilà sur la table.** There they are on the table.
> **Il y a vingt personnes dans le théâtre.** There are twenty people in the theater.
> **Les voilà au premier rang.** There they are in the first row.

D. Express in French.

1. Are there some books here? 2. Yes, there is a large book and a small (one). 3. There they are on the blue chair. 4. This story is short. 5. The other is very interesting. 6. It is difficult to begin this lesson. 7. It (i.e. the lesson) is difficult to begin. 8. I like the last story very much.[1] 9. There are also several large maps. 10. There are the maps

---

[1] The adverb follows the verb directly.

on the wall.   11. There is a box on the table.   12. There is the box, on the table.   13. I am going to send it to a friend, a French actress.   14. She is always glad to have such a[1] book.

30. Irregular present tenses

dire *to say, tell*		**lire** *to read*	
je dis	nous disons	je lis	nous lisons
tu dis	vous dites	tu lis	vous lisez
il dit	ils disent	il lit	ils lisent

écrire *to write*		**vivre** *to live, exist*	
j'écris	nous écrivons	je vis	nous vivons
tu écris	vous écrivez	tu vis	vous vivez
il écrit	ils écrivent	il vit	ils vivent

NOTE: Only three common verbs in French have a **tes** ending in the second person plural of the present tense: **être, faire,** and **dire.**   All others end in **ez.**

E. Substitution Drill.

1. *Il* lit un livre intéressant.   (*Vous, Elles, Nous, Je*)
2. *Elle* ne dit pas de telles choses.   (*Nous, Vous, Jean, Ils*)
3. *Il* vit pour manger!   (*Nous, Je, Vous, Les étudiants*)
4. *J'*écris une lettre à un vieil ami.   (*Tu, Elle, Nous, Vous*)
5. *Marie* lui dit un seul mot.   (*Je, Nous, Tu, Vous*)
6. Est-ce que *vous* lisez chaque phrase?   (*il, tu, ils, nous*)
7. *Nous* vivons avec une famille anglaise.   (*Jean, Les étudiants, Vous, Tu*)
8. *Il* m'écrit plusieurs lettres.   (*Vous, Tu, Jeanne, Ils*)
9. Que dites-*vous* de cet accident?   (*ils, on, tu, elle*)
10. Pourquoi n'écrivez-*vous* pas quelquefois?   (*il, elles, tu, ils*)

F. Express in French.

1. Is he still living?   2. We are writing them a letter.   3. They are reading it.   4. Is she writing him a card?   5. What are you saying? 6. Read that lesson now.   7. Don't write the assignment.   8. Tell it to him.   9. Let's read the story together.   10. I am going to write to him immediately.

---

[1] The article precedes in French. See **C 8.**

LECTURE

Un jour je vais chez Jacques et je lui demande: « Jacques, prête-moi ce livre que tu as sur la France, je te prie.

— Volontiers. Le voilà sur la table.

— Je vais lire quelques pages sur la vie française. Ah ! qu'il est lourd, ce livre ! Merci, je te le rends demain.

— Bon ! Ne lis pas trop, ou tu vas te donner mal à la tête. A demain ! »

C'est un gros livre, avec de jolies images. Il y a des illustrations de plusieurs rues caractéristiques,[1] avec de beaux immeubles de toutes sortes. En général, les maisons sont les unes sur les autres [2] dans les villes, et même dans les petits villages. Les maisons détachées sont assez rares, sauf dans les quartiers riches. Très souvent aussi, il faut acheter les appartements; d'ordinaire on ne les loue pas, comme ici. Dans chaque immeuble il y a un concierge ou une concierge. Cette personne s'occupe de garder [3] l'immeuble, de distribuer le courrier, et de bavarder avec les habitants.

Le livre explique que la vie française n'est pas tout à fait pareille à la vie américaine. Par exemple, les marchés où l'on achète les provisions sont souvent en plein air. Et il n'y a pas toujours un frigidaire dans l'appartement, donc on fait le marché plusieurs fois par semaine, et même tous les jours. Par conséquent, tous les fruits, tous les légumes, et toutes les viandes sont très frais. Voilà peut-être pourquoi la cuisine française est si bonne. On dit que les Français aiment faire la cuisine et aiment manger. Mais le petit déjeuner me semble vraiment petit — seulement une tasse de café au lait [4] et un petit pain, ou peut-être une tasse de chocolat avec un croissant.[5]

Je m'intéresse beaucoup à la vie française. Je vais écrire ce soir à une amie française pour lui demander de me raconter les détails de la vie là-bas. Y a-t-il vraiment du vin avec chaque repas, même pour les enfants?

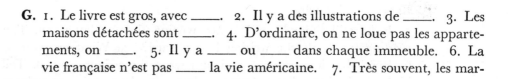

G. 1. Le livre est gros, avec ____. 2. Il y a des illustrations de ____. 3. Les maisons détachées sont ____. 4. D'ordinaire, on ne loue pas les appartements, on ____. 5. Il y a ____ ou ____ dans chaque immeuble. 6. La vie française n'est pas ____ la vie américaine. 7. Très souvent, les mar-

---

[1] **caractéristique** *typical*
[2] **les unes sur les autres** *on top of each other*, i.e., very close together.
[3] Note that French infinitives are often translated by the English present participle.
[4] **le café au lait** coffee served with a generous amount of hot milk.
[5] **le croissant** flaky breakfast roll in crescent shape.

chés sont ____. 8. On fait ____ tous les jours. 9. Voilà peut-être pourquoi ____. 10. Pour le petit déjeuner on mange ____. 11. Je m'intéresse beaucoup ____. 12. Je vais demander à une amie française ____.

VOCABULARY[1]

A demain! See you tomorrow!
chez Jacques   at, to Jim's
en plein air   outdoors
faire la cuisine   to cook
faire le marché   to shop

   acheter   to buy
   bavarder   to gossip, chat
la boîte   box, can
le chien   dog
le concierge   superintendent, caretaker
le courrier   mail
   détaché[2]   detached, separate
   distribuer   to distribute
l'eau (*f.*)   water
   garder   to guard, keep
un habitant   resident, inhabitant
une image   picture
un immeuble   house, building, property
   là-bas   there, over there
le légume   vegetable

par conséquent   consequently
plusieurs fois par semaine (jour)   several
  times a week (day)
Qu'il est lourd!   How heavy it is!
s'occuper de   to take charge of

   louer   to rent, hire
le marché   market
   même   even
le mot   word
le pain   bread; petit pain   roll
le petit déjeuner   breakfast
   peut-être   perhaps
   raconter   to tell, relate
   rendre   to give back
   sauf   except
   sembler   to seem, appear to be
   seulement   only, except
la tasse   cup
la viande   meat
le vin   wine

PATTERN SENTENCE DRILL

1. Y a-t-il un bon restaurant dans ce quartier?
_____ nouveau _____?
_____ville?
_____ immeuble _____?
_____ de nouveaux _____?

---

[1] In addition to this vocabulary, the student should know the common adjectives given in the body of this lesson.
[2] The feminine of adjectives will not be given unless irregular.

2. Il y a un bon restaurant tout près d'ici.

_____ vieux _____.

_____ maison _____.

_____ dans cette rue.

_____ petite _____.

3. Est-ce que les repas sont chers dans cet établissement?

_____ restaurant?

_____ bons _____?

_____ le pain _____?

_____ frais _____?

4. La cuisine est excellente.

__vin_____.

_____ sont _____.

_____ chers.

Les maisons _____.

5. Je suis content d'apprendre cela.

__ sommes _____.

Il _____.

_____ heureux _____.

Elle _____.

6. J'aime la cuisine française.

_____ italienne.

Nous _____.

_____ vin _____.

_____ les _____.

7. Où se trouve ce restaurant?

_____ fleuve?

___ est _____?

_____ monsieur?

_____ messieurs?

8. Le voilà de l'autre côté de la rue.

Les _____.

_____ de ce côté _____.

_____ salle.

_____ au milieu _____.

9. Qu'est-ce qu'il y a de bon?

   _____ intéressant?

   _____ ils trouvent _____?

   _____ joli?

   _____ vous avez _?

10. C'est un plat délicieux.

    _____ viande _____.

    _____ excellente.

    _____ repas _____.

    ____ des _____.

6

PATTERN SENTENCES

1. Hier Louise est allée à l'école à pied.	1. Yesterday Louise walked to school.
2. Elle s'est mise en route de bonne heure.	2. She started out early.
3. Près de la porte, elle a trouvé une montre par terre.	3. Near the door, she found a watch on the ground.
4. Elle s'est arrêtée et l'a ramassée.	4. She stopped and picked it up.
5. A l'école, elle a donné la montre au professeur.	5. At school, she gave the watch to the teacher.
6. « Où l'avez-vous trouvée? a-t-il demandé.	6. "Where did you find it?" he asked.
7. Je l'ai perdue hier après-midi ! »	7. "I lost it yesterday afternoon !"
8. Louise ne s'est pas assise tout de suite.	8. Louise did not sit down right away.
9. D'abord, elle a causé un moment avec une amie.	9. First she chatted a moment with a friend.
10. « Dis donc ! As-tu fini les devoirs?	10. "Say ! Have you finished the exercises?

54

11. Moi, je ne les ai même pas com- mencés !	11. *I* haven't even started them !
12. Je me suis lavé les cheveux [1] hier soir. »	12. I washed my hair last night."

31. Past participles

Participles are verb forms having certain characteristics of adjectives. Past participles indicate a completed state, as *done, gone, written.* The past participles of the three regular conjugations end in **é, i, u.**

donner	finir	perdre
donné *given*	**fini** *finished*	**perdu** *lost*

Past participles of irregular verbs are themselves often irregular. (Henceforth they are indicated in parentheses in the vocabularies.) Those for irregular verbs already treated are given below.

avoir **eu**	mettre **mis**	lire **lu**
être **été**	dire **dit**	vivre **vécu**
faire **fait**	écrire **écrit**	asseoir **assis**

Since the past participle is partly adjectival, it has a feminine ending in **e,** a masculine plural in **s,** and a feminine plural in **es.**

donné, donnée   donnés, données   **perdu, perdue   perdus, perdues**

Although past participles are sometimes used as simple adjectives (i.e., a *given* question, a *completed* project, a *written* answer), their principal use in both French and English is for making compound tenses.

32. *Passé composé*

Both in English and in French the past participle of a verb plus the present tense of *have* make up the past indefinite tense or *passé composé* (sometimes known as the "present perfect").

j'ai donné I have given	**ils ont eu** they have had
il a dormi he has slept	**elle a été** she has been
nous avons perdu we have lost	

Formerly, *be* as well as *have* was used in English as an auxiliary. (Cf. the King James Bible: "I *am come* that ye may have life," "For as yet he *was fallen* upon none of them," "When the angel *was departed.*") Though lost in English, this usage persists in French

---

[1] Note that the French use the plural in referring to one's hair.

in about a dozen verbs. None of these verbs, when compounded with **être**, takes a direct object, practically all being verbs of motion or change of condition. The following list of verbs compounded with **être** should be memorized.

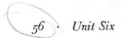

aller to go	**rester** to stay	**naître** to be born
venir to come	**tomber** to fall	**mourir** to die
entrer to come in	**arriver** to arrive	**monter** to go up
sortir to go out	**partir** to leave	**descendre** to go down
retourner to go back		

The same is true of any of these verbs with a prefix, such as **revenir, rentrer, survenir,** so long as they have no direct object. **Passer** (*to pass*) is found sometimes with **avoir,** sometimes with **être.** If any of the above verbs is used with a direct object, it takes **avoir** as auxiliary.

IMPORTANT: All reflexive verbs, whether their object is direct or not, are compounded with **être.**

>   **Je me suis caché derrière l'arbre.**   I hid behind the tree.

The only verbs in the **être** list above having irregular past participles are **venir** (**venu**), **naître** (**né**), and **mourir** (**mort**). Keep in mind that to translate *I have arrived*, French says **Je *suis* arrivé** (I *am* arrived).

Interrogative sentences in the *passé composé* show the following order:

>   **Avez-vous écouté le disque?**   Have you listened to the record?
>   **Est-elle déjà partie?**   Has she already left?
>   **Le garçon s'est-il fait beaucoup de mal?**   Did the boy hurt himself much?
>   **N'ont-ils pas terminé la réunion?**   Haven't they finished the meeting?
>   **Ne sommes-nous pas encore arrivés au sommet?**   Haven't we gotten to the top yet?
>   **Les messieurs ne se sont-ils pas entendus?**   Didn't the gentlemen come to an agreement?

In the negative, **pas** follows the auxiliary rather than the past participle.

>   **Ils n'ont pas réussi.**   They did not succeed.
>   **Elle n'est pas revenue.**   She did not come back.

The *passé composé*, which may represent either the present perfect or the simple past in English, is the correct and natural tense to translate the simple past in conversational or informal French.

Je suis venu. I came (I have come).	**J'ai entendu.** I heard (I have heard).
Nous nous sommes assis. We sat down.	**Nous sommes partis.** We left.
Elle est sortie. She went out.	**Elle a fini de bonne heure.** She finished early.

33. Agreement of past participle

Briefly, the rules of agreement are as follows.

1. As a simple adjective, or in a compound tense of one of the **être** verbs listed above, the past participle agrees like any adjective.

> **une question donnée**   a given question
> **La leçon est terminée.**   The lesson is finished.
> **Elles sont arrivées.**   They arrived.
> **Nous sommes partis.**   We left.
> **Elle est morte.**   She died. *or* She is dead.

2. In any verb which may take a direct object, agreement is with a *preceding* direct object only.   If there is no direct object, or if the direct object does not precede the verb, there is no agreement.

> **Je les ai entendus.**   I heard them.
> **Il nous a entendus.**   He heard us.
> **Où est la dame? L'avez-vous trouvée?**   Where is the lady?   Have you found her?
> **Combien de livres a-t-elle trouvés?**   How many books did she find?
> **Voici la montre qu'il m'a prêtée.**   Here is the watch that he lent me.
> BUT
> **Elle a pleuré.**   She wept.   (no object, hence no agreement)
> **Il nous a parlé.**   He spoke to us.   (Object is not direct.)
> **J'ai regardé la porte.**   I looked at the door.   (Object is direct, but does not precede.)

In reflexive verbs, agreement depends on whether the reflexive object is direct or not.

> **Elle s'est cachée.**   She hid herself.   (direct)
> **Elle s'est donné beaucoup de mal.**   She took (i.e., gave herself) a lot of trouble.   (indirect)
> **Elle s'est lavé les cheveux.**   (Direct object is **les cheveux.**)

When it is not clear whether the object is direct, it is best to make the participle agree on general principles.   The common reflexive **s'en aller** shows agreement: **nous nous en sommes allés.**

A. Substitution Drill.

   a. 1. *Louise* a lu un livre intéressant.   (*Nous, Ils, Vous, Tu*)
      2. Avez-*vous* trouvé la montre?   (*il, tu, ils, elle*)
      3. *Je* l'ai perdue ce matin.   (*Nous, Jean, Vous, Elles*)
      4. *Il* n'a pas fait le devoir.   (*Ils, Nous, Jeanne, Tu*)
      5. *Elle* me les a donnés hier.   (*Vous, Les garçons, Il, Tu*)
   b. 1. *Il* est déjà parti.   (*Elle, Nous, Vous, Jean et Pierre*)
      2. *Nous* sommes rentrés hier soir.   (*Il, Elles, Vous, Ils*)

3. N'est-*elle* pas encore arrivée?   (*ils, elles, il, nous*)
4. *Je* suis né en décembre.   (*Il, Vous, Elle, Elles*)
5. *Ils* sont venus ce matin.   (*Elle, Je, Nous, Il*)

c. 1. *Il* s'est cassé la jambe.   (*Elle, Ils, Vous, Tu*)
2. *Je* me suis habillé de bonne heure.   (*Vous, Nous, Il, Elle*)
3. *Ils* s'en sont allés tout de suite.   (*Elles, Tu, Vous, Il*)
4. *Il* ne s'est pas lavé les mains.   (*Elle, Vous, Ils, Je*)
5. A quelle heure vous êtes-*vous* couché?   (*il, nous, ils, elle*)

B. Read aloud, then restate in the *passé composé*.

1. Tu vends la maison, n'est-ce pas?
2. Nous n'allons pas en ville.
3. Quand finissez-vous le devoir?
4. Elle entre dans la salle de classe.
5. Racontez-moi l'histoire que vous lisez.
6. Jean a une bonne idée.
7. Ils la lui envoient.
8. Elle s'assied tout de suite.
9. Elle est avec son amie.
10. Écrivez-vous la lettre?

34. Irregular present tenses

dormir	sortir	servir	partir	sentir [1]
to sleep	*to go out*	*to serve*	*to leave*	*to feel*
je dors	je sors	je sers	je pars	je sens
tu dors	tu sors	tu sers	tu pars	tu sens
il dort	il sort	il sert	il part	il sent
nous dormons	nous sortons	nous servons	nous partons	nous sentons
vous dormez	vous sortez	vous servez	vous partez	vous sentez
ils dorment	ils sortent	ils servent	ils partent	ils sentent

Dormir, servir, and **sentir** are **avoir** verbs; **sortir** and **partir** are **être** verbs. The *passé composé* of the two types would therefore be as follows.

j'ai dormi	je suis sorti(e)
tu as dormi	tu es sorti(e)
il a dormi	il est sorti (elle est sortie)
nous avons dormi	nous sommes sorti(e)s
vous avez dormi	vous êtes sorti(e)(s)
ils ont dormi	ils sont sortis (elles sont sorties)

---

[1] **Sentir** is often reflexive, as in drill sentences **C** 3 and **D** 4.

NOTE: **Vous** may refer to either one person or more than one, and like **je, tu,** and **nous** may be either masculine or feminine, depending on the person or persons referred to.

C. Substitution Drill.
1. *Elle* sert le dîner.   (*Nous, Je, Vous, Ils*)
2. Partez-*vous* maintenant?   (*il, nous, tu, elles*)
3. *Je* me sens heureux.   (*Elle, Vous, Nous, Elles*)
4. *Il* ne dort pas bien.   (*Je, Nous, Vous, Elle*)
5. *Elle* sort souvent le soir.   (*Ils, Nous, Vous, Tu*)

D. Read each sentence, then restate it in the present negative, in the *passé composé* affirmative, and in the *passé composé* negative.

Example: Je pars de bonne heure.
Je ne pars pas de bonne heure.
Je suis parti de bonne heure.
Je ne suis pas parti de bonne heure.

1. Je dors tard pendant les vacances.
2. Il sert les repas.
3. Tu pars tout de suite, je suppose.
4. Elle se sent malheureuse.
5. Je sors après le dîner.
6. Vivent-ils ensemble?
7. Louise et Jeanne se mettent en route.
8. Je me dépêche de finir les devoirs.
9. Est-ce que vous avez le temps?
10. Vous êtes très sage.

LECTURE

Le professeur est arrivé en retard ce matin.   Quand il est entré dans la salle de classe il nous a dit:

« Bonjour, mesdemoiselles et messieurs. Je m'excuse d'être en retard.   Lorsque je suis sorti ce matin, l'auto a refusé de démarrer,[1] par conséquent je suis venu à pied. J'ai marché vite, mais je ne suis pas arrivé à l'heure.   Maintenant sommes-nous prêts à commencer? »

Alors la classe a commencé.   La leçon que nous avons eue aujourd'hui porte sur le passé composé.   Les verbes que le professeur nous a donnés sont « dormir » et « sortir. »   Nous les avons écrits au tableau, et le professeur les a corrigés.   Je suis

---

[1] **démarrer**   *to start* (used only with vehicle as subject)

allé au tableau avec les autres et j'ai commencé à écrire, mais tout à coup la craie est tombée par terre et s'est cassée en morceaux. Lorsque je me suis baissé pour les ramasser, j'ai laissé tomber un stylo et un crayon. Tout le monde s'est mis à rire. Puis le crayon a roulé sous le bureau du professeur. Quand je l'ai ramassé, je me suis heurté[1] la tête contre le bureau. Les autres ont ri encore plus fort.[2] Bien entendu, le professeur s'est mis en colère à cause de ce désordre.[3] Heureusement, la cloche a sonné à ce moment et a mis fin à ce cauchemar.[4]

— A propos, permettez-moi de me présenter: Maurice Dupont. Les lectures de ce livre vont vous raconter les aventures que j'ai eues en classe. J'ai commencé cet automne à étudier le français, et déjà je le trouve bien intéressant. C'est une langue que j'ai entendue parler un peu chez des amis français. Ils m'ont dit que c'est une langue utile, surtout pour voyager, et je leur ai promis de l'étudier. Je ne la trouve pas facile, et je ne la parle pas bien encore, mais je vais continuer à l'étudier, et peut-être, un jour . . .

E. 1. Ce matin le professeur ____ en retard. 2. L'auto a refusé de démarrer, par conséquent il ____ à pied. 3. Aujourd'hui la classe ____ une leçon sur le passé composé. 4. Maurice ____ au tableau pour écrire les verbes. 5. Tout à coup la craie ____ et ____. 6. Puis il a laissé tomber ____ et ____. 7. Tout le monde ____. 8. Puis Maurice ____ la tête contre le bureau. 9. Le professeur ____ à cause du désordre. 10. Cet automne Maurice a commencé ____. 11. Il l'a entendu parler un peu chez ____. 12. Il leur a promis ____.

VOCABULARY

à cause de because of
à propos by the way
bien entendu of course
chez des amis at the home of friends

mettre fin à to end, put an end to
se mettre en colère to get angry
tout à coup suddenly
un jour some day, one day

une **aventure** adventure
  se baisser to bend down
la **cloche** bell
  contre against

s'excuser[5] to apologize
facile easy
heureusement fortunately
une **idée** idea

---

[1] **se heurter la tête** *to bump one's head*   [2] **encore plus fort** *all the more*
[3] **le désordre** *confusion*   [4] **le cauchemar** *nightmare*
[5] Verbs which are cognate with English except for the infinitive ending (e.g., **excuser, continuer, mentionner**) will no longer appear in the vocabularies unless they have an extended meaning.

la **jambe** leg
  laisser to let, allow, leave; **laisser**
    tomber to drop
  malheureux unhappy, unfortunate
  marcher to walk
  permettre (**permis**) (**de**) to allow (to)
  porter to carry, wear; **porter sur**
    to deal with

  se présenter to introduce oneself
  prêt (**à**) ready (to)
  promettre (**promis**) to promise
  rire (**ri**) to laugh
  rouler to roll
  utile useful
les **vacances** holidays
  voyager to travel

PATTERN SENTENCE DRILL

1. Hier Louise est allée à l'école à pied.
  ____ Louise et Jeanne _____.
  ____ les étudiants _____.
  _____ en auto.
  _____ retournés _____.

2. Elle s'est mise en route de bonne heure.
  Elles _____.
  _____ en retard.
  _____ pour Paris.
  Je _____.

3. Près de la porte, elle a trouvé une montre par terre.
  _____ bureau _____.
  _____ Jeanne _____.
  _____laissé tomber _____.
  _____ cahier _____.

4. Elle s'est arrêtée et l'a ramassée.
  Elles _____.
  _____ regardée.
  Nous _____.
  _____ regardées.

5. Elle a donné la montre au professeur.
  ____ont_____.
  Nous _____.
  _____ devoirs_____.
  _____ étudiants.

6. Où l'avez-vous trouvée?

_____ -il _____?

___ les _____?

Quand _____?

_____ commencées?

7. Je l'ai perdue hier après-midi !

Nous_____!

__ les _____!

_____ ce matin !

_____ finies _____!

8. Louise ne s'est pas assise tout de suite.

Il _____.

_____ sont _____.

_____ couchés _____.

_____ de bonne heure.

9. Elle a causé avec une amie.

Nous _____.

_____ venus _____.

___suis _____.

_____ des ___.

10. As-tu fini les devoirs?

_____ écrit _____?

_____ lettre?

Avez _____?

__-il _____?

11. Je ne les ai même pas commencés !

Il _____!

_____ entendus !

_____ ont _____!

_____ me _____!

12. Je me suis lavé les cheveux hier soir.

Elle _____.

_____ sont _____.

_____ cet après-midi.

Nous _____.

7

Possessive Adjectives

Uses of *On*

Complementary Infinitives

Pouvoir, Vouloir, Savoir

PATTERN SENTENCES

1. Robert est venu à l'école ce matin avec sa sœur Denise.
2. Il a son cahier à lui, et elle a son cahier à elle.
3. Robert veut ouvrir la porte pour sa sœur.
4. Il a son cahier dans la main droite et ses livres dans la main gauche.
5. Ceci l'empêche d'ouvrir la porte.
6. Denise ne réussit pas à l'ouvrir non plus.
7. On a fermé la porte à clef.
8. Les enfants ne savent pas cela, et ils essayent encore de l'ouvrir.
9. Ils ne réussissent pas, et ils décident de s'arrêter.
10. « C'est inutile de continuer à tirer, dit Denise.

1. Robert has come to school this morning with his sister Denise.
2. He has *his* notebook, and she has *her* notebook.
3. Robert wants to open the door for his sister.
4. He has his notebook in his right hand and his books in his left hand.
5. This prevents him from opening the door.
6. Denise does not succeed in opening it either.
7. The door has been locked.
8. The children do not know that, and they try again to open it.
9. They don't succeed, and they decide to stop.
10. "It's useless to keep pulling," says Denise.

11. — Tu as raison, on ne peut pas faire l'impossible, répond son frère.

12. — Ce qui est désagréable, c'est qu'il va pleuvoir. »

11. "You are right, one can't do the impossible," replies her brother.

12. "The worst of it is that it is going to rain."

35. Possessive adjectives

The possessive adjectives in French are as follows:

mon (m.)		ton		son	
ma (f.)	my	ta	your	sa	his, her, its
mes (pl.)		tes		ses	

notre (sing.)		votre		leur	
nos (pl.)	our	vos	your	leurs	their

The gender and number of these possessives agree with the thing possessed, and bear no relation to the possessor.

mon frère	my brother	notre cheval	our horse
ma montre	my watch	notre maison	our house
mes souliers	my shoes	nos mouchoirs	our handkerchiefs

This principle may cause some confusion in the third person singular.

his father	son père	her mother	sa mère
her father	son père	his mother	sa mère

To specify clearly that **son, sa,** or **ses** means *his* (if it is not clear from the context), add **à lui** to the noun; for *her*, add **à elle.**

son chapeau *à lui*	*his* hat		sa montre *à lui*	*his* watch
son chapeau *à elle*	*her* hat		sa montre *à elle*	*her* watch
ses livres *à lui*	*his* books			
ses livres *à elle*	*her* books			

NOTE: Before a vowel or mute **h**, **ma, ta,** and **sa** become **mon, ton,** and **son,** even though the noun is feminine.

mon école   my school   **ton encre**   your ink   **son habitude**   his habit, her habit

A. Substitution Drill.

1. Voici mon *chapeau*. (*maison, souliers, frère, amie*)
2. Votre *professeur* est-il grand? (*maison, ami, amie, amis*)
3. Jean aime son *école*. (*professeurs, sœur, livre, auto*)
4. M. Lasalle a son livre. (*Les professeurs, L'étudiant, L'étudiante, Vous*)
5. J'attends votre *sœur*. (*sœurs, frères, ami, mère*)
6. Henri et Jacques sont venus avec leur *professeur*. (*sœur, amis, amies, parents*)

36. Definite article replacing possessive

When no confusion of ownership would result, French often uses a definite article where English uses a possessive adjective, particularly with parts of the body and articles of clothing.

Guillaume met les mains dans les poches.   William puts his hands in his pockets.
Louise se brosse les dents soigneusement.   Louise brushes her teeth carefully.
   (Here the reflexive **se** makes the ownership clear, even if logic does not already do so.)

This use of the article is not mandatory, but with reflexive constructions like the above, which are quite common, the definite article is the rule.

37. Omission of *avec*

A common type of French expression, using the definite article for the possessive, omits **avec** where we would expect to find it.

Jules part un livre à la main.   Julius leaves (with a) book in (his) hand.
Ils sont arrivés les poches pleines d'argent.   They arrived (with) their pockets full of money.

38. Uses of *on*

In English we often use an apparent "personal" pronoun or noun without referring to a definite person at all.   In the following examples, note how these various ideas are expressed in French by a single pronoun **on,** which is always followed by the third person singular of the verb.

On ne peut pas être trop prudent ces jours-ci.   One cannot be too careful these days.
On ne peut pas savoir ce qu'il pense.   You cannot know what he is thinking.
On se demande pourquoi cet homme s'en est allé si vite.   People are wondering why that man went away so quickly.
On aime être seul de temps en temps.   A fellow likes to be by himself from time to time.

A very important use of **on** is as a substitute for the passive voice, when the agent is not mentioned.

On parle anglais ici.   English *is spoken* here.
On ferme les portes à cinq heures.   The doors *are closed* at five.

On frequently becomes **l'on** if immediately preceded by a vowel sound, and not itself followed by a word beginning with **l.**

> **On peut s'asseoir si l'on veut.** One can sit down if one cares to.

B. Express in French.

1. The boy arrived book in hand. 2. The poor man broke his leg. 3. I brush my teeth in the morning and at night. 4. They say that Mr. Lenoir is very rich. 5. One doesn't say such things to a lady! 6. They're going to say that we're crazy. 7. The house hasn't been sold yet. 8. His mother and her father are dead. 9. French is spoken here. 10. He stood in front of the door, his hat in his hand.

39. Complementary infinitives with verbs

Many verbs governing a complementary infinitive do so by means of a preposition, while others are followed directly by the infinitive. The only practical way to learn the combinations is by observation and repetition. The student should commit to memory the following lists of some of the commonest verbs in three categories: (1) those followed directly by an infinitive, (2) those requiring **à,** and (3) those requiring **de.**

1. Some verbs governing an infinitive directly.

aimer	to like to	**oser**	to dare to
aller	to be going to	**pouvoir**	to be able to, **can**
compter	to expect to	**préférer**	to prefer to
désirer	to wish to	**savoir**	to know how to
espérer	to hope to	**sembler**	to seem to
laisser	to allow to, let	**vouloir**	to want to, will

EXAMPLES

> **Je vais écrire.** I am going to write.
> **Il sait nager.** He knows how to swim.
> **Pouvez-vous porter cette boîte?** Can you carry this box?
> **Voulez-vous entrer?** Will you come in?
> **Ils désirent partir.** They wish to leave.
> **Elle compte arriver bientôt.** She expects to arrive soon.
> **Laissez-moi parler!** Let me speak!

2. Some verbs requiring **à** before an infinitive.

aider à	to help to	**enseigner à**	to teach to
apprendre à	to learn to	**hésiter à**	to hesitate to
chercher à	to seek to	**inviter à**	to invite to
commencer à	to begin to	**penser à**	to think of
continuer à	to continue to	**réussir à**	to succeed in

EXAMPLES

Thomas aide son père à descendre.   Thomas helps his father to get down.
On apprend vite à parler français.   One quickly learns to speak French.
Le professeur nous enseigne à faire le devoir.   The teacher is teaching us to do the homework.
Jacques réussit enfin à mettre la grosse boîte sur le camion.   James finally succeeds in putting the big box on the truck.

3. Some verbs requiring **de** before an infinitive.

cesser de to stop, cease	**essayer de** to try to
décider de to decide to	**oublier de** to forget to
demander de to ask to	**promettre de** to promise to
se dépêcher de to hurry to	**refuser de** to refuse to
empêcher de to prevent from	

EXAMPLES

Il cesse de pleuvoir.   It stops raining.
Dépêchez-vous de descendre!   Hurry and come down!
On nous empêche de monter.   We are prevented from going up.
N'oubliez pas de fermer la porte!   Don't forget to close the door!

NOTE: **Demander** takes an indirect object:

Je demande le livre *à mon ami*.   I ask my friend for the book.
Je lui demande de me donner le livre.   I ask him to give me the book.

A number of verbs (e.g., **continuer**) may take either **à** or **de,** but generally in such cases one is more common than the other.

C. Substitution Drill.

1. *Comptez-vous* finir les phrases ce soir?   (*tu, il, ils, elle*)
2. *Ils* ne désirent pas entrer.   (*Nous, Elle, Elles, Je*)
3. *Nous* laissons partir les jeunes filles.   (*Il, Elle, Elles, On*)
4. *Elle* semble hésiter.   (*Ils, Tu, Vous, Il*)
5. Aimez-*vous* étudier les verbes?   (*tu, il, elle, elles*)
6. Oses-*tu* ouvrir cette porte?   (*vous, nous, il, ils*)

D. Answer each question affirmatively and negatively, as in the example.

Q. Est-ce que votre père vous aide à faire le devoir?
A. Oui, il m'aide à faire le devoir.
   Non, il ne m'aide pas à faire le devoir.

1. Apprenez-vous à jouer de la clarinette?   (*verb form:* J'apprends)
2. Jean cherche-t-il à apprendre l'allemand?

3. Est-ce que les garçons commencent à se battre?
4. Le professeur continue-t-il à poser des questions?
5. Est-ce qu'on nous enseigne à parler français?
6. Hésitez-vous à ouvrir la porte?
7. Est-ce qu'on vous a invité à vous asseoir?
8. Pense-t-il à lui donner l'argent nécessaire?
9. Est-ce que les jeunes gens ont réussi à s'arrêter?

E. Read aloud, then restate in the *passé composé*.

1. Il cesse de neiger.
2. Nous décidons de monter tout de suite.
3. Elle se dépêche de fermer le tiroir.
4. Essayez-vous de trouver des fleuves?
5. J'oublie de me brosser les dents.
6. Ce bruit m'empêche d'entendre la musique.
7. Georges me promet de raconter l'histoire.
8. Les jeunes filles refusent-elles de mettre les souliers?

F. Substitution Drill.

1. Nous *apprenons* à parler français.   (*commencer, cesser, continuer*)
2. Il n'*ose* pas ouvrir la porte.   (*aller, se dépêcher, essayer*)
3. J'*ai oublié* de lui donner la lettre.   (*refuser, réussir, hésiter*)
4. Elle *espère* [1] voyager en Europe.   (*penser, aimer, décider*)
5. Il m'*a promis* de finir le travail.   (*aider, laisser, empêcher*)

40. Some uses of *ce*

The neuter pronoun **ce** is used in a variety of instances in French, not all of which may be readily reduced to a rule.   Some common uses are the following.

1. In questions and answers of identity.

> **Qu'est-ce que c'est?** *or* **Qu'est-ce?** What is it?
> **C'est une fleur.**   It is a flower.
> **Qui est-ce?**   Who is it?
> **Ce sont mes amis.**   It's my friends.

---

[1] In the singular and in the third person plural of the present tense, the acute accent becomes grave. See explanation Sections 57 and 58.

NOTE: Once the person or thing has been identified, it is no longer neuter, of course, but either masculine or feminine, and may be referred to as **je, il** or **elle,** etc.

C'est une chaise. Elle est cassée. It's a chair. It is broken.
C'est votre ami. Il est ici. It's your friend. He is here.
C'est nous. Nous sommes venus vous voir. It is we. We have come to see you.

2. To repeat a word for emphasis, or to sum up an idea or situation.

Le style, c'est l'homme même. Style is man himself.
Monter en avion, c'est quelque chose que je veux faire. To fly in an airplane is something I want to do.
Paris, c'est le but de mon voyage. Paris is the goal of my trip.

3. As part of the expressions **ce qui** and **ce que,** which mean *what* in the sense of *that which.* **Ce qui** is used as subject, **ce que** as object.

Ce qui m'intéresse, c'est le prix que vous demandez. What interests me is the price you are asking.
Je sais ce que vous pensez. I know what you are thinking.

41. *Ceci* and *cela* (*ça*)

The neuter pronouns **ceci** and **cela** (usually shortened to **ça**) refer chiefly to objects not yet named (thus having no identifiable gender as yet in the sentence) or to ideas too complex to be classified as either masculine or feminine, such as a phrase or clause.

Qu'est-ce que c'est que ça? What is that?
Observez ceci, messieurs: je mets cet œuf sous ce mouchoir. Observe this, gentlemen: I put this egg under this handkerchief.
Il fait très froid dehors, et ça l'a empêché de sortir. It is very cold outside, and that kept him from going out.

G. Substitution Drill.

1. C'est un *cahier.* Il est grand. (*maison, homme, chaise, classe*)
2. Ce sont des *amis.* Ils sont de Bâton Rouge. (*étudiants, étudiantes, professeurs, amies*)
3. Ce qui est *important,* c'est que j'ai perdu mon livre de français. (*intéressant, certain, regrettable, stupide*)
4. Je ne sais pas ce que *Jean* a fait. (*Marie, tu, vous, ils*)
5. Ce que *vous* dites est vrai. (*tu, elle, elles, les garçons*)
6. Visiter Paris, c'est le but de *mon* voyage. (*son, notre, leur, ton*)

42. Irregular present tenses

pouvoir	vouloir	savoir
can, to be able	*to want, will*	*to know, know how to*
je peux (*or* puis) [1]	je veux	je sais
tu peux	tu veux	tu sais
il peut	il veut	il sait
nous pouvons	nous voulons	nous savons
vous pouvez	vous voulez	vous savez
ils peuvent	ils veulent	ils savent

Valoir (*to be worth*) is most commonly seen in the infinitive and the third person singular: present tense **il vaut.** **Falloir** (*to be necessary*) and **pleuvoir** (*to rain*) are never seen except in the infinitive and the third person singular: present tense **il faut, il pleut.**

NOTE: The construction **il faut** followed by the infinitive can mean "it is necessary," "you must," "one must," "we must," etc., according to context.

> **Vous pouvez aller au cinéma, mais il faut rentrer avant minuit.**   You may go to the movies, but you must be back before midnight.
> **Pour réussir, il faut travailler dur.**   In order to succeed, one must work hard.

All these verbs ending in **oir** have past participles ending in **u:**

pouvoir	**pu**	valoir	**valu**
vouloir	**voulu**	pleuvoir	**plu**
savoir	**su**	falloir	**fallu**

H. Substitution Drill.

1. *Je* ne peux pas faire mon devoir.   (*Elle, Nous, Ils, Jules*)
2. Pouvez-*vous* venir avec nous?   (*tu, il, elle, elles*)
3. Tu *peux* ouvrir la porte maintenant.   (*pouvons, peut, pouvez, peuvent*)
4. Voulez-*vous* visiter le musée?   (*tu, il, ils, nous*)
5. Voici ce que je *veux* faire.   (*voulons, voulez, veut, veulent*)
6. *Vous* ne savez pas ce qui est sur la carte.   (*Je, Nous, Robert, Jean et Louise*)
7. Nous ne *savons* pas faire cela.   (*sais, sait, savent, savez*)
8. Enfin *j'*ai pu finir mes leçons.   (*nous, Louis, Louise, Robert et Lucile*)
9. *Elle* n'a pas voulu monter.   (*Nous, Je, Raoul, Les messieurs*)

---

[1] The alternative form **puis** omits the **pas** in the negative.   It is commonly used instead of **peux** in the interrogative where inversion is desired: **Puis-je . . . ?**

LECTURE

Lorsque je suis entré en classe ce matin, le professeur m'a dit:

« Maurice, puis-je avoir votre cahier, s'il vous plaît?

— Oui, monsieur, le voici. Mais il faut vous dire, ce n'est pas mon cahier.

— Comment, ce n'est pas votre cahier !

— Il est à mon ami. C'est-à-dire, c'est le cahier de mon ami, mais il me l'a prêté pour aujourd'hui.

— Pourquoi cela?

— C'est très simple, monsieur. Je le lui ai demandé.

— Tiens, tiens ! Et pourquoi avez-vous fait cela? Où est votre cahier?

— Il est à la maison, sur mon bureau.

— Et pourquoi, si vous me permettez de vous poser cette question, avez-vous laissé votre cahier à la maison et emprunté son cahier à votre ami?

— C'est que dans mon propre cahier la page d'aujourd'hui est vide, monsieur.

— Alors, cela veut dire que vous n'avez pas fait votre devoir pour aujourd'hui?

— Vous avez raison, monsieur. C'est-à-dire, je ne l'ai pas écrit, mais j'ai étudié la leçon.

— N'essayez pas de me tromper, Maurice.

— Je ne veux pas vous tromper, monsieur. Posez-moi des questions sur la leçon, si vous voulez.

— Bon. Citez cinq anciennes provinces françaises, et dites-moi où elles se trouvent.

— Eh bien, il y a d'abord l'Ile-de-France, avec Paris au centre. Puis il y a la Normandie et la Bretagne, qui sont à l'ouest, sur la côte. Ensuite, vers le nord, on trouve la Picardie. Et à l'est, il y a — euh — . . . Est-ce la Champagne?

— C'est exact. Maintenant, voulez-vous me donner le nom de la province au sud-ouest de l'Ile-de-France?

— C'est le Maine, n'est-ce pas?

— C'est ça. Le Maine se trouve entre l'Ile-de-France et la Bretagne. Eh bien, je vous excuse cette fois, Maurice. Mais la prochaine fois, n'oubliez pas d'avoir votre propre cahier, et des pages bien remplies au lieu de blanches.

— C'est promis, monsieur. D'ailleurs, je promets de ne pas [1] emprunter encore une fois le cahier de mon ami.

— Êtes-vous sûr de cela?

— Très sûr, puisque Jacques part demain pour le Maine.

---

[1] The two parts of the negative frequently join together when used with an infinitive.

— Tiens, tiens ! C'est très intéressant, ça. Pensez donc: un jeune Américain dans la province du Maine.

— Ah non, monsieur, c'est l'état du Maine. Son père a un nouveau poste à Portland. »

I. 1. Lorsque Maurice est entré en classe ce matin, le professeur ____ a dit: 2. « Maurice, puis-je voir ____? » 3. Maurice répond que ce n'est pas ____ cahier. 4. Il a emprunté le cahier de ____. 5. Le cahier de Maurice est ____. 6. Maurice n'a pas ____ pour aujourd'hui. 7. C'est-à-dire, il n'a pas écrit son devoir, mais il ____. 8. Le professeur ____ des questions sur la leçon. 9. Paris est au centre de ____. 10. On trouve la Normandie et la Bretagne ____. 11. La Picardie se trouve ____ et la Champagne ____. 12. Maurice promet ____ encore une fois le cahier de son ami.

VOCABULARY

au lieu de instead of
cela veut dire that means
c'est-à-dire that is, that is to say
C'est ça. That's it.

Comment! What! What's that!
Pensez donc! Just think!
Tiens, tiens! Well, well! My, my!

ancien, ancienne old, former
l'**argent** *m.* money, silver
la **Bretagne** Brittany
brosser, se brosser to brush
le **bruit** noise
le **but** goal, aim
citer to name, cite, quote
la **côte** coast
d'ailleurs besides
la **dent** tooth
emprunter (à) to borrow (from)
ensuite then, next
un **état** state
exact correct
fermer to close, shut; **fermer à clef** to lock
la **fille** daughter, girl; **jeune fille** young lady, girl
la **fleur** flower
la **fois** time; **encore une fois** once more, again

les **gens** people
jouer to play
la **mère** mother
le **musée** museum
la **musique** music
nécessaire necessary
le **père** father
le **poste** job, position
prochain next
propre own
puisque since, as
remplir to fill
le **soulier** shoe
sûr sure
le **tiroir** drawer
le **travail** (*pl.* **travaux**) work
tromper to deceive
vide empty
visiter to visit (*of objects only*)

PATTERN SENTENCE DRILL

1. Il a son cahier à lui.
   Elle _____.
   _____ robe_____.
   ___ ses_____.
   _ ont _____.

2. Robert veut ouvrir la porte pour sa sœur.
   _____ sœurs.
   _____ peut _____.
   _____ sait _____.
   _____ frère.

3. Il a son cahier dans la main droite.
   _____ revue_____.
   Elle _____.
   _____ livre _____.
   Je _____.

4. Il a ses livres dans la main gauche.
   Je _____.
   _ avons _____.
   ___ leurs _ _____.
   Vous _____.

5. Ceci l'empêche d'ouvrir la porte.
   Cela_____.
   ___ les _____.
   ___ nous _____.
   _____ fermer _____.

6. Denise ne réussit pas à l'ouvrir non plus.
   Les garçons _____.
   _____cherchent _____.
   _____continuent _____.
   _____ les _____.

7. On a fermé la porte.
   _____ fenêtre.
   _____ les _____.
   ___ cassé _____.
   Ils _____.

8. Les enfants ne savent pas cela.
   _____ ceci.
   L'enfant _____.
   Vous _____.
   _____ voulez _____.

9. Ils essayent encore de l'ouvrir.
   _____ toujours ¹ _____.
   — oublient _____.
   _____ attendre.
   — refusent _____.

10. Ils décident de s'arrêter.
    _____ partir.
    — se dépêchent _____.
    Nous _____.
    — promettons _____.

11. C'est inutile de continuer à tirer.
    _____ impossible _____.
    _____ étudier.
    _____ essayer _____.
    _____ agréable_____.

12. Ce qui est désagréable, c'est qu'il va pleuvoir.
    _____ probable _____.
    _____neiger.
    _____ certain_____.
    _____faire beau.

---

¹ Note that **toujours** can mean "still" as well as "always."

8

Partitive

En, Y, Là

Voir, Croire, Venir, Tenir

PATTERN SENTENCES

1. Il y a beaucoup de canaux en France, n'est-ce pas?
2. Oui, il y en a beaucoup, surtout dans le nord.
3. Voit-on des canaux en Amérique aussi?
4. Oui, on en voit aux États-Unis et au Canada.
5. Mais la plupart des canaux ont perdu leur importance.
6. Au fait, quand allez-vous en Europe?
7. J'y vais cet été avec des amis. Nous allons à Londres, puis à Paris.
8. Après cela, nous allons en Espagne, et enfin à Lisbonne.
9. Pourquoi voulez-vous aller au Portugal?

1. There are many canals in France, aren't there?
2. Yes, there are a lot of them, especially in the north.
3. Do you see canals in America too?
4. Yes, you see some in the United States and Canada.
5. But most canals have lost their importance.
6. That reminds me, when are you going to Europe?
7. I am going this summer with friends. We are going to London, then to Paris.
8. After that, we are going to Spain, and finally to Lisbon.
9. Why do you want to go to Portugal?

10. On dit que le climat y est presque idéal.

11. On peut y faire de belles excursions au bord de la mer.

12. Je compte y aller un jour, mais à présent je n'ai pas assez d'argent pour voyager.

10. They say that the climate there is almost ideal.

11. You can take lovely trips there by the seashore.

12. I expect to go there some day, but right now I haven't enough money to travel.

43. Partitive

In French, nouns used in a general sense (i.e., meaning all of their kind, or considering a thing as a class) take the definite article.

> **Les arbres sont beaux.** Trees are beautiful.
> **L'argent est utile.** Money is useful.
> **Aimez-vous l'eau?** Do you like water?
> **Les œufs sont chers aujourd'hui.** Eggs are expensive today.

On the other hand, nouns referring to an unspecified number or quantity (called "partitive" nouns because meaning not all of their kind) take both **de** and the definite article.

> **A-t-il de l'argent?** Does he have money?
> **Il y a du beurre sur la table.** There is butter on the table.
> **Nous avons des fleurs dans le jardin.** We have flowers in the garden.

The presence of *some* or *any* in the English is a fairly sure sign of the partitive, especially in the predicate (i.e., after the verb).

> He brought some records. **Il a apporté des disques.**
> Do you have any tickets? **Avez-vous des billets?**
> We saw some horses in the field. **Nous avons vu des chevaux dans le champ.**

A. Substitution Drill.

1. J'aime beaucoup les *arbres*. (*enfants, vin, fleurs, viande*)
2. Avez-vous des *chevaux?* (*beurre, pommes, viande, argent*)
3. Il y a des *livres* sur la table. (*eau, beurre, crayons, pain*)
4. L'*eau* est utile. (*pain, chevaux, viande, bicyclettes*)
5. Voulez-vous de l'*eau?* (*pain, beurre, viande, crayons*)

44. Omission of article with *de*

In the partitive construction, and in one or two constructions resembling the partitive in containing **de,** the article is omitted in the following circumstances:

1. After general negation.

   Ils n'apportent pas de cadeaux. They bring no gifts.

2. After nouns and adverbs of quantity. The following list of common expressions of quantity should be memorized:

beaucoup	much, many	**autant**	as many, as much
peu	few, little	**combien**	how many, how much
plus	more	**trop**	too much, too many
moins	less, fewer	**tant**	so much, so many
assez	enough	**pas mal**	quite a lot, quite a few
une boîte	a box, a can	**un grand nombre**	a great number
un tas	a pile	**une douzaine**	a dozen

The only exceptions in this category are **bien** (*many, lots*) and **la plupart** (*most*), which follow the general rule of taking both **de** and the article.

   Il y a une boîte de disques par terre. There is a box of records on the floor.
   Je vois un tas de crayons sur la table. I see a pile of pencils on the table.
   Elle a demandé une douzaine d'œufs. She asked for a dozen eggs.
   Beaucoup de gens voyagent en France maintenant. Many people are traveling in France now.
   Peu de garçons sont venus. Few boys came.
   BUT
   Bien *des* gens jouent du piano. Many (Lots of) people play the piano.
   La plupart *des* hommes aiment les bateaux. Most men like boats.[1]

3. When an adjective precedes a plural noun, replacing the article.[2]

   de belles pommes fine apples
   de longues conversations long conversations
   de jolies filles pretty girls

4. In a phrase consisting of **de** and a noun, modifying another noun.

   une montre d'or a gold watch (a watch of gold)
   des dentelles de soie silk lace (lace of silk)
   un billet de banque a bank note

5. In certain idioms involving **de**, particularly **avoir besoin de** (*to need*) and **se servir de** (*to use*).

   Nous avons besoin de papier. We need paper.
   Il se sert d'encre pour écrire sa lettre. He uses ink to write his letter.

---

[1] **La plupart** is seldom seen with a singular complement except in the expression **la plupart du temps** *most of the time.*

[2] Not an absolute rule, as the article will sometimes be found.

Numerals, if specific, and the adjectives **quelques** (*some, a few*) and **plusieurs** (*several*) modify the noun directly, without either **de** or an article.

dix pommes   ten apples   **quarante chevaux**   forty horses
plusieurs personnes   several people   **quelques villages**   a few (some) villages

The presence of the word *the* in English means that we are not dealing with a partitive, but with something definite or specific. Whenever *the* occurs in the English, it must be expressed in French.

many children   **beaucoup *d'*enfants**
BUT
many of *the* children   **beaucoup *des* enfants**

a dozen books   **une douzaine *de* livres**
BUT
a dozen of *the* books that were delivered this morning   **une douzaine *des* livres qu'on a livrés ce matin**

B. Read the model sentence aloud, then repeat substituting the new pairs of words.

Nous avons du pain, mais nous n'avons pas de beurre.

1. _____ papier _____ encre.
2. _____ arbres _____ fleurs.
3. _____ parfum _____ parfum français.
4. _____ vin _____ lait.
5. _____ viande _____ poisson.

C. Substitution Drill.

1. J'ai remarqué un *tas* de journaux par terre.   (*douzaine, boîte, grand nombre, bien*)
2. Il y a *beaucoup* de pommes dans cette boîte.   (*peu, trop, assez, plusieurs*)
3. On nous a montré de *belles* statues dans la cathédrale.   (*jolies, vieilles, intéressantes, magnifiques*)
4. M. André est un marchand de *souliers*.   (*chevaux, parfums, fromages, tissus*)
5. Jean a besoin de *papier*.   (*bois, encre, livres, crayons*)
6. Suzanne a raconté *une* histoire.   (*trois, des, quelques, beaucoup*)

D. Insert the definite article, **de** plus the definite article, or **de** alone; or leave blank if nothing is needed.

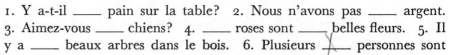

1. Y a-t-il ___ pain sur la table?   2. Nous n'avons pas ___ argent.
3. Aimez-vous ___ chiens?   4. ___ roses sont ___ belles fleurs.   5. Il y a ___ beaux arbres dans le bois.   6. Plusieurs ___ personnes sont

entrées dans l'hôtel. 7. Tiens! Voici une montre ____ or. 8. Où peut-on acheter ____ souliers? 9. Voilà dix ____ pommes de terre. 10. Nous avons besoin ____ patience. 11. J'ai assez ____ papier, mais je n'ai pas ____ encre. 12. La plupart ____ gens vont à Londres. 13. On fait ____ fromages délicieux en France. 14. Donnez-moi quelques ____ fleurs, mademoiselle. 15. Nous avons une douzaine ____ montres ____ argent. 16. Bien ____ parfums sont chers. 17. Je mange beaucoup ____ pain à midi. 18. Il y a peu ____ poissons dans le canal.

45. *En* and *y*

The partitive idea of *some* or *any*, when no noun is present, is expressed by **en,** which, like other pronoun objects, stands before the verb except in affirmative commands.

> **En avez-vous?** Do you have some (any)?
> **Ils n'en donnent pas à Jacques.** They don't give any to James.
> **Donnez-lui-en!** Give him some.

Often **en** is better rendered by *of it* or *of them*, or by omitting it entirely in English.

> **Combien en avez-vous?** How many (of them) do you have?
> **J'en ai dix.** I have ten (of them).

At times, **en** has an adverbial quality, meaning *from it* (*them*), *out of it*, or *away*. In this case, as in all others, **en** is equivalent to a **de** phrase.

> **J'ai lu ses articles, et j'en ai tiré ce renseignement.** I have read his articles, and from them I got this piece of information. (**en = de ses articles**)
> **Il est resté longtemps à Paris, mais enfin il en est parti.** He stayed a long time in Paris, but finally he left. (**en = de Paris**)

The idiom **s'en aller,** already mentioned, utilizes **en** in this same sense of *away* or *off*.

> **Le petit garçon s'en va.** The little boy goes away.

Where **en** is equivalent to a **de** phrase, **y** is equivalent to a phrase with **à** or some other preposition expressing *place where* or *motion toward*. It may be translated *to it* (*them*), *into it*, or simply *there;* or, as in the case of **en,** it may be left untranslated.

> **Puisqu'une porte de la maison est ouverte, je vais y entrer.** Since a door of the house is open, I am going to go in (there).
> **J'ai bien cherché dans vos poches, et j'y ai trouvé vos clefs.** I hunted thoroughly in your pockets, and I found your keys there.
> **Vous intéressez-vous à la chimie? Je m'y intéresse beaucoup.** Are you interested in chemistry? I am very much interested in it.
> **Allez-y, mes amis!** Go to it, my friends!

NOTE: Both **y** and **en** follow other pronoun objects.

> **Il nous y a suivis.** He followed us there.
> **Donnez-lui-en!** Give him some!

If both occur together, **en** comes last.

> **Il y en a.** There are some.

46. *Y* vs. *là*

Both **y** and **là** are used for *there* in French. In general, if the place referred to has been previously mentioned, **y** is preferred (before the verb); if not, **là** is used after the verb. **Là** is also used whenever *there* is at all emphatic.

> **Êtes-vous dans la classe de M. Dufour? Oui, j'y suis.** Are you in Mr. Dufour's class? Yes, I am.
> **Où sont mes souliers? Ils sont là dans le coin.** Where are my shoes? They are there in the corner.
> **Où avez-vous mis mes livres? Là, sur la table.** Where did you put my books? There, on the table.

E. Answer the following questions in a complete expression using **en, y,** or **là.** The word or words in parentheses will provide the clue to your answer.

> *Example:* Combien de pommes avez-vous? (dix)
> J'en ai dix.

1. Avez-vous du papier? (oui)
2. A-t-il des stylos? (non)
3. Allez-vous au cinéma? (oui)
4. Êtes-vous dans la maison? (oui)
5. Combien de chevaux ont-ils? (cinq)
6. Combien de crayons vous a-t-il donnés? (toute une boîte) [1]
7. Où est mon livre? (sur la chaise)
8. Qu'avez-vous appris dans ce livre? (beaucoup)
9. Allez-vous en France cet été? (Oui, j'espère)
10. Où va-t-on bâtir l'école? (de l'autre côté de la rue)

47. *En* and *à* with geographical names

In general, *to* or *in* with countries is **en** [2] if the name of the country is feminine singular; otherwise **au** or **aux** is used. Most European countries are feminine singular, while most countries of the Western Hemisphere are masculine.

---

[1] With **en,** the past participle never shows any agreement, remaining invariable in its simplest form.
[2] Not to be confused with the partitive **en** discussed above. The two bear no relationship whatsoever.

en Belgique to (in) Belgium	**au Mexique** to Mexico
en Allemagne to Germany	**au Canada** to Canada
en Angleterre to England	**aux États-Unis** to the United States

Continents are uniformly feminine singular and, therefore, take **en.**

en Afrique to Africa   **en Europe** to Europe   **en Amérique** to America

To, *at*, or *in* with cities is usually **à.**

à Paris   **à Londres**   **à New-York**   **à Rome**   **à Lisbonne**

If the name of the city contains an article, it is retained with **à.**

au Havre in Le Havre	**à la Haye** at The Hague
au Mans in Le Mans	**à la Rochelle** to La Rochelle

NOTE :   For those names taking **à** + article, *of* or *from* is expressed by **de** + article.
For those taking **en,** the article in the **de** phrase is usually omitted.

du Havre   from Le Havre   **d'Europe**   of Europe

F. Read aloud, supplying **à, en, au,** or **aux.**

1. Nous allons _____ Angleterre cet été. 2. Allez-vous _____ Canada?
3. Jean est _____ Bruxelles maintenant. 4. Quand va-t-il _____ Suisse?
5. Elle est allée _____ Lisbonne, et puis _____ Paris. 6. La famille va
souvent _____ États-Unis. 7. Je ne suis pas allé _____ Australie, mais je
suis allé _____ Asie et _____ Afrique. 8. Les étés sont très chauds _____
Espagne.

48. Irregular present tenses

voir	**croire**	**venir**	**tenir**
to see	*to believe*	*to come*	*to hold*
je vois	je crois	je viens	je tiens
tu vois	tu crois	tu viens	tu tiens
il voit	il croit	il vient	il tient
nous voyons	nous croyons	nous venons	nous tenons
vous voyez	vous croyez	vous venez	vous tenez
ils voient	ils croient	ils viennent [1]	ils tiennent [1]
PAST PART.	PAST PART.	PAST PART.	PAST PART.
vu	**cru**	**venu**	**tenu**

---

[1] Note doubling of **n,** in third person plural only.

ANGLETERRE

MER DU NORD

Londres

BELGIQUE

ALLEMAGNE

Rhin

Pas de Calais

Calais

FLANDRE

Lille

ARTOIS

LUXEM-BOURG

Arras

LA MANCHE

PICARDIE

Amiens

GUERNESEY

JERSEY

le Havre

Rouen

Reims

LORRAINE

ILE-DE-FRANCE

Strasbourg

Caen

NORMANDIE

Seine

Paris

Nancy

ALSACE

VOSGES

Brest

LE PERCHE

Chartres

CHAMPAGNE

Rhin

BRETAGNE

Mont-Saint-Michel

MAINE

BEAUCE

Troyes

Rennes

le Mans

ORLÉANAIS

FRANCHE-COMTÉ

SUISSE

Orléans

Dijon

Besançon

JURA

Angers

Tours

Loire

BOURGOGNE

Nantes

ANJOU

SOLOGNE

TOURAINE

NIVERNAIS

Bourges

Nevers

Saône

Geneve

POITOU

BERRY

BEAUJOLAIS

BRESSE

Mt. Blanc

Poitiers

Moulins

ALPES

la Rochelle

BOURBONNAIS

SAVOIE

OCÉAN ATLANTIQUE

AUNIS

Guéret

LYONNAIS

Chambery

MARCHE

Limoges

ANGOUMOIS

FOREZ

Lyon

ITALIE

SAINTONGE

LIMOUSIN

Clermont-Ferrand

Grenoble

Angoulême

AUVERGNE

St-Étienne

DAUPHINE

PÉRIGORD

Bordeaux

GUYENNE

Dordogne

MASSIF CENTRAL

VIVARAIS

COMTE DE NICE

ET GASCOGNE

Rhône

Nice

MONACO

LANDES

Garonne

CÉVENNES

Avignon

COMTAT VENAISSIN

Cannes

PAYS BASQUE

Auch

Toulouse

LANGUEDOC

Nîmes

Aix

PROVENCE

Bayonne

ARMAGNAC

Pau

BÉARN

Montpellier

Marseille

Toulon

PYRÉNÉES

Carcassonne

ESPAGNE

COMTE DE FOIX

Perpignan

ROUSSILLON

MER MÉDITERRANÉE

FRANCE

Miles

0   25   50   75   100

0   50   100   150

Kilomètres

G. Substitution Drill.

1. Que voyez-*vous* dans le tiroir? (*il, ils, tu, elle*)
2. *Je* ne vois pas de cadeaux. (*Nous, Vous, Elles, Jacques*)
3. *A-t-il* vu le château? (*Avez, Ont, As, Avons*)
4. *Je* crois qu'il est parti. (*Elle, Nous, Charles, Les enfants*)
5. Y croyez-*vous* vraiment? (*elle, ils, tu, on*)
6. *Elle* a cru tout ce qu'il a raconté. (*Nous, Ils, On, Mes parents*)
7. Vient-*il* demain soir? (*tu, vous, ils, elle*)
8. *Elles* sont venues voir le monument. (*Nous, Pierre, Danielle, Pierre et Danielle*)
9. *Georges* tient son journal à la main. (*Louise, Nous, Je, Les messieurs*)
10. *Elle* tient l'enfant dans les bras. (*La mère, je, il, vous*)

LECTURE

La plupart des étudiants ne sont pas encore arrivés dans la salle de classe quand le professeur y entre et se met à dessiner une carte de France sur le tableau.

« Aujourd'hui, dit-il enfin, nous allons parler encore de la France, mais cette fois nous allons faire attention aussi à ses voisins. Dans le passé, la France a eu des difficultés avec quelques-uns des pays d'Europe, comme vous le savez. »[1]

Je réponds tout de suite: « Ah oui, monsieur, par exemple la dernière guerre mondiale. Je m'y intéresse beaucoup parce que mon père a été en France pendant la guerre et il m'en a souvent parlé.

— Tiens! Racontez-nous ce qui s'est passé.

— Avec plaisir. Vous savez, j'espère, que la France, les États-Unis, la Russie et l'Angleterre, ainsi que plusieurs autres pays, se sont alliés[2] contre l'Allemagne, l'Italie et le Japon. Alors mon père a participé[3] à l'invasion de la France comme sergent[4] d'infanterie,[5] et enfin il est même entré en Allemagne.

— Mais, dit Guillaume, vous ne nous avez pas dit s'il est arrivé en France le premier jour où[6] les alliés ont traversé la Manche. C'est ça surtout que je veux apprendre.

---

[1] **comme vous le savez** *as you know*
[2] **s'allier** *to ally oneself*
[3] **participer** *to participate*
[4] **le sergent** *sergeant*
[5] **l'infanterie** *infantry*
[6] Here, **où** means "when."

— Oui, il y est arrivé le 6 juin 1944, avec les premiers soldats, sur une plage de Normandie.

— Sans blague ! dit Georges.   Combien de bateaux ont participé à l'invasion?

— Je n'en suis pas sûr, mais il y en a eu un grand nombre, de toutes sortes.

— Est-ce que les alliés ont engagé plus d'hommes que les Allemands?

— Je crois que oui; en tout cas, ils ont réussi à tenir la plage.

— Et votre père, a-t-il reçu des blessures? demande Louise.

— Ah oui ! Le soir il a essayé d'ouvrir une boîte de haricots [1] et il s'est coupé le doigt. »

H. 1. Le professeur arrive dans la salle de classe avant la plupart _____. 2. Il _____ entre et dessine une carte de France sur le tableau. 3. Les étudiants vont parler de la France, et aussi ils vont _____ ses voisins. 4. Dans le passé, la France a eu des difficultés avec _____. 5. Le père de Maurice a été en France _____. 6. Le professeur demande à Maurice de raconter _____. 7. Pendant cette guerre, plusieurs pays du monde se sont alliés contre _____. 8. Le père de Maurice _____ l'invasion de la France. 9. Guillaume demande s'il _____ en France le premier jour. 10. Maurice répond qu'il _____ le 6 juin, 1944. 11. Les alliés ont employé un grand nombre _____ et _____ dans l'invasion. 12. Le père de Maurice _____ le doigt.

VOCABULARY

ainsi que as well as, in the same manner as
avec plaisir gladly
avoir besoin de to need

en tout cas anyhow
faire attention to pay attention
je crois que oui I believe so

un **arbre** tree
le **bateau** boat, ship
bâtir to build
le **beurre** butter
la **bicyclette** bicycle
la **blessure** wound
le **bras** arm
le **cadeau** gift, present
la **cathédrale** cathedral
le **château** castle

couper: se couper to cut
dessiner to draw
la **difficulté** trouble, difficulty
le **doigt** finger
l'**encre** (*f.*) ink
le **fromage** cheese
la **guerre** war; **guerre mondiale** world war
le **lait** milk
magnifique magnificent

---

[1] **les haricots** *beans*

le **marchand** dealer, salesman
l'**or** (*m.*) gold
le **papier** paper
parce que because
le **parfum** perfume
se passer to happen, occur
le **poisson** fish
la **pomme** apple; **pomme de terre** potato

quelqu'un someone; (*pl.*) **quelques-uns** some
recevoir (**reçu**) to receive
le **soldat** soldier
le **tissu** fabric, tissue, cloth
traverser to cross
le **voisin,** la **voisine** neighbor

PATTERN SENTENCE DRILL

1. Il y a beaucoup de canaux en France, n'est-ce pas?
   _____châteaux _____?
   _____ un grand nombre _____?
   _____ Italie _____?
   _____ plus _____?

2. Il y en a beaucoup, surtout dans le nord.
   _____ un grand nombre _____.
   _____ assez _____.
   _____ ouest.
   _____ tant _____.

3. Voit-on des canaux en Amérique aussi?
   _____ châteaux _____?
   _____Asie _____?
   Trouve _____?
   _____Afrique _____?

4. On en voit aux États-Unis et au Canada.
   _____ Mexique.
   _____ trouve _____.
   Nous _____.
   _____ Suisse _____.

5. La plupart des canaux ont perdu leur importance.
   Bien _____.
   _____ histoires _____.
   _____ intérêt.
   Plusieurs _____.

6. Quand allez-vous en Europe?
   _____ Australie?
   _____ vas _____?
   _____ -on _____?
   _____ Angleterre?

7. J'y vais cet été avec des amis.
   _____ hiver _____.
   _____ voisins.
   Elle _____.
   __ allons _____.

8. Nous allons à Londres, puis à Paris.
   _____ Marseille _____.
   Ils _____.
   _____ Lyon.
   Jean _____.

9. Après cela, nous allons en Espagne, et enfin à Lisbonne.
   _____ Suisse _____.
   _____ vont _____.
   _____ puis _____.
   Avant _____.

10. Pourquoi voulez-vous aller au Portugal?
    _____ Belgique?
    _____ -il _____?
    _____ veulent _____?
    Quand _____?

11. On dit que le climat y est presque idéal.
    Jean _____.
    _____ toujours ___.
    _____ agréable.
    _____ les gens _____.

12. On peut y faire de belles excursions au bord de la mer.
    _____ à la campagne.
    _____ promenades _____.
    Nous _____.
    _____ longues _____.

13. Je compte y aller un jour.
    Jules _____.
    _____voyager ___.
    Nous _____.
    Les enfants _____.

14. Je n'ai pas assez d'argent pour voyager.
    ___ avons _____.
    Elle _____.
    _____ l'acheter.
    _____ temps _____.

9

Adverbs

Comparisons

Disjunctive Pronouns

Naître, Connaître,
Courir, Prendre

PATTERN SENTENCES

1. Je m'endors facilement, surtout en classe.
2. Je m'endors plus facilement encore quand on lit à haute voix.
3. Plus on lit, plus j'ai sommeil.

4. Mais vous lisez tout aussi mal que les autres.
5. Connaissez-vous le poème que le professeur a lu aujourd'hui?
6. Il est meilleur que le poème d'hier, je crois.
7. En fait, c'est le meilleur poème du livre.
8. Je connais plus de trente poèmes maintenant.
9. Ce cours devient de plus en plus intéressant.
10. Moi, je le trouve moins intéressant que le cours de l'année passée.

1. I fall asleep easily, especially in class.
2. I fall asleep still more easily when someone is reading aloud.
3. The more they read, the sleepier I get.

4. But you read just as poorly as the rest.
5. Do you know the poem the professor read today?
6. It is better than yesterday's poem, I think.
7. In fact, it is the best poem in the book.
8. I know more than thirty poems now.

9. This course is getting more and more interesting.
10. *I* find it less interesting than last year's course.

11. Mais M. Lasalle est le professeur le plus gentil de l'école.
12. A vrai dire, j'aime beaucoup travailler avec lui.

11. But Mr. Lasalle is the nicest teacher in the school.
12. To tell the truth, I like working with him.

49. Formation and position of adverbs

The French adverbial ending corresponding to English *ly* (*swiftly*, *lightly*) is **ment,** generally added to the feminine of the adjective, or to the masculine if it ends in a vowel.

fort, forte	strong	**fortement**	strongly
franc, franche	frank	**franchement**	frankly
infini, infinie	infinite	**infiniment**	infinitely
facile	easy	**facilement**	easily

Most adjectives (of more than one syllable) ending in **ent** and **ant** change **nt** to **m** before adding **ment.**

prudent	careful	**prudemment**	carefully
courant	current	**couramment**	currently
évident	evident	**évidemment**	evidently

The adverbs corresponding to **bon, mauvais,** and **petit** do not follow the general rule.

bon, bonne	good	**bien**	well
mauvais, mauvaise	bad	**mal**	badly
petit, petite	little (size)	**peu**	little (quantity)

Some adverbs do not correspond to any adjective at all.

beaucoup many, much   **souvent** often   **volontiers** gladly

With exceptions, the position of adverbs in French is similar to that of adverbs in English. Most frequently the adverb follows the verb it modifies. In compound tenses, common adverbs such as **beaucoup, bien, déjà, trop, jamais, toujours** are placed between the auxiliary and the past participle.

Il parle bien. He speaks well.
Il a bien parlé. He spoke well.

A. Read the sentences aloud with the adverb corresponding to the adjective in parentheses.
1. Il a parlé (long) à l'enfant.
2. (Heureux) on est arrivé de bonne heure.
3. Raymond est (récent) rentré d'un long voyage.
4. Le professeur a répondu (franc) à l'élève.
5. Marchons (lent).

6. (Vrai), je ne crois pas ce que vous racontez.
7. Jacques a réussi (facile) à vendre l'auto.
8. Simone est (évident) très contente.
9. En fait, elle est (tel) contente qu'elle veut embrasser sa mère.
10. Il a (rapide) lu la leçon.

50. Comparison of adjectives and adverbs

The comparative of an adjective is formed by adding **plus** to the positive.

beau	beautiful	**plus beau**	more beautiful
grand	large	**plus grand**	larger

The only common exception to this rule is **bon,** whose comparative is **meilleur.** (**Mauvais** has an irregular comparative **pire,** which is stronger, but less common, than the regular comparative **plus mauvais.**)

French has no real superlative in common use. Most comparatives become practical superlatives by the simple addition of a definite article or a possessive adjective.

bon	good	**meilleur**	better	**le meilleur**	the best, the better
petit	small	**plus petit**	smaller	**le plus petit**	the smallest
son plus long poème	his longest poem			**notre meilleur essai**	our best try

Comparatives and superlatives agree like ordinary adjectives.

une plus belle femme   a more beautiful woman
les plus jolies filles   the prettiest girls
sa meilleure œuvre   his best work

If a superlative *follows* the noun, as very often happens, another article, or else a possessive adjective, must be supplied before the noun.

le roi le plus puissant   the most powerful king
les gens les plus fatigués   the weariest people
sa pièce la plus récente   his most recent play

In general, comparative and superlative forms follow the rules of position applying to the simple adjective.[1] Thus we have **un meilleur exemple, le plus beau garçon;** but **la leçon la plus facile** and **le livre le plus intéressant.**

---

[1] The student should review the list of adjectives which precede the noun as stated in Unit 5.

The adjective **bon** and its comparative **meilleur** have not only feminine forms (**bonne, meilleure**) but special neuter forms **bien** and **mieux,** which are used as predicate adjectives when the subject is one of the neuter pronouns **ce, ceci,** or **cela** (**ça**).

> **C'est très bien, ça.**   That's really good.
> **Ceci est mieux que cela.**   This is better than that.[1]

Diminishing comparison (done with **moins** instead of **plus**) is much more common in French than in English.

> **Elle n'est pas moins coupable que son frère.**   She is no less guilty than her brother.
> **Elle est beaucoup moins âgée que sa sœur.**   She is much younger (less old) than her sister.

Comparisons of equality are made with **aussi . . . que,** often accompanied by **tout** (*just*). In the negative, **aussi** usually becomes **si.**

> **Elle est aussi âgée que son amie.**   She is as old as her friend.
> **Il est tout aussi adroit que vous.**   He is just as clever as you.
> **Raoul n'est pas si grand que Paul.**   Ralph is not as tall as Paul.

Adverbs are compared like adjectives. However, since they possess neither gender nor number, they have but one form for each degree.

poliment politely   **plus poliment** more politely   **le plus poliment** most politely
mal badly   **plus mal** worse   **le plus mal** worst

The comparative of **bien** is **mieux,** which is identical with the neuter of **meilleur.**

> **Il l'a fait mieux que son frère.**   He did it better than his brother.

Also irregular are **peu, moins, le moins** [2] (*little, less, least*) and **beaucoup, plus, le plus** (*much, more, most*).

> **Nous avons moins de temps que vous.**   We have less time than you.
> **Il a plus d'argent que d'esprit.**   He has more money than wit.

SPECIAL USAGES

1. Before a number, *than* is expressed by **de** rather than **que.**

> **plus de douze francs**   more than twelve francs
> **moins de seize personnes**   less than sixteen people

---

[1] Occasionally these "neuter" forms appear, with special meanings, even when the subject is personal. E.g. **Elle est bien.** *She is good looking.* **Êtes-vous bien (mieux)?** *Are you comfortable (more comfortable)?* Perhaps originally these forms were adverbs accompanying an adjective which has since disappeared (i.e., **bien faite, bien installé,** or the like).

[2] **Moins** has a corresponding adjective form **moindre,** which may be considered an alternate comparative of **petit,** and refers not to size but rather to quantity or intensity. It is seldom used except in the superlative.

Le sujet n'a pas le moindre intérêt.   The subject isn't interesting in the least.

2. *As much as* is **autant que.**

    Il n'a pas autant d'argent que vous. He hasn't as much money as you.

3. When the second part of a comparison is unexpressed, *more* is frequently **davantage** rather than **plus.**

    Je n'en sais pas davantage. I don't know any more about it.
    Jules a mille francs, mais vous en avez davantage. Julius has a thousand francs, but you have more.

4. After a superlative, *in* is **de.**

    le plus haut bâtiment *du* **monde** the highest building *in the* world
    la plus jolie fille *de la* **classe** the prettiest girl *in the* class

5. *The more . . . the more* is **plus . . . plus;** *the less . . . the less* is **moins . . . moins.**

    Plus je le connais, plus je l'admire. The more I know him, the more I admire him.

6. *More and more* is **de plus en plus;** *less and less* is **de moins en moins.**

    Il devient de plus en plus paresseux. He is getting lazier and lazier.

B. Read the following phrases aloud, then form the comparative and superlative as in the example.

    Example: une bonne pomme; une meilleure pomme, la meilleure pomme
        un livre intéressant; un livre plus intéressant, le livre le plus intéressant

1. un petit chien; _____ , _____
2. une vieille dame; _____ , _____
3. une œuvre intéressante; _____ , _____
4. une jolie femme; _____ , _____
5. une leçon difficile; _____ , _____
6. une bonne idée; _____ , _____
7. un problème compliqué; _____ , _____
8. un homme sage; _____ , _____
9. un élève diligent; _____ , _____
10. une gentille personne; _____ , _____

C. Complete the following sentences according to the pattern given.

    a. *Pattern:* Cette robe est belle, mais l'autre est plus belle.

1. Cette salle est froide, _____ .
2. Ces pommes sont bonnes, _____ .
3. Ce papier est cher, _____ .
4. Cette machine est lourde, _____ .
5. Ces garçons sont grands, _____ .

b. *Pattern:* Jules a marché vite, mais Charles a marché plus vite.

1. Roger est tombé souvent, mais Raoul _____.
2. Martin marche lentement, mais Guy _____.
3. Émile a bien chanté, mais Victor _____.
4. Claude travaille peu, mais Claudette _____.
5. Le professeur parle beaucoup, mais sa femme _____.

D. Express in French.

1. Louis sings better than Louise. 2. It's better[1] to go on foot. 3. Here is his best book.[2] 4. I have a better idea. 5. We have the least difficult lessons this week. 6. This cheese is as expensive as the other. 7. It is the longest river in the world. 8. Does that classroom have more than six windows? 9. Roger has less than ten francs. 10. He has as much money as we. 11. She walks more quickly than her friend. 12. This house is not as big as the others. 13. These neighbors are more agreeable than the Duponts. 14. That story is less interesting than *Les Misérables*. 15. The more I think about it, the more I hesitate. 16. They have less money than you. 17. It's the easiest story in the book. 18. It's the most beautiful dress in the shop.

51. Disjunctive pronouns

The pronoun objects already studied stand normally just before the verb and are said, therefore, to be "conjunctive" (i.e., "joined with" the verb). Another set, called "disjunctive," often does not stand before the verb, but rather apart from it. While the conjunctive pronouns are mainly weak or unaccented forms, the disjunctives are relatively strong forms, capable of bearing considerable stress.

moi	**nous**
toi	**vous**
lui, elle, soi	**eux, elles**

NOTE: **Soi** is purely reflexive, and seldom used except when the subject is **on**.

The disjunctives are used as follows:

1. Alone.

« **Qui est là? — Moi!** » "Who is there?" "I!"

2. In identification expressions with **être**.

« **Est-ce vraiment mon ami Jean? — C'est lui.** » "Is it really my friend John?" "It's he."

---

[1] Use **Ce** for *It*.
[2] Use **œuvre**.

3. In a compound subject.

Elle et lui vont au théâtre.   She and he go to the theater.

NOTE: If the two elements are not both in the third person, they are sometimes summed up by a conjunctive pronoun to make the verb agreement clear.

Lui et moi, (nous) allons en ville.   He and I are going to town.
Vous et elle, (vous) pouvez rester avec moi.   You and she can remain with me.

4. To add force to a subject or object.   Sometimes **-même** or **-mêmes** may be added, expressing *–self* or *–selves* where no reflexive is used.

Sa femme va souvent à l'opéra, mais *lui*, (il) [1] ne l'aime pas.   His wife often goes to the opera, but *he* does not like it.
Comment est-ce qu'on ne l'a pas vue, *elle?*   How is it they didn't see *her?*
Il l'a fait lui-même.   He did it himself.
Ils ont ouvert la porte eux-mêmes.   They opened the door themselves.

5. As the object of a preposition (by far the commonest use).

Nous travaillons avec eux.   We work with them.
Il le fait pour moi.   He is doing it for me.

6. In comparisons.

Elle est moins âgée que lui.   She is younger than he.
Je suis tout aussi coupable que toi.   I am just as guilty as you.

7. Replacing a conjunctive object after an affirmative command (first and second person singular only).

Montrez-moi le mot!   Show me the word!   (replaces **me**)
Lave-toi bien!   Wash yourself well!   (replaces **te**)

NOTE: Third person objects remain conjunctive in form, but are stressed in speech.

Regardez-le! *Look at him!*   **Arrêtez-les!** *Stop them!*
Réveillez-la! *Wake her up!*   **Parlez-leur!** *Speak to them!*

E. Express in French.

1. Are you going with him? 2. Lend me some money, please. 3. Look at him. 4. *I* didn't do it. 5. You are bigger than she. 6. He and they want to go away together. 7. Your father and I are [2] good friends.[3] 8. You and he are going [2] to be happy. 9. He wrote the poem for me.

---

[1] In this, as also in the two preceding examples, if the conjunctive pronoun (**nous, vous, il**) is omitted, no comma is needed.

[2] Be very careful of the verb agreement, which must be precise.

[3] *good friends* **de bons amis**

10. The ladies think he wrote it for them.   11. It is he who arrived.
12. The gentlemen are leaving, and I am going with them.   13. Go to
bed, James![1]   14. Louise's friend thinks of her often.   15. Tell me the
story.   16. It is I who did[2] it.   17. You and he are coming[2] with me.
18. *She* is leaving, but *he* is staying.   19. We are as old as those boys,
but we aren't as tall as they.   20. Get dressed at once, James![1]

52. Irregular present tenses

naître	**connaître**	**courir**	**prendre**
to be born	*to know, be acquainted with*	*to run*	*to take*
je nais	je connais	je cours	je prends
tu nais	tu connais	tu cours	tu prends
il naît	il connaît	il court	il prend
nous naissons	nous connaissons	nous courons	nous prenons
vous naissez	vous connaissez	vous courez	vous prenez
ils naissent	ils connaissent	ils courent	ils prennent
PAST PART.	PAST PART.	PAST PART.	PAST PART.
né	**connu**	**couru**	**pris**

NOTE: Compounds (e.g. **renaître** *to revive*, **reconnaître** *to recognize*, **parcourir** *to run through*, **comprendre** *to understand*, and the like) are conjugated like the verbs above.

F. Substitution Drill.

1. Connaissons-*nous* ce monsieur?   (*vous, tu, il, ils*)
2. *Je* ne l'ai pas reconnu tout de suite.   (*Ils, Elle, Nous, Robert*)
3. Es-*tu* né aux États-Unis?   (*il, elle, ils, elles*)
4. Quelquefois *vous* courez d'ici à l'école.   (*je, nous, Jules, les frères*)
5. Aujourd'hui j'*ai* couru plus vite que d'ordinaire.   (*avons, ont, avez, as*)
6. *Tu* prends ton déjeuner de bonne heure, n'est-ce pas?   (*Vous, Suzanne, Les enfants, Jacques*)
7. Pour aller au musée, *j'ai pris* le métro.[3]   (*Nous, On, Les jeunes filles, M. Dumont*)

LECTURE

Ce matin le professeur entre brusquement dans la salle de classe. Sans même attendre le silence, il annonce qu'il va nous donner une dictée. Puis il nous donne

---

[1] Use familiar form.
[2] Be very careful of the verb agreement, which must be precise.
[3] **le métro**   (Paris) *subway*

du papier, et nous nous mettons à écrire des phrases qu'il lit dans un livre qu'il a apporté avec lui.

Pendant qu'il lit, il marche de long en large. Sa voix, à vrai dire, est assez monotone.[1] Quant à moi, bien fatigué d'avoir mal dormi, je commence à avoir sommeil et je ferme les yeux. Tout à coup j'entends une voix derrière moi:

« Maurice, Maurice ! Attention, ou tu vas t'endormir ! »

Heureusement c'est la voix d'une des étudiantes et je me mets à écouter moins distraitement.[2] Le professeur est en train de continuer la dictée. Je prends mon crayon et j'écris. C'est un poème de Paul Verlaine qu'il nous lit maintenant, mais cette fois il y met du sentiment. D'abord je ne le comprends pas très bien. Mais à mesure que j'écoute le poème, je commence à y trouver du sens. Il commence ainsi:

Il pleure dans mon cœur
Comme il pleut sur la ville.
Quelle est cette langueur [3]
Qui pénètre [4] *mon cœur?*

O bruit doux de la pluie
Par terre et sur les toits!
Pour un cœur qui s'ennuie,
O le chant de la pluie!

La lecture finie, je donne ma dictée au professeur. « Ce cours devient de plus en plus intéressant, lui dis-je. Il y a une chose que j'ai certainement apprise aujourd'hui, monsieur.

— Je suis bien heureux de le savoir. Évidemment vous faites des progrès. Qu'est-ce que c'est que vous avez appris?

— C'est que plus je connais la littérature française, plus je suis content d'étudier le français, malgré mes difficultés avec la grammaire. »

G. 1. Le professeur entre ____ dans la salle de classe. 2. Il annonce qu'il va ____ à la classe. 3. Les étudiants ____ des phrases qu'il lit. 4. Maurice, fatigué d'avoir mal dormi, commence à ____. 5. Tout à coup il entend ____. 6. Le professeur est ____ continuer la dictée. 7. C'est un poème de ____. 8. D'abord Maurice ne le comprend pas

[1] **monotone** *monotonous* [2] **distraitement** *absent-mindedly* [3] **la langueur** *listlessness* [4] **pénétrer** *to penetrate*

_____. 9. A mesure qu'il écoute le poème, _____. 10. Le poème commence par la phrase: « _____. » 11. Le professeur demande à Maurice ce qu'il a _____. 12. Plus il connaît la littérature française, _____ d'étudier le français.

VOCABULARY

à mesure que as, in proportion as
attention! look out! careful!
de long en large up and down
en train de in the act of, in the process of

faire des progrès to improve, make progress
quant à as for, as to

annoncer to announce
apporter to bring
brusquement abruptly
le **chant** singing, melody
chanter to sing
le **cœur** heart
compliqué complicated
comprendre (**compris**) to understand
la **dictée** dictation
embrasser to kiss, embrace
ennuyer to bore, annoy; **s'ennuyer** to be bored, become weary
franc, franche frank
lent, lente slow

longuement at length
malgré in spite of
le **monde** world
une **œuvre** work
pendant que while
pleurer to weep, cry
la **pluie** rain
reconnaître (**reconnu**) to recognize
le **sens** meaning
le **sentiment** feeling
tellement so
le **toit** roof
la **voix** voice
les **yeux** (*sing.* **œil**) (*m.*) eyes

PATTERN SENTENCE DRILL

1. Je m'endors facilement, surtout en classe.
   _____ souvent _____.
   _____ théâtre.
   Vous _____.
   _____ même _____.

2. Je m'endors plus facilement encore quand on lit.
   _____rapidement _____.
   Ils _____.
   _____ chante.
   Nous_____.

3. Plus on lit, plus j'ai sommeil.
   ___ je _____.
   _____mange _____.
   _____ faim.
   Moins _____.

4. Connaissez-vous le poème que le professeur a lu?
   _____ -ils _____?
   _____ histoire _____?
   _____ lues?
   _____ -elle _____?

5. Il est meilleur que le poème d'hier.
   _____plus long_____.
   Ils _____.
   _____ poèmes_____.
   _____moins _____.

6. C'est le meilleur poème du livre.
   _____plus court_____.
   _____ histoire _____.
   ___sont _____.
   _____ longues _____.

7. Vous lisez tout aussi mal que les autres.
   _____parlez _____.
   _____vite _____.
   _____ moi.
   René _____.

8. Je connais plus de trente poèmes maintenant.
   _____ vingt_____.
   Nous _____.
   _____ à présent.
   _____ moins _____.

9. Ce cours devient de plus en plus intéressant.
   ___classe _____
   _____de moins en moins _____.
   ___classes _____.
   _____ difficiles.

10. Moi, je le trouve moins intéressant que le cours de l'année passée.

    Lui _____.

    _____ ils _____.

    _____ plus _____.

    _____ les _____.

11. Mais M. Lasalle est le professeur le plus gentil de l'école.

    _____ la personne _____.

    _____ diligente _____.

    _____mes amis _____.

    _____ les étudiants _____.

12. A vrai dire, j'aime beaucoup travailler avec lui.

    _____ vais_____.

    _____ moins_____.

    _____ eux.

    _____ nous _____.

10

Future

Future Perfect

E–Stem Verbs

Chez

PATTERN SENTENCES

1. Qu'allez-vous faire cet été?

2. J'irai à la campagne dès que j'aurai fini mes classes.

3. Je vais chez mon oncle, qui a une ferme.

4. Ah bon! Présentez-lui mes respects quand vous le verrez.

5. Lorsque vous arriverez chez votre oncle, l'aiderez-vous dans les champs?

6. Je ferai de mon mieux; je travaillerai dur.

7. On se lève de bonne heure à la ferme, n'est-ce pas?

8. Je me lèverai probablement au lever du soleil.

9. D'abord je m'occuperai des poules.

10. On les appelle et on leur jette du grain.

---

1. What are you going to do this summer?

2. I am going to the country as soon as school is out.

3. I'm going to the home of my uncle, who has a farm.

4. How nice! Give him my regards when you see him.

5. When you get to your uncle's, will you help him in the fields?

6. I'll do my best; I'll work hard.

7. They get up early on the farm, don't they?

8. I'll probably get up at sunrise.

9. First I'll look after the hens.

10. You call them and you throw them some grain.

100

11. Reviendrez-vous chez vous à la fin de l'été?

12. Oui, mais j'espère rester à la ferme aussi longtemps que possible.

11. Will you come back home at the end of the summer?

12. Yes, but I hope to stay on the farm as long as possible.

53. Future tense

The future tense (*futur*) in French is essentially a union of the infinitive of the verb with the present tense of **avoir.** It is formed, in regular verbs, by adding the present of **avoir** (minus the **av** in the first and second persons plural) to the infinitive, or to as much of it as ends in **r: donner–, finir–, perdr–.**

donner	finir	perdre
je donner**ai**	je finir**ai**	je perdr**ai**
tu donner**as**	tu finir**as**	tu perdr**as**
il donner**a**	il finir**a**	il perdr**a**
nous donner**ons**	nous finir**ons**	nous perdr**ons**
vous donner**ez**	vous finir**ez**	vous perdr**ez**
ils donner**ont**	ils finir**ont**	ils perdr**ont**

54. Irregular future stems

The endings of the future never vary, but stems are often irregular in irregular verbs. Of the irregular verbs already studied, the following have irregular stems for the future.

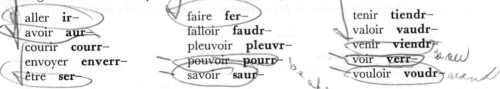

aller **ir–**	faire **fer–**	tenir **tiendr–**
avoir **aur–**	falloir **faudr–**	valoir **vaudr–**
courir **courr–**	pleuvoir **pleuvr–**	venir **viendr–**
envoyer **enverr–**	pouvoir **pourr–**	voir **verr–**
être **ser–**	savoir **saur–**	vouloir **voudr–**

Asseoir may have either of two stems: **asseoir–** or **assiér–,** of which **assiér–** is probably most often used.

aller	s'asseoir
j'irai *I shall (will) go*	je m'assiérai *I will sit down*
tu iras *you will go*	tu t'assiéras
il ira	il s'assiéra
nous irons	nous nous assiérons
vous irez	vous vous assiérez
ils iront	ils s'assiéront

A. Substitution Drill.

1. *Tu* trouveras l'hôtel sans difficulté. (*Il, Je, Vous, Elles*)
2. Partirez-*vous* bientôt? (*tu, elle, ils, nous*)

3. Vendrons-*nous* la ferme? (*vous, tu, il, ils*)
4. *Il* n'aura pas le courage de le faire. (*Nous, Je, Georges, Elles*)
5. Sera-t-*elle* ici avant midi? (*nous, tu, vous, ils*)

B. Reply in a simple sentence, using the future tense.

1. Iras-tu chez ton oncle?
2. Voudrez-vous une maison plus grande?
3. Viendra-t-elle la prochaine fois?
4. Finiront-ils cet après-midi?
5. Est-ce que je me coucherai de bonne heure à la ferme?

C. Restate in the future.

1. Marguerite est chez elle.
2. Nous courons rapidement.
3. Pleut-il?
4. Combien vaut-il?
5. Je tiens ma promesse.
6. Je peux le faire bientôt.
7. Il faut partir demain.
8. Ils voient les Alpes cet été.
9. Nous venons de bonne heure.
10. Il veut rester à la maison.
11. Je sais faire ce travail.
12. Ils s'asseyent tout de suite.
13. Allez-vous chez votre nièce?
14. Vous faites un exercice sur le futur.
15. Nous envoyons une lettre à notre ami.

55. Future perfect

Combining the future of **avoir** or **être** with the past participle of a verb produces the future perfect (*futur antérieur*). Two examples follow.

faire	aller
j'aurai fait *I ~~will~~ have done*	je serai allé(e) *I will have gone*
tu auras fait	tu seras allé(e)
il aura fait	il sera allé
nous aurons fait	nous serons allé(e)s
vous aurez fait	vous serez allé(e)(s)
ils auront fait	ils seront allés

56. Uses of future and future perfect

The future is used where we would use it in English. In addition, it is used where English uses the present, in a clause introduced by a time conjunction (**quand, lorsque, dès que,** or **aussitôt que**) if the main verb is future in either form or sense.

He will come when he *is* ready. **Il viendra quand il *sera* prêt.**
Do your lessons when you *get* home. **Faites vos devoirs lorsque vous *arriverez* chez vous.**

Sometimes with these same conjunctions, in a similar construction, we find the future perfect.

Dès que (or **aussitôt que**) **vous *serez arrivé*, fermez la porte à clef.** As soon as you *have arrived*, lock the door.

Vous viendrez me voir quand vous *aurez fini* vos devoirs. You will come to see me when you *have finished* your assignments.

The present tense, or a construction with **aller** plus the infinitive, often supplants the future, as in English.

N'oubliez pas que je *viens* vous voir demain. Don't forget that I *am coming* to see you tomorrow.

Nous *avons* nos examens de fin d'année cet après-midi. We *are having* our finals this afternoon.

Elle *va travailler* dur cette fois. She *is going to work* hard this time.

Simple conditions use a combination of present and future, as in English.

Si vous *allez* en ville, vous *verrez* le défilé. If you *go* into town, you *will see* the parade.

S'il *vient* me voir, je lui *donnerai* un conseil. If he *comes* to see me, I *shall give* him a piece of advice.

D. Substitution Drill.

1. *Je* serai arrivé de bonne heure. (*Elles, Vous, Jacques, Tu*)
2. *Je* me serai déjà assis. (*Nous, La femme, Les garçons, Vous*)
3. *J'*aurai oublié son nom lorsqu'il reviendra. (*Vous, Son professeur, Elles, Tu*)
4. *Le petit garçon* se sera couché quand elle rentrera. (*Nous, Vous, Les étudiants, Tu*)
5. *Vous* pourrez vous asseoir quand vous aurez fini. (*Les jeunes filles, Je, Tu, L'étudiant*)

E. Express in French.

1. They will choose their presents right away. 2. We will be able to go out now. 3. When he comes, I'll be here. 4. If he comes, I'll be here. 5. Write these sentences when you have the time. 6. Write these sentences if you have the time. 7. As soon as we have left,[1] do your reading. 8. We'll be going to France soon. 9. We are going to see the Arc de Triomphe, I guess.[2] 10. If you see it, you will like it. 11. When you see it, you will like it. 12. I will have left before ten-thirty. 13. She will have finished her work already. 14. The girls will not have arrived yet.

[1] Use **partir.**
[2] "Guess" in this sense is **croire.**

57. *E*-stem verbs

Verbs of CONJUGATION I having an unaccented **e** as the last vowel of the stem (**lever, acheter**) are called "**e**-stem verbs." When this **e** is followed by an ending with a silent **e**, the **e** of the stem becomes **è** (**je lève, tu achètes, ils mènent**). The exceptions to this rule are **jeter** and **appeler** and their compounds, which double the consonant before a silent **e** ending (**je jette, tu rejettes, ils appellent**).

lever	**jeter**
to lift	*to throw*
je lève	je jette
tu lèves	tu jettes
il lève	il jette
nous levons	nous jetons
vous levez	vous jetez
ils lèvent	ils jettent

These spelling changes occur not only in the present (including the subjunctive, which we shall be studying presently), but also in the future and conditional. In the future (and in the conditional, which is taken up in Unit 12), it will occur in every person, both singular and plural, because here the **e** of the original stem is followed by the **e** of the future stem throughout the whole tense.

je lèverai *I will lift*	je jetterai *I will throw*
tu lèveras	tu jetteras
il lèvera	il jettera
nous lèverons	nous jetterons
vous lèverez	vous jetterez
ils lèveront	ils jetteront

58. False *e*-stems

A special case involves what may be called "false **e**-stem verbs," which have an acute accent (´) on the **e** of the stem in the infinitive, such as **céder** (*to give up, yield*), **espérer** (*to hope*). In these cases, the accent becomes grave (`) in the present tense before a mute **e** syllable, but not in the future or conditional.

je cède, j'espère
BUT
je céderai, j'espérerai

F. Substitution Drill.

1. *Il mène une vie active.* (*Tu, Ils, Nous, Vous*)
2. *Nous rejetons cette théorie.* (*Je, Elle, Elles, Le professeur*)
3. *Je me rappelle bien cet incident.* (*Nous, Vous, Juliette, Les garçons*)

4. *Vous* espérez voir le président.   (*Nous, Cécile, Jean et Paul, Je*)

5. *Anatole* se promènera en ville.   (*Je, Louise, Nous, Les jeunes filles*)

6. Probablement *elle* préférera la robe noire.   (*vous, ces dames, nous, je*)

7. *Je* m'appelle Lefèvre.   (*Ce monsieur, Nous, Mes amis, Vous*)

G. Express in French.

1. I always get up early.[1] 2. I'll get up tomorrow at six. 3. He throws me the ball. 4. They are calling their friends. 5. She prefers to stay here. 6. Where will you buy your hat? 7. They hope to go to Spain. 8. He buys houses. 9. Throw some grain to the hens! 10. I'll leave as soon as he calls me. 11. She will prefer to go with him. 12. They raise their hands.[2] 13. He gives up the bicycle. 14. But the next time, he will not give it up. 15. He leads a hard life. 16. We get up late mornings.

59. The preposition *chez*

The preposition **chez** requires special attention in its uses, which are best illustrated by examples.

chez eux at (to) their house	**chez Delmonico** at Delmonico's (restaurant)
chez moi at (to) my house	
Je vais chez moi. I am going home.	**chez Victor Hugo** in Victor Hugo (i.e., in his works)
chez les Brun at (to) the Browns'	
chez Cartier at Cartier's (store)	**chez les Indiens** among the Indians

IMPORTANT: The preposition **chez** is never used without a personal object. It must not be used alone or at the end of a sentence. If its object is a pronoun, the latter will be disjunctive.

H. Express in French.

1. She is going home. 2. He is going home. 3. The men are going home. 4. We shall go to the Duponts'. 5. I buy my hats at Charpentier's.

LECTURE

Quand j'aurai assez d'argent, j'irai en Europe. J'ai surtout envie d'aller en France. Notre professeur en a tant parlé que j'ai déjà le sentiment de la bien connaître. D'abord, il faudra aller à Paris, et puis en province. Je visiterai sûrement

---

[1] Put "always" between "get up" and "early."

[2] "Hands" will be singular if each person is raising but one hand, otherwise plural. Use definite article instead of possessive adjective.

Grenoble, la ville où notre professeur a fait ses études. On dit que sa situation dans les Alpes est des plus belles. Dans le Midi, je verrai Carcassonne, cette ville fortifiée [1] qui a l'air de sortir tout droit du Moyen Age. Je pourrai visiter aussi le Mont-Saint-Michel,[2] autre monument médiéval, que je connais déjà par une belle affiche [3] au mur de la classe.

Lorsque j'irai là-bas, je voyagerai en auto car notre professeur nous a dit que c'est le meilleur moyen pour voir le pays de près. Dans mon auto j'irai de ville en ville et de province en province. Le professeur nous a dit que les routes sont bonnes, construites souvent sur d'anciennes voies [4] romaines extrêmement solides. Cela me fera plaisir de réfléchir que les anciens Romains, peut-être Jules César lui-même, se sont servis de ces routes. On dit que le Midi surtout est plein de vestiges [5] romains, et qu'on trouve partout des monuments qui datent du Moyen Age. Je suis sûr que je m'amuserai beaucoup en France, car de toutes les matières, je préfère l'histoire.

Dès que j'aurai fini mes voyages en France, j'irai en Suisse et en Belgique, où l'on parle français aussi. Je tiendrai à visiter Bruges en Belgique, car mon amie Hélène y a des parents.[6] Après avoir étudié le français, je saurai probablement me tirer d'affaire chez eux. Sinon, ces gens sauront peut-être parler anglais.

Aussitôt que j'aurai vu tout ce qu'il faut voir en Suisse et en Belgique, j'irai aux Pays-Bas, en Allemagne, en Italie et en Espagne, peut-être même au Portugal.

Mais je rêve. Me voici toujours devant mon bureau, chez moi, avec le devoir de demain à moitié terminé. C'est aujourd'hui lundi le douze décembre de ma première année à l'université. Il vaut mieux finir mes exercices sur le futur, et laisser les voyages pour l'avenir.

I. 1. Quand Maurice aura assez d'argent, il ____. 2. Il a surtout envie ____. 3. D'abord, il faudra aller ____ et puis ____. 4. Carcassonne est une ____ du Midi. 5. Maurice voyagera en auto, car c'est le meilleur moyen ____. 6. Dans l'auto, il ira ____ et ____. 7. On trouve beaucoup de vestiges romains dans ____. 8. Maurice tiendra à visiter Bruges, car ____. 9. Il espère savoir ____ chez eux. 10. Il ira dans d'autres pays après avoir vu ____ en Suisse et en Belgique. 11. Mais en ce moment-ci, Maurice est ____. 12. Il ____ laisser les voyages pour l'avenir.

---

[1] **fortifié** *fortified*
[2] **le Mont-Saint-Michel** ancient abbey on summit of fortified rock off Normandy coast.
[3] **une affiche** *poster*
[4] **la voie** *way, highway*
[5] **les vestiges** *vestiges, remains*
[6] Here, "relatives."

VOCABULARY

à moitié terminé   half finished
après avoir étudié   after having studied
avoir envie de   to feel like, want to
avoir le sentiment (l'impression) de   to have the feeling of
de ... en ...   from ... to ..., from one ... to another
des plus belles   one of the most beautiful

en ce moment   at this moment, now
faire des études   to study, go to school
faire plaisir (à)   to please
il vaut mieux   it's better, one had better
se tirer d'affaire   to get along, manage
tenir à   to be anxious to
tout ce qu'il faut voir   all there is to see
tout droit   directly, straight

s'amuser   to have a good time
s'appeler   to be named, be called
aussitôt que   as soon as
l'**avenir** (*m.*)   future
la **balle**   ball
céder   to give up, yield
construire (**construit**)   to build, construct
la **matière**   matter, subject
mener   to lead
le **Midi**   the South (of France)
le **moyen**   means
le **Moyen Age**   Middle Ages
noir   black

partout   everywhere
les **Pays-Bas**   Netherlands
plein (**de**)   full (of)
se promener   to take a walk, ride
la **promesse**   promise
rappeler   to remind; **se rappeler**   to remember, recall
réfléchir   to reflect, think
rejeter   to reject
rêver   to dream
romain   Roman; un **Romain**   a Roman
la **route**   road, route
sinon   if not, otherwise

PATTERN SENTENCE DRILL

1. Qu'allez-vous faire cet été?
   — vas _____?
   _____ lire _____?
   _____ hiver?
   _____ -ils _____?

2. J'irai à la campagne dès que j'aurai fini mes classes.
   Nous _____.
   _____en France _____.
   _____ aussitôt que _____.
   Il _____.

3. Je vais chez mon oncle, qui a une ferme.

   Ils _____.

   _____ parents _____.

   _____ chevaux.

   Marie _____.

4. Présentez-lui mes respects quand vous le verrez.

   _____-leur _____.

   _____ nos _____.

   _____ lorsque _____.

   _____ trouverez.

5. Lorsque vous arriverez chez votre oncle, l'aiderez-vous dans les champs?

   _____ tu _____?

   Quand _____?

   _____ amis _____?

   _____ Pierre _____?

6. Je ferai de mon mieux; je travaillerai dur.

   Jacques _____.

   _____ étudiera_____.

   _____ beaucoup.

   Nous _____.

7. On se lève de bonne heure à la ferme.

   _____ chez M. Bourget.

   Nous _____.

   _____ tard _____.

   Ils _____.

8. Je me lèverai probablement au lever du soleil.

   Nous _____.

   _____quelquefois _____.

   _____ cinq heures du matin.

   Jacques_____.

9. D'abord je m'occuperai des poules.

   _____ il _____.

   _____ cheval.

   Plus tard _____.

   _____ vous _____.

10. On les appelle et on leur jette du grain.
    Nous _____.
    ____ le _____.
    _____donnons ____.
    _____ cadeaux.

11. Reviendrez-vous chez vous à la fin de l'été?
    _____ -ils _____?
    _____ commencement___?
    _____ hiver?
    Iront _____?

12. J'espère rester à la ferme aussi longtemps que possible.
    Nous_____.
    _____ en ville _____.
    Elles _____.
    _____ chez nous _____.

11

Negatives

Interrogative Pronouns and Adjectives

Verbs in *vrir* and *ffrir*

PATTERN SENTENCES

1. Qu'est-ce qu'il faut voir à la Nouvelle-Orléans?
2. Quoi! Vous ne l'avez jamais visitée?
3. Jamais. Quelle sorte de ville est-ce?
4. Ce n'est pas du tout une ville ordinaire.
5. Le Vieux Carré, le quartier français, n'a guère changé depuis le temps de Napoléon.
6. Ce quartier n'est qu'un écho du passé qui n'existe plus.
7. Qu'est-ce qui le rend donc si particulier?
8. Nul endroit n'offre un aspect plus pittoresque, avec ses maisons antiques et ses vieilles balustrades en fer.
9. Aujourd'hui le quartier n'est ni français ni tout à fait américain.

1. What must one see in New Orleans?
2. What! You have never visited it?
3. Never. What sort of city is it?
4. It's not at all an ordinary city.
5. The Vieux Carré (Old Square), the French Quarter, has hardly changed since the time of Napoleon.
6. This quarter is but an echo of the past that no longer exists.
7. What makes it so special, then?
8. No spot offers a more picturesque aspect of old-fashioned houses and old iron railings.
9. Today the quarter is neither French nor entirely American.

10. Personne ne doit manquer d'aller dans un des restaurants célèbres.
11. Lequel préférez-vous?
12. Moi, je préfère dîner chez Antoine, car je ne connais aucun restaurant avec plus d'ambiance.

10. Nobody should fail to go to one of the famous restaurants.
11. Which one do you prefer?
12. Personally I prefer to dine at Antoine's, for I don't know any restaurant with more atmosphere.

60. Negatives

Besides **ne ... pas,** the commonest negatives are the following.

ne ... point not a bit		**ne ... personne** nobody	
ne ... pas du tout not at all		**ne ... plus** no longer, no more	
ne ... jamais never		**ne ... ni ... ni** neither ... nor	
ne ... guère scarcely		**ne ... aucun(e)**	not any, no ...
ne ... rien nothing		**ne ... nul(le)**	

EXAMPLES

Nous ne dirons rien. We shall say nothing.
Il ne chante plus. He no longer sings.
Je n'en ai guère. I have scarcely any.

A partitive after **ne ... ni ... ni** takes neither **de** nor an article.

Ils n'ont ni or ni argent. They have neither gold nor silver.

Quasi-negative is **ne ... que,** which may be translated *nothing but,* but is usually rendered by *only*.

Il n'a que des inquiétudes. He has nothing but worries.
Je n'ai que cinq francs sur moi. I have only five francs with me.

Rien and **personne** are often used as the subject, as is also **aucun(e)** (which may be either adjective or pronoun). In this case, the order of the negative is reversed, but the **ne** always remains before the verb.

Rien ne m'est arrivé. Nothing happened to me.
Personne n'est encore parti. Nobody has left yet.
Aucune idée ne m'est venue. No idea came to me.

NOTE: **Personne** takes masculine agreement when it means *nobody*. When it means *person* (as in **une belle personne**) it is feminine.

In a compound tense, the auxiliary becomes negative rather than the participle.

Il n'aura pas vu la photographie. He will not have seen the photograph.
Nous n'avons point résisté. We did not resist a bit.

On the other hand, **que** is placed immediately before the word or phrase it qualifies, while **personne,** when object, always follows the participle.

> **Il n'a fait que raconter des plaisanteries.**   He did nothing but tell jokes.
> **Il n'y a dans ce livre que deux histoires.**   There are in this book only two stories.
> **Nous n'avons vu personne.**   We did not see anybody.

A. Express in French.

1. I heard nothing.   2. No one came.   3. James has neither brother nor sister.   4. He has never worked hard.   5. I don't see anybody.   6. I hardly have the time.   7. He doesn't like cheese at all.   8. There are only three trees in front of the house.   9. We have no more money.   10. There is nothing to eat.[1]   11. I have no idea of the time.   12. That house is no longer new.   13. I am only a poor student.   14. She said nothing and saw no one.

61. Interrogative pronouns

The interrogative pronouns in their simplest form are as follows.

> **qui?**   who, whom? (all uses)
> **que?**   what? (predicate nominative, or object of verb)
> **quoi?**   what? (object of preposition, or used alone)

As an interrogative, **qui** may refer only to persons.   It may be the subject, the object of a verb, or the object of a preposition.

> **Qui est là?**   Who is there?
> **Qui avez-vous vu?**   Whom have you seen?
> **De qui parlez-vous?**   Of whom are you talking?

As interrogatives, **que** and **quoi** may refer only to things, and may never be used as the subject.

> **Que voyez-vous?**   What do you see?
> **Qu'est-ce?   Qu'est-ce que c'est?**   What is it?
> **A quoi pensez-vous?**   Of what are you thinking?
> **Quoi?** [2] **Vous n'avez pas d'argent?**   What?   You have no money?

Inasmuch as neither of the words for *what* may be used as subject, we must for that purpose employ the locution **qu'est-ce qui?**

> **Qu'est-ce qui vous ennuie?**   What is bothering you?   (What is it that is bothering you?)
> **Qu'est-ce qui est arrivé?**   What happened?

---

[1] Use **à** before the infinitive.
[2] **Quoi** is as much interjection as interrogative pronoun in this use.

Similar long forms exist for the other uses, too — e.g., **qui est-ce qui** (for subject **qui**), **qui est-ce que** (for object **qui**), and **qu'est-ce que** (for **que**) — but only the last is common.

> **Qu'est-ce que c'est?** What is it? (equivalent to **Qu'est-ce?**)
> **Qu'est-ce que vous avez vu?** What did you see? (equivalent to **Qu'avez-vous vu?**)
> **Qu'est-ce que c'est que cela?** What is that?

Since the long forms carry with them their own inversion, they are followed by normal declarative order.

> **Qu'est-ce que *vous voyez?*** (short form **Que** *voyez-vous?*)

B. Restate each of the following as a direct question, then answer in a complete sentence.

> *Example:* Demandez à Jacques ce qu'il voit dans la rue.
> Jacques, qu'est-ce que vous voyez dans la rue?
> Je vois une auto dans la rue.

1. Demandez-moi ce qui m'intéresse.
2. Demandez à Marie ce qu'elle fait le soir.
3. Demandez-lui ce qui se trouve dans cette ville.
4. Demandez à Jean ce qu'il a fait chez son oncle.
5. Demandez à Jacques qui il voit dans la rue.
6. Demandez-lui ce qu'elle regarde par la fenêtre.
7. Demandez-lui qui elle regarde par la fenêtre.
8. Demandez-lui qui la regarde par la fenêtre.

C. Using an interrogative pronoun, ask a question for which each of the following would be a suitable answer.

1. Jacques est à la porte.
2. Je vois la ferme là-bas.
3. Il y a un cadeau dans la boîte.
4. C'est un livre de français.
5. Nous parlons de Jean.
6. Je pense à ce qui est arrivé hier.

62. Interrogative adjectives

Interrogative adjectives have a form for each gender and number: **quel, quelle, quels, quelles.**

> **Quel roman?** What (Which) novel?
> **Quelle chanson?** What song?
> **Quels garçons?** Which boys?
> **Quelles jeunes filles?** Which girls?

Standing next to their noun, as above, they mean *what* or *which*. Used alone before the verb **être,** with their noun following the verb, they resemble pronouns, and if the noun refers to a person, may be translated *who*.

> **Quel est ce monsieur?** Who is that gentleman?
> **Quelle est cette dame?** Who is that lady?

In this use, they have the sense of "What sort of man is he?" or "What is the position or occupation of that man?" rather than merely asking for his name.

63. *Lequel* forms

Occasionally we meet a real pronoun form of **quel,** which is **lequel.** It too has four forms: **lequel, laquelle, lesquels, lesquelles.** As an interrogative, it means *which one*, *which ones*, or simply *which*, and is used when a choice is called for.

> **Voici deux couteaux. Lequel préférez-vous?** Here are two knives. Which one do you prefer?
> **Voilà trois fourchettes. Laquelle est la plus longue?** There are three forks. Which is the longest?
> **Lesquelles de ces cuillers voulez-vous employer?** Which (ones) of these spoons do you want to use?

All of the forms, except **laquelle,** combine like definite articles with **à** and **de: auquel, auxquels, auxquelles; duquel, desquels, desquelles.**

> **Auquel de ces hommes a-t-il donné l'argent?** To which (one) of these men did he give the money?
> **Duquel de ces livres avez-vous besoin?** Which of these books do you need?

D. Substitution Drill.
1. Quel *livre* avez-vous là? (*clef, fourchettes, journaux*)
2. Quel est le *monsieur* dans la salle de classe? (*dame, hommes, jeunes filles*)
3. Voici deux *couteaux*. Lequel est à vous? (*cuillers, cahiers, bicyclettes*)
4. A laquelle de ces *dames* pensez-vous? (*hommes, arbres, fermes*)
5. Desquelles de ces *fourchettes* a-t-il besoin? (*cuillers, couteaux, mouchoirs*)

64. Verbs in *vrir* and *ffrir*

Verbs ending in **vrir** and **ffrir** (the common ones are **ouvrir, couvrir, offrir, souffrir**) have two peculiarities: (1) their past participle ends in **ert,** and (2) their present tense follows the pattern of CONJUGATION I instead of CONJUGATION II.

ouvrir	couvrir	offrir	souffrir
to open	*to cover*	*to offer*	*to suffer*
j'ouvre	je couvre	j'offre	je souffre
tu ouvres	tu couvres	tu offres	tu souffres
il ouvre	il couvre	il offre	il souffre
nous ouvrons	nous couvrons	nous offrons	nous souffrons
vous ouvrez	vous couvrez	vous offrez	vous souffrez
ils ouvrent	ils couvrent	ils offrent	ils souffrent
PAST PART.	PAST PART.	PAST PART.	PAST PART.
ouvert	**couvert**	**offert**	**souffert**

E. Substitution Drill.

1. *Je* vous offre la maison pour l'été. (*Nous, Il, Ils, Elle*)
2. *Il* ouvre la porte pour les dames. (*Vous, Elle, Nous, Je*)
3. *Elle* a couvert le bureau de livres. (*Nous, On, Tu, Ils*)
4. *J'*ouvrirai la fenêtre tout de suite. (*Elle, Jacques, Nous, Vous*)
5. *Il* n'a jamais souffert de sa vie. (*Je, Nous, Vous, Tu*)
6. *Nous* leur offrirons du café. (*Elle, Je, Vous, On*)
7. Est-ce qu'*il* souffre beaucoup? (*vous, tu, elles, elle*)
8. *Ils* couvrent la terre de fleurs. (*On, Nous, Je, Elle*)

F. Express in French.

1. Who is that man? 2. Which of the two boys is your brother? 3. Of the four girls, which one is the prettiest? 4. To which of the men did you offer the money? 5. Who has suffered more than I? 6. Which people are coming today? 7. What do you see in front of the house? 8. What! You haven't finished your lessons? 9. What happened to you? 10. With which (ones) of those maps did he cover the wall? 11. I will offer you two books. Which ones do you want? 12. Which of the doors shall I open?

LECTURE

Un jour le professeur a décidé de nous interroger au sujet de nos maisons. « Qui veut essayer de décrire sa maison en français? » demande-t-il. D'abord personne ne répond. « Il ne faut pas avoir peur, continue-t-il. Je ne demande que des renseignements généraux. Par exemple, quelle sorte de maison habitez-vous, Maurice?

— Moi, monsieur? Mais[1] une maison toute ordinaire, je vous assure. Certainement ce n'est guère un palais.

— Ça ne fait rien. Décrivez-la. Commencez par l'extérieur.

— Eh bien, devant la maison il y a une pelouse,[2] et derrière, un jardin potager[3] où l'on cultive des légumes comme la laitue, les tomates et les haricots verts.

— Et la maison elle-même?

— La maison est en briques. Elle est assez vieille maintenant, et couverte de lierre.[4] Pour y entrer il n'y a qu'une marche à monter et une petite véranda à traverser.

— Et à l'intérieur, qu'est-ce qu'on trouve?

— La porte d'entrée s'ouvre sur un vestibule qui traverse la maison jusqu'au fond. Dans ce vestibule il y a un escalier qui monte au premier étage.[5]

— Avant de monter, dites-nous quelles sont les pièces qui se trouvent au rez-de-chaussée.

— Eh bien, d'un côté il y a le salon, assez grand et plein de meubles anciens, car ma mère a la passion des antiquités.[6] Du salon on passe par une porte assez large dans la bibliothèque, qui sert aussi de bureau à mon père. Le jour, cette pièce est bien éclairée par deux portes-fenêtres, qui donnent sur le jardin à côté de la maison. Dans ce jardin il y a un vieux puits[7] qu'on n'emploie plus et qui est actuellement couvert d'une grosse pierre.

— Quittons le jardin et rentrons dans la maison.

— De l'autre côté du vestibule il y a la salle à manger, et par derrière, la cuisine. De la cuisine on peut descendre par un escalier dans la cave.

— Qu'est-ce qui se trouve au premier étage?

— Au premier il n'y a que les chambres à coucher, avec des lits, des armoires[8] et ainsi de suite, et la salle de bains.

— Est-ce qu'il y a aussi un deuxième[9] étage?

— Il y a un grenier,[10] où il n'y a rien que des choses trop vieilles même pour ma mère. Nous n'y allons presque jamais.

---

[1] Here, **mais** means *why* rather than *but*.
[2] **la pelouse** *lawn*
[3] **le jardin potager** *vegetable garden*
[4] **le lierre** *ivy*
[5] **Le premier étage** in French is the second floor. The ground floor is **le rez-de-chaussée**.
[6] **une antiquité** *antique*
[7] **le puits** *well, pit*
[8] **une armoire** *clothes closet, wardrobe*
[9] When **ième** is added to a numeral, it becomes an ordinal.
[10] **le grenier** *attic*

— Bon. C'est assez pour aujourd'hui. Vous avez si bien répondu, Maurice, qu'une autre fois vous pourrez nous faire un cours au sujet de la cuisine.

— Merci mille fois, monsieur. Oh, pourquoi n'ai-je pas eu le bon sens de ne pas ouvrir la bouche? »

Questions

Answer the following questions in complete sentences, basing your responses on the *Lecture*. Practice each until you can give the complete answer unhesitatingly without referring to the *Lecture*.

1. Sur quel sujet le professeur décide-t-il d'interroger la classe? 2. Qui répond d'abord à la question du professeur? 3. Quelle sorte de maison Maurice habite-t-il? 4. Qu'est-ce qu'il y a devant la maison? 5. Quels légumes cultive-t-on dans le jardin potager? 6. Est-ce que la maison est en pierre ou en briques? 7. De quoi la maison de Maurice est-elle couverte? 8. Combien de marches y a-t-il devant la maison? 9. Qu'est-ce qu'on trouve dans le vestibule? 10. Quelles pièces se trouvent au rez-de-chaussée? 11. Lesquelles se trouvent au premier? 12. Est-ce qu'on monte souvent au grenier?

VOCABULARY

à côté de beside, by
au sujet de about, concerning
avoir la passion de to be crazy about
avoir peur to be afraid
ça ne fait rien that makes no difference
donner sur (s'ouvrir sur) to open on, look out on

d'un côté on one side, on the one hand
et ainsi de suite and so on
faire un cours to give a lecture
par derrière behind that
servir de to serve as
tout(e) ordinaire quite ordinary

arriver to happen
la **bibliothèque** library
la **bouche** mouth
la **brique** brick
la **cave** cellar
la **chambre à coucher** (often simply **chambre**) bedroom
la **clef** key

le **couteau** knife
la **cuiller** spoon
la **cuisine** kitchen
décrire (décrit) to describe
éclairer to light, illuminate
une **entrée** entrance; **porte d'entrée** front door
un **escalier** stairway

un **étage**   floor, story
le **fond**   back, bottom, end
la **fourchette**   fork
habiter   to dwell, live
interroger   to question
le **jardin**   garden
la **laitue**   lettuce
large   wide, broad
le **lit**   bed
la **marche**   step (of stair)
le **meuble**   piece of furniture; (*pl.*) furniture
mille   thousand
le **mouchoir**   handkerchief
le **palais**   palace

passer   to pass, go through
la **pièce**   room, piece
la **pierre**   stone
la **porte-fenêtre**   French door, French window
quitter   to leave
les **renseignements** (*m.*)   information
la **salle à manger**   dining room; **salle de bains**   bathroom
le **salon**   living room
le **sens**   sense, direction; **bon sens**   common sense
le **sujet**   subject
la **tomate**   tomato

PATTERN SENTENCE DRILL

1. Qu'est-ce qu'il faut voir à la Nouvelle-Orléans?
   _____ France?
   _____ faire_____?
   Que _____?
   _____ visiter _____?

2. Vous ne l'avez jamais visitée?
   Il _____?
   _____ vue?
   _____ guère ___?
   _____ as _____?

3. Ce n'est pas du tout une ville ordinaire.
   _____ plus _____.
   _____intéressante.
   ___ sont_____.
   _____ livres _____.

4. Le Vieux Carré n'a guère changé depuis le temps de Napoléon.
   _____ maison _____.
   _____ Moyen Age.
   _____ jamais _____.
   _____ monuments _____.

5. Ce quartier n'est qu'un écho du passé.
   _____ vestige _____.
   Ces _____.
   ___rues _____.
   ___palais _____.

6. Qu'est-ce qui le rend donc si particulier?
   _____ beau?
   _____ fait _____?
   _____ belle?
   _____ les _____?

7. Nul endroit n'offre un aspect plus pittoresque.
   ___ ville _____.
   _____ agréable.
   _____ climat _____.
   _____ moins _____.

8. Aujourd'hui le quartier n'est ni français ni américain.
   Par conséquent _____.
   _____ la cuisine _____.
   _____ anglaise.
   _____ les gens _____.

9. Personne ne doit manquer d'aller dans un des restaurants célèbres.
   _____ cafés _____.
   Vous ne devez pas _____.
   _____hésiter _____.
   _____entrer _____.

10. Je ne connais aucun restaurant avec plus d'ambiance.
    _____maison _____.
    _____ antiquités.
    Nous _____.
    _____ meubles.

12

Imperfect
(and Pluperfect)

Conditional
(and Conditional Perfect)

*Plaire, Rire,
Suivre, Produire*

PATTERN SENTENCES

1. Que feriez-vous si vous étiez artiste?

2. Je ferais des portraits de gens riches, aussi deviendrais-je riche moi-même.

3. Mais peut-être ne vous achèteraient-ils rien.

4. Oh, si j'avais assez de talent, ils préféreraient mes portraits.

5. Mon grand-père était artiste quand il était jeune.

6. A peine avait-il fini une peinture qu'on l'achetait.

7. Il m'a dit qu'une fois il avait commencé une nature morte.

8. Elle représentait une grande assiette avec un oiseau et un poisson morts dessus.

9. Il venait de sortir pour un moment quand ma grand-mère l'a vendue à un client.

---

1. What would you do if you were an artist?

2. I would do portraits of rich people, and so would get rich myself.

3. But maybe they would not buy anything from you.

4. Oh, if I had enough talent, they would prefer my portraits.

5. My grandfather was an artist when he was young.

6. He would scarcely have finished a painting when someone would buy it.

7. He told me that once he had begun a still life.

8. It represented a big plate with a dead bird and fish on it.

9. He had just gone out for a moment when my grandmother sold it to a customer.

10. « S'il l'avait bien regardée, a dit mon grand-père, il aurait remarqué que l'oiseau n'avait point de queue.

11. — Je crois que cela lui plaît d'avoir une œuvre inachevée, a-t-elle répondu.

12. En tout cas, il a beaucoup ri, et quand il est sorti il riait toujours. »

10. "If he had looked at it carefully," said my grandfather, "he would have noticed that the bird had no tail at all."

11. "I guess he likes having an unfinished painting," she replied.

12. "In any case, he laughed uproariously, and when he went out he was still laughing."

65. Imperfect tense

To express an action or situation which covered an indefinite period of time in the past, or was recurrent or habitual, French uses the imperfect tense (*imparfait*), which may be translated in various ways.[1] The endings are identical for all verbs, whether regular or irregular, and the stem may be found, in all verbs but **être**, by dropping the **ons** from the first person plural of the present tense.

donn ons **fais** ons **av** ons **finiss** ons **all** ons **mange** ons **commenç** ons

The endings, which are all pronounced alike except the first and second persons plural, are:

ais	ions
ais	iez
ait	aient

pouvoir *can, to be able*	**nager** *to swim*	**placer** *to place, put*
je pouvais	je nageais	je plaçais
tu pouvais	tu nageais	tu plaçais
il pouvait	il nageait	il plaçait
nous pouvions	nous nagions	nous placions
vous pouviez	vous nagiez	vous placiez
ils pouvaient	ils nageaient	ils plaçaient

NOTE: The **e** after the **g** and the cedilla under the **c** are needed to keep these consonants soft before **a,** and are dropped from the first and second persons plural because **g** and **c** are naturally soft before **i.**

Être alone has a stem (**ét–**) not found in the present tense.

j'étais	nous étions
tu étais	vous étiez
il était	ils étaient

---

[1] See Section 67.

66. Pluperfect tense

Combining the imperfect of **avoir** or **être** with the past participle of a verb produces the pluperfect tense (*plus-que-parfait*).

finir

j'avais fini *I had finished*
tu avais fini
il avait fini
nous avions fini
vous aviez fini
ils avaient fini

venir

j'étais venu *I had come*
tu étais venu
il était venu
nous étions venus
vous étiez venu(s)
ils étaient venus

se tromper *to be mistaken*

je m'étais trompé *I had been mistaken*
tu t'étais trompé
il s'était trompé
nous nous étions trompés
vous vous étiez trompé(s)
ils s'étaient trompés

A. Read aloud, then reread first in the imperfect tense and then in the pluperfect.

1. Ils commencent à lire l'histoire.
2. Il souffre beaucoup du froid.
3. Mangez-vous le dîner?
4. Je ne comprends pas la question.
5. Nous sommes dans le salon.
6. Vous n'avez plus d'argent.
7. Elle garde toujours ses meubles anciens.
8. Il travaille dur à la ferme.
9. Je me lève de bonne heure.
10. Ils ne partent jamais avant minuit.

67. Imperfect or *passé composé*?

The imperfect, contrary to the *passé composé*, depicts an action or condition whose limits are unexpressed or undefined in time, as "The sky was blue," "The man lived on Thirty-first Street," "Peanuts were selling for thirty cents a pound." It also expresses what used to be true, or what habitually happened. English uses various locutions to convey these concepts, in addition to using a plain past tense: "He *used to go* to school in the winter," "She *generally ate* her lunch in the diner," "John *kept dropping* his pipe," "Jones *would* often *drop in* for a cup of tea," "The boys *were* always *fooling around* the sand pile." In all these cases, French would use the imperfect of the verb, adding like English an occasional adverbial expression to enhance the feeling of continuity or habituality. In translating from the French, the student should strive for the English verb form which best fits the context.

Il *faisait* froid. It *was* cold.

Jean *portait* son meilleur complet. John *was wearing* his best suit.

Quand il *demeurait* à côté de nous, *j'allais* le voir tous les jours. When he *lived* next to us, I *would go* and see him every day.

L'enfant *répétait toujours* les mêmes paroles. The child *kept repeating* the same words.

Often the imperfect occurs in the same sentence with the *passé composé*, in which case it is the imperfect that tells what was going on when something happened, while the *passé composé* tells what happened.

Quand nous sommes arrivés, il pleuvait. When we arrived, it was raining.

Pendant qu'il était dans le magasin, quelqu'un a volé sa bicyclette. While he was in the store, somebody stole his bicycle.

B. Express in French.

1. He was beginning his lunch when I entered. 2. It was very cold that day. 3. He kept coming back every day. 4. I was hungry. 5. She had offered me some vegetables. 6. It was three o'clock when they closed the doors. 7. We had come on time. 8. You were choosing a bicycle when we arrived. 9. They were traveling fast. 10. Did they open the windows from time to time? 11. Had she already left? 12. You had not read your lesson, I guess. 13. We used to swim every day. 14. She was afraid of dogs.

68. Conditional

In a sentence like "If he were here, I would give him a piece of my mind," *would give* is said to be in the "conditional tense" (*conditionnel*). This tense is formed in French by simply combining the imperfect endings with the future stem.

donner

je donner**ais** *I would give*
tu donner**ais**
il donner**ait**
nous donner**ions**
vous donner**iez**
ils donner**aient**

faire

je fer**ais** *I would make*
tu fer**ais**
il fer**ait**
nous fer**ions**
vous fer**iez**
ils fer**aient**

69. Conditional perfect

The compound form of this tense, called "conditional perfect" (*conditionnel passé*), consists of the conditional of **avoir** or **être** plus the past participle of the verb: **j'aurais parlé** (*I would have spoken*), **je serais tombé** (*I would have fallen*).

70. Uses of conditional and conditional perfect

The principal use of the conditional and conditional perfect is in the conclusion of "if" sentences, in which the "if clause" stands in the imperfect or pluperfect, respectively.

Si le garçon finissait son travail avant cinq heures, je le payerais. If the boy should finish his work before five o'clock, I would pay him.
Si j'étais riche, je voyagerais. If I were rich, I'd travel.
Si mon père avait été ici, l'accident ne serait pas arrivé. If my father had been here, the accident would not have happened.
Il aurait accompli son œuvre s'il avait vécu. He would have fulfilled his work if he had lived.
Si Jean s'était levé plus tôt, il serait arrivé à l'heure. If John had gotten up earlier, he would have arrived on time.

Another common use of the conditional is in the verb of an indirect statement, when the main verb is in a past tense.

Il m'a promis qu'il viendrait. He promised me he would come.
Ils ont demandé s'il chanterait. They asked if (whether) he would sing.
Elles se demandaient si elles auraient le temps. They wondered if (whether) they would have time.

A third use of the conditional is in the "softened statement," where it is the main verb.

Je voudrais vous demander un service. I would like to ask a favor of you.
J'aimerais vous accompagner. I would love to accompany you.
Que voudriez-vous faire? What would you like to do?
Il vaudrait mieux dire la vérité. It would be better to tell the truth.

C. Substitution Drill.

1. Si Jean venait à votre soirée, *je* viendrais aussi. (*nous, Marie, la famille, ses frères*)
2. Si *elle* n'était pas fatiguée, elle ferait son devoir. (*il, je, les étudiants, nous*)
3. On a dit qu'*elle* l'apporterait. (*elles, nous, vous, il*)
4. *Je* voudrais bien visiter Paris. (*Jean, Nous, Suzanne, Lucie et Berthe*)
5. Aurait-*elle* aimé venir avec nous? (*tu, vous, il, ils*)
6. *Je* serais allé en ville si j'avais eu la voiture. (*Nous, Jacques, Mes amis, Mon amie*)

7. Si *vous* étiez venu plus tôt, vous auriez vu le président.   (*il, tu, nous, ces messieurs*)

8. Si *tu* te dépêchais un peu, tu pourrais finir ton travail.   (*vous, Pierre, nous, les dames*)

9. Je me demandais s'*il* passerait par ici.   (*vous, ils, on, tu*)

10. Si *vous* n'étiez pas fâché, pourquoi n'êtes-vous pas venu hier soir?   (*tu, Jean, Jeanne, ils*)

71. Special cases of inversion

It is customary to invert verb and subject after **peut-être** (*perhaps*), **à peine** (*scarcely, hardly*), and **aussi** (*and so*).   Note that when **aussi** begins a clause, it always has the meaning *and so*, and is not to be confused with **aussi** meaning *also*.

Peut-être étaient-ils déjà partis.   Perhaps they had already left.
A peine était-elle arrivée que le téléphone a sonné.   Hardly had she arrived when the telephone rang.
J'avais déjà vu le film, aussi ai-je refusé son invitation.   I had already seen the film, and so I refused his invitation.

72. *Venir de*

The idiom **venir de,** almost never used in the infinitive form itself, is invariably followed by the infinitive.   In this construction, **venir** can be only in the present or imperfect.   In the present, the translation is *just, have just,* or *has just,* followed by a past participle in English.

Ils viennent de partir.   They (have) just left.
Elle vient d'arriver.   She (has) just arrived.

In the imperfect, the translation is *had just.*

Nous venions de commencer.   We had just begun.
Quand nous nous sommes approchés de la gare, l'heure venait de sonner.   When we approached the station, the hour had just struck.

73. Special use of *il y a*

Used before a time expression, **il y a** frequently means *ago.*   In this usage, the main verb will normally be in a past tense.

Le monsieur est sorti il y a longtemps.   The gentleman left a long time ago.
Vous n'étiez pas si heureux il y a quinze ans.   You were not so happy fifteen years ago.
Il y a vingt ans, la guerre venait de commencer.   Twenty years ago, war had just begun.

D. Express in French.

1. Perhaps he will come soon. 2. Scarcely had she left when they arrived. 3. We have just bought some furniture. 4. The gentlemen had just dined when I entered the dining room. 5. He left for London ten days ago. 6. They arrived late, and so they didn't see him after all. 7. I just got up five minutes ago. 8. In fact, that happened a long time ago. 9. Four years ago, I had just arrived in Paris. 10. He had scarcely begun to read when he fell asleep.

74. Irregular present tenses

plaire	**rire**	**suivre**	**produire**
to please	*to laugh*	*to follow*	*to produce*
je plais	je ris	je suis	je produis
tu plais	tu ris	tu suis	tu produis
il plaît	il rit	il suit	il produit
nous plaisons	nous rions	nous suivons	nous produisons
vous plaisez	vous riez	vous suivez	vous produisez
ils plaisent	ils rient	ils suivent	ils produisent
PAST PART.	PAST PART.	PAST PART.	PAST PART.
plu	**ri**	**suivi**	**produit**

Like **produire** are **conduire** (*to drive, lead*), **réduire** (*to reduce*), and **construire** (*to build*).

E. Substitution Drill.

1. *Nous* suivons le couloir jusqu'au fond. (*Vous, Il, Je, Les garçons*)
2. *Il* produit toutes sortes de meubles. (*Nous, Vous, Ils, On*)
3. Est-ce que *le salon* vous plaît?[1] (*les fleurs, la salle à manger, le parfum, nous*)
4. Maintenant *vous* riez, mais demain vous allez pleurer. (*il, nous, tu, elles*)
5. Combien de *parfum* a-t-on produit? (*mouchoirs, encre, bouteilles, fromage*)
6. *Nous* avons beaucoup ri. (*Vous, Tu, Ils, Elle*)
7. *La chambre* ne lui plaisait[1] point. (*Les cadeaux, Vous, Cette idée, Sa conduite*)
8. Si *je* pouvais, je les suivrais. (*Nous, Il, Ils, Vous*)

---

[1] Note that **plaire** takes an indirect object, and is often used to express "liking": **Est-ce que cela lui plaît?** *Does he like it?*

LECTURE

Aujourd'hui notre classe a été plus intéressante que d'ordinaire. La semaine dernière le professeur avait dit qu'il nous ferait voir quelques exemples d'art français, aussi a-t-il apporté en classe des projections [1] sur l'histoire de la peinture française. Moi, qui pensais [2] plaire au professeur, j'ai demandé si je pourrais l'aider, et il m'a dit que je pourrais changer les projections pendant qu'il les commentait. Il a commencé par quelques tableaux de deux peintres du dix-septième siècle, Poussin et Le Lorrain. Comme je n'avais jamais étudié l'histoire de l'art, je ne connaissais point ces peintres classiques avec leurs paysages si tranquilles. J'ai surtout aimé un tableau de Poussin où on voit des bergers [3] devant un monument en pierre, et un autre du Lorrain qui représente un port de mer au coucher du soleil. A voir ces tableaux, on dirait que le monde était bien tranquille, et que personne n'avait de souci. Ou la vie était différente dans ce temps-là, ou on ne lisait pas les journaux. Peut-être n'y avait-il pas de journaux alors. Je me le demande . . .

Ensuite le professeur nous a montré quelques tableaux du siècle suivant, mais les œuvres de Boucher, de Fragonard, de Watteau et de Greuze m'ont laissé un peu froid. En réalité, la peinture du dix-huitième siècle ne m'a guère intéressé, sauf quelques œuvres de Chardin. La technique de ce peintre, selon notre professeur, a devancé [4] l'impressionisme du dix-neuvième siècle. Mais probablement, la raison pour laquelle je l'ai préféré aux autres c'est que ses tableaux sont presque toujours des natures mortes. Puisque la classe de français est à onze heures du matin, j'ai toujours faim avant la fin de l'heure, et ces peintures m'ont fait penser à mon déjeuner.

Les impressionnistes ont beaucoup plu à la classe, surtout aux jeunes filles, qui ont préféré Monet parce que les couleurs qu'il emploie rendent la nature si belle. Quant à moi, il faut dire que je confonds souvent Monet avec un autre artiste impressionniste qui s'appelle Manet. A mon avis, l'un ou l'autre aurait bien fait de changer de nom. S'ils l'avaient fait, ils auraient évité beaucoup de confusions à des étudiants tels que moi.

Nous n'avons pas eu assez de temps pour tout ce que nous avions à voir. A peine le professeur avait-il commencé à nous montrer des projections de l'art contemporain que la sonnette a mis fin à l'heure. Moi, je n'en étais pas du tout fâché, car j'avais peur de ne pas comprendre cet art moderne. J'ai lu quelque part qu'une fois des juges ont donné le prix à un tableau qui était à l'envers !

---

[1] **la projection** *photographic slide*
[2] **Pensais** is first person singular to agree with **qui,** which in turn refers to **moi.**
[3] **le berger** *shepherd*   [4] **devancer** *to anticipate*

Questions

1. Qu'est-ce que le professeur a apporté en classe aujourd'hui? 2. Pourquoi est-ce que Maurice voulait aider le professeur? 3. De quel siècle sont Poussin et Le Lorrain? 4. Qu-est-ce qu'on voit dans le tableau du Lorrain? 5. A voir ces tableaux, quelle impression a-t-on de ce siècle? 6. Qu'est-ce que Maurice se demande, au sujet de ce temps-là? 7. Que pense-t-il des peintres du dix-huitième siècle en général? 8. Pourquoi Maurice aime-t-il les tableaux de Chardin? 9. A quelle heure est la classe de Maurice? 10. Lequel a été le peintre préféré des jeunes filles, Monet ou Manet? 11. Pourquoi le professeur n'a-t-il pas fait voir des exemples d'art moderne? 12. Pourquoi Maurice n'en était-il pas fâché?

VOCABULARY

à l'envers upside down
à mon avis in my opinion
avoir à to have to, must
changer de nom to change names, change
  one's name

faire voir to show
je me (le) demande I wonder
par ici this way

un **an** year
la **bouteille** bottle
  commenter to comment on, explain
la **conduite** behavior
  confondre to confuse
  contemporain contemporary
le **coucher du soleil** sunset
la **couleur** color
le **couloir** corridor
  se demander to wonder
  éviter to avoid
  fâché angry; **être fâché de** to be
   sorry about
le **juge** judge
  ou . . . ou either . . . or
le **paysage** landscape

le **peintre** painter
le **port de mer** seaport
le **prix** prize, price
  quelque part somewhere
la **raison** reason
  selon according to
le **siècle** century
la **soirée** party, evening
la **sonnette** bell, buzzer
le **souci** anxiety, worry
  suivant following, next
le **tableau** picture, painting
  tel que such as, as
  tranquille calm, peaceful
la **voiture** car

PATTERN SENTENCE DRILL

1. Que feriez-vous si vous étiez artiste?
   _____ -tu _____?
   _____ peintre?
   ____ ferait _____?
   _____ sculpteur?

2. Je ferais des portraits de gens riches.
   _____ beaux enfants.
   Il _____.
   __ achèterait _____.
   _____ natures mortes.

3. Aussi deviendrais-je riche moi-même.
   _____ -nous _____.
   _____ célèbres _____.
   Peut-être_____.
   _____ eux-mêmes.

4. Mais peut-être ne vous achèteraient-ils rien.
   _____ me _____.
   _____ -on ____.
   _____ pas beaucoup.
   _____ interrogerait _____.

5. Si j'avais assez de talent, ils préféreraient mes portraits.
   _____ aimeraient _____.
   _____œuvres.
   __ il _____.
   _____ nous _____.

6. Mon grand-père était artiste quand il était jeune.
   _____ pauvre _____.
   _____ étudiant.
   ____ grand-mère _____.
   _____ belle _____.

7. A peine avait-il fini une peinture qu'on l'achetait.
   _____ tableau _____.
   _____ prenait.
   _____ commencé _____.
   _____ -je _____.

8. Une fois il avait commencé une nature morte.
   _____ fini _____.
   _____ paysage.
   ___ jour _____.
   _____ je _____.

9. Il venait de sortir quand ma grand-mère l'a vendue.
   _____ partir _____.
   Je _____.
   _____ on _____.
   _____ cassée.

10. S'il l'avait bien regardée, il aurait vu l'oiseau.
    _____ clef.
    _____ cherchée _____.
    _____ trouvé _.
    _ vous _____.

11. Je crois que cela lui plaît d'avoir une œuvre inachevée.
    _____ célèbre.
    _____ acheter _____.
    _____ portrait _____.
    _____ leur _____.

12. Quand il est sorti il riait toujours.
    _____. elle _____.
    _____ sont _____.
    _____ causaient ___.
    _____ entrées_____.

13

Relative Pronouns

Special Use of *à*

Boire, Devoir, Recevoir, Apercevoir

Special Uses of *Devoir*

PATTERN SENTENCES

1. Où est le livre que je lisais hier soir?

2. Vous voulez dire le livre dont nous parlions, vous et moi?

3. Oui, le livre à la couverture bleue.

4. Ah, je sais le livre auquel vous pensez.

5. C'est une histoire dont je connaissais le titre, mais je ne l'ai pas lue.

6. Je suppose que je devrais la lire un de ces jours.

7. En fait, j'aurais dû la lire il y a longtemps.

8. Quand je l'aurai finie, vous aussi, vous devrez la lire.

9. Merci, mon vieux. Je suivrai votre conseil avec plaisir.

10. A propos, est-ce que nous devons lire *l'Étranger* pour demain?

---

1. Where is the book I was reading last night?

2. You mean the book you and I were talking about?

3. Yes, the book with the blue cover.

4. Ah, I know the book you are thinking of.

5. It's a story whose title I knew, but I haven't read it.

6. I suppose I should read it one of these days.

7. In fact, I should have read it long ago.

8. When I have finished it, you will have to read it yourself.

9. Thanks, old man. I shall follow your advice with pleasure.

10. By the way, are we supposed to read *The Stranger* for tomorrow?

131

11. D'après le professeur, nous devions le lire pour aujourd'hui.

11. According to the professor, we were supposed to read it for today.

12. Zut alors ! J'ai dû mal comprendre ce qu'il a dit.

12. Darn ! I must have misunderstood what he said.

75. Relative pronouns

Relative pronouns refer to an antecedent, usually a noun or pronoun already mentioned, as in "The man who just passed is my uncle," where *who* is the relative pronoun, and *man* the antecedent to which it refers. Common relative pronouns in French are **qui, que,** and **dont,** all of which may refer to either persons or things.

Qui is subject.

> **la femme *qui* est dans la rue**   the woman *who* is in the street
> **la montre *qui* est cassée**   the watch *which* is broken
> **les chiens *qui* courent là-bas**   the dogs *that* are running over there

Que is direct object (often omitted in English, never in French).

> **les chevaux *que* je préfère**   the horses I prefer
> **le monsieur *que* j'ai remarqué**   the gentleman (*whom*) I noticed

Dont always contains **de.** It means *of which, of whom,* or *whose,* and occasionally, *in which* (with **manière, façon**).

> **la maison *dont* je parle**   the house *of which* I am speaking
> **l'argent *dont* j'ai besoin**   the money I need (*of which* I have need)
> **la manière *dont* il parle**   the manner *in which* he speaks
> **la façon *dont* nous l'avons reçu**   the way *in which* we received him

NOTE: **Dont** is always followed by straight declarative order (subject, verb, complement), no matter what the English may be, and the noun following retains its article.

> **le garçon dont *le père est si grand***   the boy whose *father is so tall*
> **la femme dont *j'aime la fille***   the woman whose *daughter I love*

Notice that in the last example, English puts subject after object, whereas French order is normal.

The pronoun **qui,** which is normally subject, may, for persons only, be used as the object of a preposition.

> **le médecin *à qui* je pense**   the doctor I am thinking of (*of whom* I am thinking)
> **l'ami *pour qui* j'ai fait cela**   the friend *for whom* I did that

Another very common relative is **où,** which may refer only to nouns of place or time. Its fundamental meaning is *in which, on which,* or *to which,* but it is frequently translated *where* or *when.*

la maison où	} je suis né	the house where	} I was born
le jour où		the day when	

A. Combine the following pairs of sentences by means of *qui* or *que.*

> *Examples:* a. Voici un étudiant. Il est dans ma classe.
> Voici un étudiant qúi est dans ma classe.
>
> b. J'ai vu le monsieur. Vous me l'aviez indiqué.
> J'ai vu le monsieur que vous m'aviez indiqué.

1. Je connais la ferme. Elle est à votre oncle.
2. Voici le cadeau. On me l'a donné pour Noël.
3. J'ai entendu un bruit. Il n'est pas familier.
4. Avez-vous trouvé la faute? Elle est dans la première phrase.
5. J'admire la vue. On l'a du sommet.
6. Nous aimons le fromage. Vous l'avez apporté.
7. Voilà la petite fille. Elle a chanté pour nous.
8. Je vais vous raconter une histoire. Je viens de l'entendre.

B. Combine by means of **dont,** a preposition plus **qui,** or **où.**

> *Example:* Voici l'œuvre. Nous en avons parlé.
> Voici l'œuvre dont nous avons parlé.

1. Voilà la dame. Je lui ai parlé.
2. Est-ce le même endroit? Je vous en ai donné la description.
3. Nous avons visité la maison. Victor Hugo y est mort.
4. Vous connaissez l'homme. Georges lui a donné la clef.
5. Voulez-vous me montrer la revue? Vous y avez vu l'article.
6. C'est la même personne. On a bâti cette maison pour elle.
7. Qui est cette dame? Je vous ai vu avec elle hier soir.
8. Voilà le juge. Je connais sa fille.

76. *Lequel* as relative

The four **lequel** forms (**lequel, laquelle, lesquels, lesquelles**), already met as interrogatives, occur also as relative pronouns. All but **laquelle** combine like definite articles with **à** and **de: auquel, auxquels, auxquelles; duquel, desquels, desquelles.** They may refer to either persons or things.

la maison à laquelle il pensait   the house of which he was thinking
la dame pour laquelle on a appelé un taxi   the lady for whom they called a taxi
les événements auxquels il faisait allusion   the events to which he was alluding

Unless another preposition is present, **dont** is generally used rather than the **duquel** forms.

> **le garçon pour la mère duquel on a donné le concert**   the boy for whose mother they gave the concert
> BUT
> **le garçon dont la mère a donné le concert**   the boy whose mother gave the concert

C. Substitution Drill.

1. Voici l'*histoire* à laquelle je pensais.   (*histoires, tableau, tableaux*)
2. L'*ami* pour lequel nous avons commandé ce repas n'est jamais venu. (*femme, femmes, amis*)
3. On peut voir la *salle* par laquelle il a passé.   (*couloir, couloirs, rues*)
4. Voici le *livre* dans lequel on trouve sa philosophie.   (*histoire, articles, histoires*)

77. Special use of *à*

The preposition **à** is often used to express purpose or characteristic.

PURPOSE

> **une machine à écrire**   a typewriter
> **une table à thé**   a tea table
> **une tasse à café**   a coffee cup
> BUT
> **une tasse de café**   a cup of coffee

CHARACTERISTIC

> **un homme à barbe blanche**   a man with a white beard
> **l'homme à la barbe blanche**[1]   the man with the white beard
> **une poêle à longue queue**   a long-handled frying pan

D. Complete each of the following sentences by filling in the blank with **à, de,** or **à** plus the article.

1. Je préfère une maison ____ grandes fenêtres. 2. La maison ____ grandes fenêtres est à moi. 3. Voyez-vous cette dame ____ chapeau blanc? 4. Avez-vous rencontré la jeune fille ____ chapeau blanc? 5. Mettez ce linge dans la machine ____ laver, s'il vous plaît. 6. Cette tasse ____ thé est cassée. 7. Puis-je vous offrir une tasse ____ thé?

---

[1] Note that if the noun being described is preceded by the indefinite article, **à** alone is used, whereas if the noun is preceded by the definite article or by a form of **ce**, the definite article is used with **à** in the descriptive phrase.

8. Le garçon _____ cheveux blonds est mon frère.   9. Je ne connais que la dame _____ robe bleue.   10. Il prend toujours un verre _____ vin avec le dîner.

78. Irregular present tenses

boire	devoir	recevoir	apercevoir
to drink	*to owe, ought*	*to receive*	*to notice*
je bois	je dois	je reçois	j'aperçois
tu bois	tu dois	tu reçois	tu aperçois
il boit	il doit	il reçoit	il aperçoit
nous buvons	nous devons	nous recevons	nous apercevons
vous buvez	vous devez	vous recevez	vous apercevez
ils boivent	ils doivent	ils reçoivent	ils aperçoivent
PAST PART.	PAST PART.	PAST PART.	PAST PART.
bu	**dû**	**reçu**	**aperçu**

Future stems of **devoir, recevoir,** and **apercevoir** are irregular: **devr–, recevr–apercevr–.**

E. Substitution Drill.

1. Buvons-*nous* du café ou du thé ce soir?   (*il, ils, vous, tu*)
2. Dois-*tu* laisser la porte ouverte?   (*vous, nous, je, elle*)
3. Quand reçoit-*on* des cadeaux?   (*ils, vous, elle, tu*)
4. *J'*aperçois une lumière à la fenêtre.   (*Nous, Elle, Ils, Vous*)
5. Combien est-ce que *je* vous dois?   (*nous, il, ils, Jeanne*)

F. Read aloud, then restate in tenses called for.

1. Ils aperçoivent la faute.   (future, *passé composé*)
2. Je reçois le visiteur dans le salon.   (conditional, pluperfect)
3. Nous buvons de l'eau.   (imperfect, *passé composé*)
4. Elle boit du lait.   (*passé composé*, future)
5. Vous devez partir.   (conditional, conditional perfect)

79. Special uses of *devoir*

Because the various translations of **devoir** involve defective English verbs, no single verb suffices to cover its shades of meaning.   Besides its original meaning of *owe*, we have the following.

PRESENT   *am to, is to, are to, am supposed to, must*

A quelle heure est-ce que je dois y être?   At what time am I (supposed) to be there?

Vous devez y être à cinq heures précises.   You are to be there at five sharp.
Alors, je dois partir tout de suite.   Then I must leave right away.
La salle est vide.   Nous devons être en retard.   The hall is empty.   We must be late.

IMPERFECT (same as present except for time)
Je devais arriver à minuit.   I was (supposed) to arrive at midnight.

PASSÉ COMPOSÉ   *must have, had to*
J'ai dû tomber du lit, car me voici par terre.   I must have fallen out of bed, for here I am on the floor.
Il a dû chercher une lampe.   He had to hunt up a lamp.

FUTURE   *shall have to, will have to*
Demain nous devrons nous lever de bonne heure.   Tomorrow we shall have to get up early.

CONDITIONAL   *ought to, should* (perhaps the most important single use of **devoir**)
Je devrais étudier maintenant, je suppose.   I ought to study now, I suppose.
Vous ne devriez pas manger si vite, vous savez.   You should not eat so fast, you know.

CONDITIONAL PERFECT   *ought to have, should have*
Il aurait dû le savoir.   He should have known it.
Nous n'aurions pas dû partir du théâtre si tôt.   We ought not to have left the theater so early.

Note that in every instance **devoir,** whatever the English might lead you to expect, is followed by the infinitive in French, without any intervening preposition.

    G. Express in French.
        1. I suppose I should do my homework now.   2. You should have done it long ago.   3. When I have written these sentences, you will have to correct them.   4. By the way, when is Robert supposed to be here?   5. He was supposed to be here an hour ago.   6. He must have forgotten to come.

    H. Substitution Drill.
        1. *Le monsieur a dû venir trop tôt.*   (*Les messieurs, Je, Nous*)
        2. *Nous* devions étudier la leçon suivante.   (*Jules, Je, Les enfants*)
        3. *Vous ne devriez pas travailler si dur.*   (*Tu, Nous, Ils*)
        4. *J'aurais dû suivre cette route.*   (*Nous, Vous, On*)
        5. *Tu dois être au bureau demain à huit heures.*   (*Vous, Nous, Jean*)
        6. Devrait-*elle* faire la demande en personne?   (*nous, vous, il*)

LECTURE

Ce matin le professeur m'a rappelé que je devais continuer la description de ma maison commencée il y a quelques jours.

« Nous ne devrions pas négliger notre vocabulaire pratique, dit-il à la classe, aussi vais-je confier à Maurice la tâche de nous indiquer, s'il peut le faire, le nom des meubles du salon, de la salle à manger et de la cuisine.

— J'essayerai, monsieur, mais c'est une tâche pour laquelle je ne suis pas très bien préparé.

— On verra. Par exemple, quels meubles trouve-t-on d'habitude dans le salon?

— D'habitude on y trouve quelques fauteuils, peut-être une ou deux chaises ordinaires, et un divan devant lequel se trouve parfois une table à thé. Souvent aussi il y a un piano avec son tabouret. Et puis on doit avoir des lampes pour lire.

— Très bien. Et la salle à manger?

— Dans la salle à manger on trouve une grande table autour de laquelle il y a plusieurs chaises, et un buffet où l'on range la vaisselle et l'argenterie, aussi bien que le linge de table.

— C'est tout pour la salle à manger?

— Oui, sauf le lustre au-dessus de la table.

— Soit! [1] Entrons dans la cuisine.

— Avec plaisir. Seulement ici on trouve tant de choses que si j'essayais de les nommer toutes, je n'en finirais pas. D'ailleurs il y a beaucoup d'objets dont je ne sais pas le nom en français.

— N'importe. Allez-y !

— Eh bien, ce qu'il y a de plus important c'est sans doute le fourneau à gaz ou à l'électricité, qui s'appelle aussi une cuisinière, je crois. Puis il y a l'évier où on lave la vaisselle. Ensuite, dans la plupart des maisons américaines au moins, le frigidaire. Naturellement il y a aussi des placards pour mettre la vaisselle.

— Et les ustensiles?

— Quant aux ustensiles, je ne connais que la casserole et la poêle, mais je sais qu'on appelle l'ensemble des ustensiles la batterie de cuisine.

— Bon. Eh bien, cela suffit pour aujourd'hui, je pense. Et puisque nous parlons de poêles, et que [2] vous avez si bien répondu aujourd'hui, Maurice, je vais vous faire un petit cadeau.

---

[1] **Soit** as an exclamation pronounces the **t**.

[2] When two clauses would be introduced by the same conjunction, the second conjunction is often replaced by **que** alone.

— Oh, merci, monsieur.

— C'est une invitation à dîner ce soir dans un petit restaurant qui s'appelle la Vieille Poêle à Frire. J'ai reçu l'invitation hier, mais je suis tellement occupé ce soir que je ne peux pas accepter. Mais, je vous fais ce cadeau à une condition. Voulez-vous l'accepter?

— Oh, je l'accepte volontiers, avec ou sans condition. C'est aujourd'hui le vingt-neuf du mois, et il me reste [1] si peu d'argent que même si vous me demandiez de tout commander en français, j'accepterais.

— Ce n'est pas loin de ce que j'allais vous demander, Maurice. Je veux dire que vous devrez nous donner demain en classe un compte rendu de votre repas, en français bien entendu. »

Questions

1. Quand Maurice a-t-il commencé sa description de la maison? 2. D'après le professeur, qu'est-ce que nous ne devrions pas négliger? 3. Quelle tâche le professeur donne-t-il à Maurice? 4. Dans quelle pièce trouve-t-on des fauteuils? 5. Qu'est-ce qu'il y a parfois devant le divan? 6. Que range-t-on dans le buffet? 7. Qu'est-ce qui éclaire la salle à manger? 8. Qu'est-ce qu'il y a de plus important dans la cuisine? 9. Comment appelle-t-on l'ensemble des ustensiles? 10. Quel est le cadeau que le professeur fait à Maurice? 11. Pourquoi ne peut-il pas accepter l'invitation lui-même? 12. Qu'est-ce que Maurice doit faire en classe le lendemain?

VOCABULARY

Allez-y! Go to it!
au-dessus de above, over
au moins at least
aussi bien que as well as
autour de around
la batterie de cuisine kitchen utensils
d'habitude = **d'ordinaire**

l'**argenterie** (*f.*) silverware
la **casserole** saucepan
commander to order

il me reste si peu d'argent I have so little money left
je n'en finirais pas I would never finish
n'importe no matter
sans doute no doubt, doubtless
Soit! All right, O.K.

le **compte rendu** report, account
confier to entrust
la **cuisinière** stove, cook

---

[1] An example of the impersonal use of **il**. See idiom in Vocabulary.

la **demande**   request
le **divan**   sofa
un **ensemble**   ensemble, total
un **évier**   sink
le **fauteuil**   armchair, easy chair
le **fourneau**   stove
   frire (**frit**)   to fry
le **gaz**   gas
le **linge**   linen
   loin   far
le **lustre**   chandelier
   négliger   to neglect
   Noël (*m.*)   Christmas
   nommer   to name
un **objet**   object
   occupé   busy

   parfois   sometimes
le **placard**   cupboard
la **poêle**   frying pan
   pratique   practical
   ranger   to arrange, put away, store
   rencontrer   to meet, encounter
le **sommet**   summit
   suffire (**suffi**) to suffice, be enough (*obj.*
      is indirect)
le **tabouret**   stool
la **tâche**   task, job
le **thé**   tea
un **ustensile**   utensil
la **vaisselle**   dishes, china
le **verre**   glass
la **vue**   view

PATTERN SENTENCE DRILL

1. Où est le livre que je lisais hier soir?
   _____ histoire _____?
   _____ il _____?
   _____ écriviez ____?
   _____ la semaine dernière?

2. Vous voulez dire le livre dont nous parlions?
   _____ livres _____?
   _____ Jean _____?
   _____ avait besoin?
   Tu _____?

3. Oui, le livre à la couverture bleue.
   _____ bizarre.
   _____titre _____.
   _____ poème _____.
   _____ extraordinaire.

4. Je sais le livre auquel vous pensez.
   _____ livres _____.
   _____elle _____.
   _____ histoires_____.
   Nous _____.

5. C'est une histoire dont je connaissais le titre.

___était_____.

_____ sujet.

_____ nous _____.

_____ livre _____.

6. Je devrais la lire un de ces jours.

Tu_____.

_____ les _____.

_____ finir _____.

Vous _____.

7. J'aurais dû la lire il y a longtemps.

_____ un an.

Nous _____.

_____ plusieurs jours.

Paul _____.

8. Quand j'aurai fini l'histoire, vous aussi, vous devrez la lire.

_____ Pierre _____.

_____ je _____.

_____ lettre _____.

_____ Marie _____.

9. Je suivrai votre conseil avec plaisir.

_____ son _____.

_____ regret.

Nous _____.

_____ exemple _____.

10. Est-ce que nous devons lire *l'Étranger* pour demain?

_____je _____?

_____mardi?

_____ finir_____?

_____ vous _____?

11. D'après le professeur, nous devions le lire pour aujourd'hui.

_____ mon ami _____.

_____je _____.

_____ les _____.

_____ vous _____.

12. J'ai dû mal comprendre ce qu'il a dit.

Vous———————————————.

————————————————je —.

——————— entendre ———————.

———————————————demandé.

14

Present Subjunctive

Past Subjunctive

Uses of Subjunctive

PATTERN SENTENCES

1. Il faut que je vous dise ce qui m'est arrivé hier.
2. Je voulais acheter une auto d'occasion pour que nous ayons, ma sœur et moi, un moyen d'aller au collège.
3. D'un côté, mon père désirait que j'achète une voiture qui ne soit pas trop chère.
4. De l'autre côté, ma mère avait peur que je ne revienne avec une guimbarde.
5. « Pour que tu ne sois pas seul, me disent mes parents, nous allons t'accompagner. »
6. Quoique j'aie déjà une idée de l'auto que je désire, je ne dis rien.
7. Papa demande que nous essayions un modèle bon marché que je n'aime pas du tout.

1. I must tell you what happened to me yesterday.
2. I wanted to buy a used car so that my sister and I would have a means of getting to school.
3. On the one hand, my father wanted me to buy a car that was not too expensive.
4. On the other hand, my mother was afraid I would come back with a jalopy.
5. "So that you will not be alone," my parents say to me, "we are going to go with you."
6. Although I already have an idea of the car I want, I don't say anything.
7. Dad asks that we try a low-priced model that I don't like at all.

8. Avant même que nous ne traversions le pont, le moteur s'arrête.

8. Before we even cross the bridge, the motor stops.

9. Maman veut que je prenne une jolie conduite intérieure, mais le prix en est exorbitant.

9. Mother wants me to take a pretty sedan, but the price of it is exorbitant.

10. Je finis par acheter la voiture de mon choix.

10. I end up by buying the car of my choice.

11. Mes parents sont contents que je l'aie achetée.

11. My parents are glad I bought it.

12. « C'est la meilleure voiture que j'aie jamais vue ! » dit papa.

12. "It's the best car I ever saw!" Dad says.

80. Subjunctive mood

The subjunctive mood (*subjonctif*), almost extinct in spoken English except for such expressions as "He asked that I be here" and "If he were here, I would tell him a thing or two," remains very much alive in French, although it is less common than the indicative. Its formation is much simpler than that of the indicative, for two reasons: (1) the endings are far more regular; (2) it has but four tenses, of which only two normally occur outside of literature. The present subjunctive, with the exception of **avoir** and **être,** has but one set of endings for all verbs. They resemble the present indicative endings of **donner** with the simple addition of an **i** in the first and second plural:

e	ions
es	iez
e	ent

The stem, for all regular and most irregular verbs, may be found by dropping the **ent** of the third person plural of the present indicative.

ils donn ent	**ils finiss** ent	**ils perd** ent	**ils prenn** ent

PRESENT SUBJUNCTIVE OF THE THREE REGULAR CONJUGATIONS

je donne	je finisse	je perde
tu donn**es**	tu finiss**es**	tu perd**es**
il donne	il finisse	il perde
nous donn**ions**	nous finiss**ions**	nous perd**ions**
vous donn**iez**	vous finiss**iez**	vous perd**iez**
ils donn**ent**	ils finiss**ent**	ils perd**ent**

Verbs whose stem for the first and second persons plural differs from that of the third person plural in the indicative will normally show the same change in the subjunctive.[1]

---

[1] Among these, the student should review **voir, croire, venir, prendre, devoir,** and **recevoir.**

boire

INDICATIVE	SUBJUNCTIVE
je bois	je boive
tu bois	tu boives
il boit	il boive
nous **buv**ons	nous **buv**ions
vous **buv**ez	vous **buv**iez
ils boivent	ils boivent

This includes verbs which change **i** to **y**.

envoyer

j'envoie	nous en**voy**ions
tu envoies	vous en**voy**iez
il envoie	ils envoient

81. Irregular present subjunctive of *avoir* and *être*

avoir	**être**
j'aie	je sois
tu aies	tu sois
il ait	il soit
nous ayons	nous soyons
vous ayez	vous soyez
ils aient	ils soient

A. Substitution Drill.

1. Il faut que *nous* arrivions ce soir.   (*elle, vous, ils, tu*)
2. Il demande qu'*elles* finissent avant minuit.   (*elle, vous, je, nous*)
3. Je désire qu'*on* vende la maison.   (*vous, tu, il, ils*)
4. Elle est contente que *tu* reçoives les cadeaux.   (*vous, nous, les garçons, son ami*)
5. J'ai fait cela pour que *vous* ayez le temps de finir ce travail.   (*tu, Jean, les jeunes filles, nous*)
6. Il faut qu'*elle* prenne l'argent.   (*nous, ils, tu, vous*)
7. Le professeur voudrait que *sa femme* soit riche.   (*ses enfants, l'université, vous, je*)
8. Il faut que *Lucien* se lève [1] tout de suite.   (*tu, les deux amis, nous, je*)
9. Est-ce qu'on veut que *j'*appelle [1] les enfants?   (*nous, ils, il, vous*)
10. Il faudra qu'*elle* vienne les voir à l'hôpital.   (*elles, tu, vous, nous*)

---

[1] As in the indicative, the placing of the accent or the doubling of the consonant in **e**-stem verbs takes place only before a mute **e** syllable.

82. Past subjunctive

Combining the present subjunctive of **avoir** and **être** with the past participle of a verb produces the past subjunctive (*passé du subjonctif*), which corresponds to the *passé composé* of the indicative.

j'aie donné	je sois venu
tu aies donné	tu sois venu
il ait donné	il soit venu
nous ayons donné	nous soyons venus
vous ayez donné	vous soyez venu(s)
ils aient donné	ils soient venus

B. Read aloud, then restate with the italicized verb in the past subjunctive.

1. Quoiqu'elle *perde* son poste, elle est heureuse.
2. Quoiqu'ils *trouvent* l'argent, ils ne sont pas contents.
3. J'ai voulu que nous *arrivions* avant eux.
4. C'est le plat le plus cher que je *voie* sur le menu.
5. Êtes-vous content que nous *venions?*

83. Uses of subjunctive

The subjunctive is rarely used in the main clause of a sentence, standing generally in a subordinate clause introduced by **que** (or a compound of **que,** such as **pour que** or **bien que**), where it is dependent upon a verb, adjective, or other expression requiring qualification in some manner. There is usually a kind of oblique, doubtful, or contingent quality about the subjunctive which is not difficult to recognize. Three common uses of the subjunctive are as follows.

1. In a subordinate clause governed by an expression of desire, command, necessity, or emotion such as regret, joy, and the like.[1]

Je veux qu'il finisse ses devoirs tout de suite. I want him to finish (that he finish) his lessons immediately,

Elle est contente qu'il revienne à la maison pour les vacances. She is glad that he is coming home for vacation.

Il faut que vous partiez demain. You must (It is necessary that you) leave tomorrow.

Il demande que nous soyons prêts à l'heure. He asks that we be ready on time.

J'ai peur que nous (n')arrivions trop tard. I am afraid that we shall arrive too late.

---

[1] Although **espérer** (*to hope*) would seem to fit this category, it is *not* followed by the subjunctive.

NOTE: After certain expressions with negative implications — such as expressions of fearing, preventing, avoiding; **avant que,** *before;* **à moins que,** *unless* — many French speakers retain a **ne** (from Latin *ne,* "lest") before the verb which follows **que.** Unless **pas** is added after the verb, the clause is not negative in meaning. See Pattern Sentences 4 and 8.

2. In an adjective clause modifying a doubtful, negative, or superlative antecedent.

> **Je cherche un homme qui apprenne à conduire une auto.** I am looking for a man who is learning to drive a car.
> **Connaissez-vous une femme qui ait plus de bijoux que Mme X?** Do you know of a woman who has more jewels than Mrs. X?
> **Il n'y a pas d'étudiant qui ait réussi à cet examen sans travailler.** There is no student who has passed this examination without working.
> **C'est la plus jolie fille que je connaisse.** She is the prettiest girl I know.

3. In adverbial clauses introduced by certain conjunctions, most common of which are **pour que** and **afin que** (*so that, in order that*); **bien que** and **quoique** (*although*); **à moins que** (*unless*); **avant que** (*before*); and (except in a completed past event) **jusqu'à ce que** (*until*).

> **Il a fait ceci pour que nous le respections plus.** He did this so that we would respect him more.
> **Bien qu'il soit riche, il aime les pauvres.** Although he is rich, he loves the poor.
> **Restez ici jusqu'à ce que le dîner soit prêt.** Stay here until dinner is ready.

IMPORTANT: a. The subjunctive does not follow the ordinary time conjunctions **pendant que** and **tandis que** (*while*), **dès que** and **aussitôt que** (*as soon as*), and **lorsque** (*when*); nor the causals **parce que** (*because*) and **puisque** (*since*).

> **Lorsque la leçon est finie, nous quittons la classe.** When the lesson is finished, we leave the class.
> **Puisque vous êtes prêt, qu'attendons-nous?** Since you are ready, what are we waiting for?

b. The subjunctive does not occur in conditions, even when the English equivalent would have it. For instance, "If he *were* here, I'd tell him a thing or two" would not take the subjunctive in French, but the usual imperfect indicative.

> **C.** Complete the following sentences with the proper form of the verb indicated.
>> a. 1. Maurice voit que le restaurant (être) plein de monde.
>> 2. Maurice a peur que le restaurant ne (être) plein de monde.
>> 3. Je vous décris le restaurant pour que vous (avoir) une idée de son originalité.

4. J'ai un dictionnaire qui (contenir) la plupart des mots que nous étudions.

5. Je cherche un dictionnaire qui (contenir) plus de mots encore.

6. Il faut que Maurice (finir) son devoir.

7. Il n'y a pas de restaurant qui (avoir) plus d'originalité.

8. Le professeur demande que l'élève (écrire) le poème.

9. Nous regrettons que vous ne (boire) [1] pas de café, car ce café est le meilleur que nous (connaître).

10. Y a-t-il des restaurants qui (être) plus intéressants que la Vieille Poêle à Frire?

11. Bien qu'il (servir) peu de gens, il les (servir) bien.

12. Nous voudrions que vous (envoyer) une lettre et que Maurice (envoyer) une carte.

13. J'espère que vous (se lever) de bonne heure demain.

14. Il est possible qu'elle (finir) [1] déjà.

15. Le professeur est content que Maurice (répondre) [1] si bien.

b. 1. Ils partent demain, parce qu'ils (finir) [1] leur travail.

2. Aussitôt qu'ils (arriver) à la maison, ils se coucheront.

3. Bien qu'elle (lire) [1] le livre, elle a oublié l'histoire.

4. Je lui ai laissé le dictionnaire pour qu'il (chercher) les mots difficiles.

5. Puisque vous (avoir) le temps, vous pourrez me chercher une cravate.

6. C'est l'homme le plus riche que je (connaître).

7. Je ne connais aucun homme qui (être) plus riche que lui.

8. Il est dommage qu'il (partir).

9. Il faut que je le (voir) avant qu'il ne (partir).

10. Quoique nous (se coucher) [1] de bonne heure hier soir, nous sommes fatigués aujourd'hui.

LECTURE

J'ai bien dîné à la Vieille Poêle à Frire, et le lendemain, avant même de commencer la leçon, le professeur a demandé que je fournisse non seulement un compte rendu du repas mais aussi une description du restaurant.

---

[1] Use compound tense.

« J'avais peur que vous ne me demandiez cela, lui ai-je dit. A vrai dire, ce restaurant ne peut guère rivaliser avec [1] Delmonico. Pourtant il est intéressant, bien qu'il ne soit pas élégant. Le propriétaire l'a rempli d'antiquités, pour que le décor soit en harmonie avec le nom, je suppose. Cela aurait plu à ma mère, qui se serait sentie tout à fait chez elle. Dommage qu'elle n'ait pas été avec moi ! Vraiment je ne connais pas de restaurant qui soit si plein de vieux meubles.

— J'espère au moins que le repas était bon.

— Oh oui, monsieur. Je vous raconterai le tout en détail, pour que vous ayez une idée plus exacte de la Vieille Poêle à Frire. Lorsque j'y suis entré, on m'a demandé d'attendre quelques minutes, car il y avait beaucoup de monde et peu de places. En fait, il n'y avait aucune table qui soit libre à ce moment-là. Heureusement il n'a pas fallu que j'attende longtemps, car deux ou trois personnes se sont bientôt levées, et alors le propriétaire m'a demandé: « Voulez-vous que je vous mette à côté de la cheminée, ou préférez-vous une place près de la fenêtre là-bas? » Puisqu'il faisait sombre dehors et qu'il n'y avait rien à voir, j'ai choisi la table à côté de la cheminée.

— Est-ce qu'on avait déjà mis le couvert?

— Oui, c'est-à-dire qu'on avait remplacé la nappe sale par une nouvelle, et qu'un moment après on a apporté un couteau, une fourchette et une cuiller, ainsi qu'une assiette et une tasse à café, et ensuite un verre d'eau et une serviette, suivis d'un panier de pain. Puis on a commencé à me passer une série de plats appétissants.

— Ma foi, n'a-t-on même pas attendu que vous commandiez quelque chose?

— Non. Évidemment ce qui fait l'originalité de l'établissement c'est qu'il est sans façon. Afin que vous vous imaginiez être à la campagne, on passe les plats au lieu de vous servir individuellement.

— Il n'y a pas de menu, alors?

— Si,[2] il y en a un, et on peut manger au prix fixe ou à la carte.[3] Mais les plats qu'on passe sont si abondants et si variés que cela ne vaut pas la peine de commander à la carte.

— Qu'est-ce que vous avez mangé donc?

— Je ne peux pas tout me rappeler, mais je me souviens qu'il y avait une grande assiette pleine de hors-d'œuvre,[4] deux ou trois espèces de poisson salé, une salade de laitue et du rosbif avec des pommes frites.

---

[1] **rivaliser avec** *to rival*

[2] *Yes*, in contradiction of a *negative* statement or question, is often **si** rather than **oui**.

[3] **manger au prix fixe ou à la carte** Eat a more or less set combination of dishes at a fixed price or order from the menu.

[4] **Hors-d'œuvre** does not change in the plural.

— Le rosbif était-il bien cuit ou saignant?

— Au choix. Ou si on n'aimait pas le rosbif, il y avait du jambon.

— Et comme dessert?

— Comme dessert, on avait le choix entre différentes tartes aux fruits et plusieurs sortes de gâteaux. Ou bien [1] on pouvait prendre des fruits [2] ou du fromage, à la française.

— Ma foi, je commence à regretter qu'un rendez-vous m'ait empêché d'y aller moi-même.

— J'aurais voulu que vous soyez avec moi, monsieur. Et même, pour vous montrer ma reconnaissance, je vais vous promettre quelque chose.

— Quoi? Que vous travaillerez davantage?

— Je vous promets, monsieur, que si je reçois une invitation à dîner à la Vieille Poêle à Frire, je vous la rendrai volontiers. »

Questions

1. Qu'est-ce que le professeur a demandé que Maurice fournisse à la classe? 2. Quelle sorte de restaurant est la Vieille Poêle à Frire? 3. De quoi est-il rempli? 4. Qui aurait dû être avec Maurice? 5. Pourquoi a-t-il fallu que Maurice attende quelques minutes? 6. Pourquoi Maurice n'a-t-il pas choisi la table près de la fenêtre? 7. Qu'est-ce qu'on a mis comme couvert? 8. Pourquoi passe-t-on les plats au lieu de servir individuellement? 9. Pourquoi ne vaut-il pas la peine de commander à la carte? 10. Qu'est-ce que Maurice a mangé? 11. Qu'est-ce que le professeur commence à regretter? 12. Comment Maurice va-t-il montrer sa reconnaissance?

VOCABULARY

à la française in the French manner, French style
au choix at your choice
beaucoup de monde a lot of people
Ma foi! My goodness!

ou bien or else
plein de monde crowded
sans façon informal, free and easy
valoir la peine to be worthwhile, worth the trouble

---

[1] See idioms in Vocabulary.
[2] Note that **fruit** is generally used in the plural unless it means a single fruit.

appétissant tasty, appetizing
la **cheminée** chimney, fireplace
contenir (contenu) to contain
le **couvert** table setting (cf. English "cover charge"); **mettre le couvert** to set the table
la **cravate** necktie
cuire to cook; **bien cuit** well done
dehors outside, outdoors
dommage too bad, a pity
une **espèce** kind, type
fournir to provide, furnish
le **gâteau** cake
un **hôpital** hospital
le **jambon** ham
libre free
la **nappe** tablecloth

le **panier** basket
pourtant however, but
la **reconnaissance** gratitude
regretter to regret
remplacer to replace
le **rendez-vous** appointment (business or social)
le **rosbif** roast beef
saignant rare (of meat)
salé salty, salted
la **série** series
la **serviette** napkin
se souvenir (de) to remember
la **tarte** pie, tart; **tarte aux fruits** fruit pie
varié varied, various

PATTERN SENTENCE DRILL

1. Il faut que je vous dise ce qui m'est arrivé hier.
   _____leur_____.
   _____ nous _____.
   _____ce matin.
   _____ elle_____.

2. Je voulais acheter une auto pour que nous ayons un moyen d'aller au collège.
   _____ ils _____.
   _____ bicyclette _____.
   Nous _____.
   _____ tu _____.

3. Mon père désirait que j'achète une voiture qui ne soit pas trop chère.
   _____ nous _____.
   _____ assiettes _____.
   _____ maman _____.
   _____ fauteuil _____.

4. Ma mère avait peur que je ne revienne avec une guimbarde.
   _____ Georges _____.
   _____ voulait empêcher _____.
   _____ vous _____.
   _____ maladie sérieuse.

5. Pour que tu ne sois pas seul, nous allons t'accompagner.
   _____ vous _____.
   _____ venir chez vous.
   _____ fâché _____.
   _____ elle _____.

6. Quoique j'aie une idée de l'auto que je désire, je ne dis rien.
   _____ veux _____.
   _____ nous _____.
   _____ frigidaire _____.
   _____ maman_____.

7. Papa demande que nous essayions un modèle bon marché.
   _____ je _____.
   _____ autos _____.
   _____ d'occasion.
   _____ les garçons _____.

8. Avant que nous ne traversions le pont, le moteur s'arrête.
   _____ ils _____.
   _____ les voitures _____.
   _____ rue _____.
   _____ papa _____.

9. Maman veut que je prenne une jolie conduite intérieure.
   _____ nous _____.
   _____ modèle récent.
   _____ voudrait _____.
   _____ elles _____.

10. Je finis par acheter la voiture de mon choix.
    Nous _____.
    _____ tableau_____.
    _____ami.
    _____ choisir _____.

11. Mes parents sont contents que je l'aie achetée.
_____ vous _____.
_____ fâchés_____.
M. Lefèvre _____.
_____ son fils _____.

12. C'est la meilleure voiture que j'aie jamais vue !
_____ nous _____ !
_____ autos françaises _____ !
_____ premières _____ !
_____ Jacques _____ !

15

Irregular Subjunctives
Further Uses of Subjunctive
Irregular Imperatives
Present Participle

PATTERN SENTENCES

1. Bonsoir, Jeanne. Allez-vous à la réunion du Cercle Français demain soir?

2. Je ne sais pas, Paul. Maman a invité des amis, et il faut que je sois à la maison pour le dîner.

3. Mais ne pourriez-vous pas venir après? La réunion ne commence pas avant sept heures et demie.

4. Je ne crois pas que nous ayons fini le dîner à temps. C'est l'anniversaire de papa, vous savez.

5. Je comprends. Tout de même, il est possible que vous finissiez plus tôt, n'est-ce pas?

6. Oui, c'est possible. Mais vous savez que M. Lasalle n'aime pas qu'on vienne en retard aux réunions du cercle.

1. Hello, Jean. Are you going to the French Club meeting tomorrow night?

2. I don't know, Paul. Mother has invited some friends, and I have to be at home for dinner.

3. But couldn't you come afterwards? The meeting doesn't begin until seven thirty.

4. I don't think we will have finished dinner in time. It's dad's birthday, you see.

5. I see. Even so, it is possible you'll finish sooner, isn't it?

6. Yes, it's possible. But you know Mr. Lasalle doesn't like people to come late to club meetings.

153

7. Ça m'est égal qu'il soit fâché ! Je viendrai vous chercher en auto.

8. Oh, chic ! J'essayerai d'être prête à sept heures et quart.

9. Ça ne vous fait rien que nous prenions Roger et Louise en passant?

10. Mais non ! Tant mieux ! Mais pensez-vous qu'ils aient l'intention de venir?

11. Je le crois. Étant la secrétaire, Louise ne peut pas manquer cette réunion.

12. C'est vrai. A demain soir, alors ! Mais ne soyez pas impatient si je ne suis pas prête.

7. I don't care if he's mad ! I'll come for you in the car.

8. Oh, swell ! I'll try to be ready by a quarter past seven.

9. Do you mind if we pick up Roger and Louise on the way?

10. Why no. So much the better. But do you think they mean to come?

11. I think so. Being the secretary, Louise can't miss this meeting.

12. True. See you tomorrow night, then. But don't be impatient if I'm not ready.

84. Irregular subjunctives

Faire, pouvoir, savoir, vouloir, and **aller** have irregular stems for the present subjunctive. The first three verbs have uniform stems throughout the tense.

faire **fass–**   pouvoir **puiss–**   savoir **sach–**

Vouloir and **aller,** on the other hand, like **venir, prendre, devoir,** and **recevoir,** show alternation of stem.

vouloir	aller
je veuille	j'aille
tu veuilles	tu ailles
il veuille	il aille
nous **voul**ions	nous allions
vous **voul**iez	vous alliez
ils veuillent	ils aillent

NOTE: Like **aller** is **il faut,** whose subjunctive is **il faille.**

    A. Substitution Drill.

       1. Il est possible que *je* fasse ce travail en trois heures. (*vous, nous, les hommes, Jean*)

       2. Il est peu probable que *nous* puissions ouvrir cette porte. (*vous, je, tu, les enfants*)

       3. M. Lasalle est content que *je* sache le présent du subjonctif. (*nous, Maurice. les étudiants, vous*)

4. Mme Lasalle est surprise que *nous* voulions offrir un cadeau au professeur. (*vous, tu, je, les élèves*)

5. On demande que *tu* ailles voir l'ambassadeur. (*nous, vous, il, ils*)

85. Further uses of the subjunctive

In addition to the uses of the subjunctive already cited, two others are relatively
common.

1. In a clause following a verb of thinking or believing in the negative or interrogative,
when strong doubt is implied by the speaker.

> **Je ne crois pas que ces pommes soient bonnes.** I don't believe these apples are
> good.
> **Pensez-vous qu'il pleuve ce soir?** Do you think it will rain tonight?

2. In the third person imperative, usually with **que,** and with subject expressed.

> **Qu'il vienne demain !** Have him come tomorrow.
> **Que la petite fille me dise la réponse !** Let the little girl tell me the answer.
> **Qu'il boive son café et s'en aille !** Let him drink his coffee and go away.

NOTE: English, having no third person imperative, uses *have* or *let* plus the infinitive
to express this type of command. One exception is of the type **Vive la reine !**
Long live the queen!

86. Irregular imperatives

Être, avoir, and **savoir** use partially modified forms of the present subjunctive for
their ordinary command forms.

être	avoir	savoir
Sois!	Aie!	Sache!
Soyons!	Ayons!	Sachons!
Soyez!	Ayez!	Sachez!

Vouloir has but one imperative commonly used, this being also a modified subjunctive:
Veuillez. Always initial in a clause, and always followed by the infinitive of a verb,
it provides a somewhat formal way of saying *Please.*

> **Veuillez me donner une liste de . . .** Please give me a list of . . .
> **Veuillez me passer le sel et le poivre.** Please pass me the salt and pepper.

> **B.** Read aloud, then reread substituting the words in parentheses for those
> in italics, and using the indicative or subjunctive as required.
>
> 1. *Je remarque* qu'il fait son devoir. (*Il faut, Je pense*)
> 2. *Il croit* que j'ai rempli ce questionnaire comme il faut. (*Il ne croit pas,
> Vous savez*)

3. *On me dit* que vous vendez votre maison. (*Nous regrettons, Votre père voudrait*)
4. *Je suppose* que votre cousine est déjà partie. (*Nous sommes fâchés, J'ai entendu dire*)
5. *Si* tu prends ton temps, tu finis par arriver. (*Lorsque, Quoique*)
6. *Il est certain* que ce savant a raison. (*Je pense, Pensez-vous*)
7. *Sans doute* je suis le premier à utiliser ce système. (*On m'a dit que, Il est possible que*)
8. *Il est évident* qu'il faut insister sur ce point. (*Je regrette, Je sais*)
9. *Si* elle va chez elle, je la verrai bientôt. (*Puisque, Bien que*)
10. *Je suis sûr* que les jeunes filles se sont couchées à dix heures. (*Il est impossible, Il est certain*)
11. *Il est clair* que nous ne savons pas cette leçon. (*Il est évident, Il est regrettable*)
12. Nous le faisons *parce que* nous voulons vous aider. (*bien que, quoique*)
13. *Il est vrai* qu'il peut résumer cette philosophie. (*Je suis sûr, Je doute*)
14. *Voici* un savant qui veut perfectionner cette méthode. (*Nous cherchons, Il n'y a pas de*)

87. Present participle

Present participles are verb forms ending in *ing* in English, such as *going, coming*. The French present participle ends in **ant**, the stem being normally the first person plural of the present indicative, minus **ons**.

all ons   **allant**   **pren** ons   **prenant**   **finiss** ons   **finissant**

Three verbs have stems which cannot be found in the present indicative:

avoir **ay–**   être **ét–**   savoir **sach–**

Their present participles are:

ayant   **étant**   **sachant**

The present participle is used with no preposition except **en**. **En** with the present participle is usually translated *on, while*, or *by*, occasionally by *in*. All prepositions other than **en** are followed by the infinitive.

En arrivant ce matin, elle s'est mise à étudier. On arriving this morning, she began to study.
Elle est tombée en courant. She fell while running.
En écrivant on apprend à écrire. By writing you learn to write.
En commandant ce livre, demandez d'abord le prix. In ordering this book, first ask the price.
BUT
Il a commencé par raconter une histoire. He began by telling a story.

Notice that in practically every instance with **en,** the action of the participle takes place at the same time as that of the main verb. Often the continuity of the action is enhanced by the use of **tout,** which usually does not need translating.

> **Il a continué à parler tout en mangeant.** He kept right on talking while eating.
> **Tout en restant poli, il a insisté pour ne pas payer l'addition.** While remaining polite, he insisted on not paying the check.

The present participle often occurs without **en,** in which case the action frequently takes place just before that of the verb, or, if no action is involved, the condition expressed by the participle already exists.

> **Laissant son pistolet sur la table, il a sauté par la fenêtre.** Leaving his pistol on the table, he leaped out the window.
> **Se levant brusquement, elle sort en courant.** Getting up abruptly, she runs out.
> **Étant malade, la pauvre femme ne pouvait faire autrement.** Being ill, the poor woman could not do otherwise.

In the uses described above, the participle is invariable. Used as a simple adjective, however, it agrees like any adjective.

> **eau courante** running water
> **une découverte étonnante** an astounding discovery

C. Combine the two sentences into one by making the first a phrase with a present participle, following the pattern.

a. *Pattern:* En passant à côté de notre ami, nous lui avons dit bonjour.

1. Elle sort du restaurant. Elle rencontre son ami.
2. Il traduit le livre. Il trouve beaucoup de phrases utiles.
3. Nous nous approchons du palais. Nous remarquons qu'il est en ruines.
4. Ils préparaient leurs devoirs. Ils se sont rendu compte de leur ignorance.
5. On conduit trop vite. On court le risque d'avoir un accident.

b. *Pattern:* Remarquant le garçon, elle l'a appelé.

1. Elle est malade. Elle n'est pas venue ce soir.
2. Nous avons le temps. Nous allons visiter le musée.
3. Il a aperçu la porte. Il est entré.
4. Nous avons compris la situation. Nous sommes partis sans dire un mot.
5. Il savait bien la leçon. Il l'a récitée avec assurance.

D. Express in French.

1. The boy succeeds in finishing the assignment. 2. We begin by opening our books. 3. He had the idea of building the wall. 4. Do they have any intention of reading those books? 5. Don't leave without seeing your uncle.

LECTURE

En arrivant ce matin nous avons vu au tableau: « Avis à la classe de français ! Le professeur sera en retard de quelques minutes. En l'attendant, veuillez chercher dans votre Larousse [1] les noms de quelques savants français, et expliquer en une ou deux phrases pourquoi chacun est illustre. »

Prenant mon Larousse, j'ai commencé à parcourir la partie biographique. J'ai eu des difficultés, mais j'ai fini par écrire ceci:

Descartes est le fondateur [2] de la méthode scientifique, qu'on peut résumer ainsi: « Pour atteindre à la vérité, il faut une fois pour toutes se défaire de toutes les opinions que l'on a reçues et reconstruire de nouveau, depuis le fondement, [3] tout le système de ses connaissances. »

Lavoisier était un illustre chimiste français qui a fondé la chimie moderne sur la loi de la conservation de la matière: « Rien ne se perd, rien ne se crée. » [4]

Pasteur était un savant français dont les travaux sur la rage [5] et les maladies contagieuses ont complètement changé la médecine.

Curie (Pierre et sa femme Marie). On leur doit la découverte du radium, qui a changé nos idées sur la source de l'énergie et la constitution de la matière.

Pascal. On lui doit des lois physiques importantes et une remarquable collection de réflexions sur le christianisme réunies sous le titre de *Pensées.*

Ampère a trouvé la loi de l'électricité d'après laquelle deux fils électriques s'attirent ou se repoussent [6] suivant que les courants vont dans le même sens ou dans le sens contraire. Son nom sert à désigner l'intensité des courants électriques.

Niepce est l'inventeur de la photographie, que *Daguerre* a perfectionnée. On connaît ce dernier par le mot *daguerréotype,* qui veut dire une image fixée sur une plaque [7] sensible.

---

[1] Standard French dictionary and reference work.
[2] **le fondateur** *founder*
[3] **le fondement** *foundation, base*
[4] **Rien ne se perd, rien ne se crée** *Nothing is lost, nothing is created*
[5] **la rage** *rabies*   [6] **se repousser** *to repel each other*   [7] **la plaque** *plate*

Michelet, illustre historien français, est né à Paris. Dans son *Histoire de France* et son *Histoire de la Révolution*, il a essayé de faire de l'histoire une véritable résurrection du passé.

Taine, philosophe, historien et critique français, a essayé d'appliquer la méthode des sciences naturelles aux productions les plus diverses de l'esprit humain. Parmi d'autres livres, il a écrit *Philosophie de l'art* et *Origines de la France contemporaine*.

Comte, mathématicien et philosophe français, né à Montpellier, est l'auteur du *Cours de philosophie positive*, une des œuvres importantes de la philosophie du dernier siècle.

Le professeur est arrivé, et je lui ai rendu mon devoir. Il y a jeté un coup d'œil.

« Maurice, m'a-t-il dit, vous m'étonnez. Vous avez fait ceci très, très bien. Pourquoi ne réussissez-vous pas comme ça tous les jours?

— Ah, monsieur, ai-je répondu, si nous pouvions toujours avoir assez de temps pour préparer notre devoir en classe, comme je serais heureux ! C'est une méthode tout à fait scientifique. Rien ne se perd, l'esprit de travail devient contagieux, et je deviens une vraie source d'énergie. Vive la science !

— C'est une bonne théorie, Maurice, mais malheureusement il faut garder notre temps en classe pour la leçon. Comment avez-vous trouvé une telle liste en si peu de temps?

— Oh, j'ai fait des recherches. D'abord, après avoir cherché dans le Larousse, j'ai jeté un coup d'œil dans le couloir, où par hasard un professeur passait. C'est lui qui m'a donné les deux premiers noms. Puis j'ai remarqué en passant devant votre bureau un livre qui s'appelait *Hommes illustres de la France moderne*. Enfin, aussi par hasard, j'ai aperçu une liste de noms que vous aviez laissée sur le bureau.

— Maurice, m'a dit le professeur, vous irez loin. J'espère que ce sera toujours dans le bon chemin. »

Questions

1. Qu'est-ce que la classe a dû faire en attendant le professeur? 2. Qui est le fondateur de la méthode scientifique? 3. Quels travaux Pasteur a-t-il faits? 4. Quelle est la loi de la conservation de la matière? 5. A qui doit-on la découverte du radium? 6. Que veut dire le mot *daguerréotype*? 7. Comment le professeur a-t-il regardé le devoir de Maurice? 8. Quelle « méthode tout à fait scientifique » rendrait Maurice heureux? 9. Pourquoi ne peut-on pas préparer tous les devoirs en classe? 10. Qui a donné à Maurice les premiers noms de sa liste? 11. Comment Maurice a-t-il

remarqué le livre *Hommes illustres de la France moderne?* 12. Qu'est-ce que le professeur a dit au sujet de l'avenir de Maurice?

VOCABULARY

comme il faut proper, properly
comme je serais heureux! how happy I would be!
de nouveau, à nouveau anew, again
entendre dire que to hear that
il est peu probable it is very unlikely
jeter un coup d'œil to glance

par hasard by chance
passer à côté de to pass by
se défaire de (défait) to get rid of
se rendre compte de to realize
suivant que according to whether
une fois pour toutes once and for all

appliquer to apply
s'approcher (de) to approach
atteindre (atteint) (à) to attain, reach
attirer to attract; **s'attirer** to attract each other
un **auteur** author
un **avis** notice, warning
chacun(e) each one
le **chemin** road; **le bon chemin** the right road
la **chimie** chemistry
le **chimiste** chemist
clair clear, bright
la **connaissance** acquaintance, knowledge; (*pl.*) knowledge
le **courant** current
la **découverte** discovery
désigner to designate
douter to doubt
l'**esprit** (*m.*) mind, spirit, wit
étonner to astonish, astound

le **fil** wire, thread
fonder to found
illustre famous, illustrious
la **loi** law
malade sick, ill
parcourir (parcouru) to run through
parmi among
la **partie** part
la **pensée** thought
perfectionner to perfect, improve
le **philosophe** philosopher
physique physical
la **recherche** search; (*pl.*) research
reconstruire (reconstruit) to reconstruct, rebuild
résumer to sum up, summarize
le **savant** scientist, learned man
sensible sensitive
traduire (traduit) to translate
utiliser to utilize, use
la **vérité** truth

PATTERN SENTENCE DRILL

1. Il faut que je sois à la maison pour le dîner.

   _ est important _____.

   _____ nous _____.

   _____ chez nos amis_____.

   _____ anniversaire.

2. La réunion ne commence pas avant sept heures et demie.

   La cérémonie _____.

   _____ finit _____.

   _____minuit et demi.

   ____cérémonies _____.

3. Je ne crois pas que nous ayons fini le dîner à temps.

   Elle _____.

   _____ vous _____.

   _____ pense _____.

   _____ lecture_____.

4. Il est possible que vous finissiez plus tôt, n'est-ce pas?

   _____nous _____?

   ____nécessaire _____?

   _____ arrivions _____?

   _____ à l'heure _____?

5. M. Lasalle n'aime pas qu'on vienne en retard.

   _____ veut _____.

   _____ ils _____.

   Je _____.

   _____ vous _____.

6. Ça m'est égal qu'il soit fâché.

   _____ vous_____.

   __ lui _____.

   _____en retard.

   _____ nous _____.

7. Ça ne vous fait rien que nous prenions Roger et Louise en passant?

   _____ te _____?

   _____je _____?

   _____laisse _____?

   _____ lui _____?

8. Pensez-vous qu'ils aient l'intention de venir?

   _____ -elle _____?

   _____ vous _____?

   _____ parler?

   _____ nous _____?

9. Étant la secrétaire, Louise ne peut pas manquer cette réunion.

   _____ présidente _____.

   _____ Louis _____.

   _____ veut _____.

   _____le train.

10. Ne soyez pas impatient si je ne suis pas prête.

    _____ il _____.

    _____ préparé.

    __ soyons _____.

    _____ fâchés _____.

16

Passé Simple

Depuis, Depuis Quand,
Il y a

PATTERN SENTENCES

1. Un vieillard demeurait dans un village canadien depuis son enfance.
2. Un jour il décida de visiter Québec, la capitale de sa province.
3. Il fit le long voyage dans sa vieille auto.
4. Ne trouvant pas de place dans les grands hôtels, il dut descendre dans une petite auberge.
5. Le propriétaire s'intéressa tout de suite à cette voiture antique.
6. Il demanda au vieillard depuis quand il l'avait.
7. Ce dernier répondit: « Je l'ai depuis vingt-cinq ans.
8. — On peut dire que vous conduisez depuis longtemps, poursuivit le propriétaire.
9. — Il y a plus de quarante ans que je conduis une machine, dit le vieillard.
10. Pendant trente ans j'avais voyagé en voiture à cheval.

1. An old man had lived in a Canadian village since his childhood.
2. One day he decided to visit Quebec, the capital of his province.
3. He made the long trip in his old car.
4. Finding no room in the big hotels, he had to put up at a tiny inn.
5. The proprietor took an immediate interest in this antique car.
6. He asked the old man how long he had had it.
7. The latter replied: "I have had it for twenty-five years."
8. "I'd say you have been driving for a long time," continued the proprietor.
9. "For more than forty years now I have been driving a machine," said the old fellow.
10. "For thirty years I had made my trips by horse and carriage.

11. J'ai acheté ma première voiture il
y a trente-cinq ans.

12. Et j'en ai toujours une depuis ce
temps-là, » finit-il.

11. I bought my first car thirty-five
years ago.

12. And I have had one ever since," he
concluded.

88. *Passé simple:* Conjugation I

In historical and literary writing, the *passé composé* is seldom used except where conversation is being quoted or where English would use the present perfect. Instead,
an action in the past is expressed by the *passé simple*, sometimes called "*passé défini*"
or "past definite." In this purely literary tense, which developed out of the Latin
"perfect," verbs of CONJUGATION I stand apart from all others. The stem vowel is **a,**
which changes in the third person plural to **è.** For this reason, it is preferable to
include the vowel in the endings rather than in the stem. The endings for CONJUGA-
TION I are as follows:

ai	âmes
as	âtes
a	èrent

The stem may be found by dropping the **er** from the infinitive. Following are two
typical verbs of CONJUGATION I.

donner		aller	
je donnai	*I gave*	j'allai	*I went*
tu donnas		tu allas	
il donna		il alla	
nous donnâmes		nous allâmes	
vous donnâtes		vous allâtes	
ils donnèrent		ils allèrent	

There are no irregular first conjugation verbs in the *passé simple.*

89. *Passé simple:* verbs other than Conjugation I

There is a common set of endings for all verbs outside the first conjugation.

s	^mes
s	^tes
t	rent

The stem, which must be learned individually for irregular verbs, will, with the
exception of **venir** and **tenir** and their compounds, always end in **i** for regular verbs,

and either **i** or **u** for irregular verbs. Following are two regular verbs and three irregular verbs. Note that the endings are the same for all.

finir	**perdre**	**pouvoir**
je finis	je perdis	je pus
tu finis	tu perdis	tu pus
il finit	il perdit	il put
nous finîmes	nous perdîmes	nous pûmes
vous finîtes	vous perdîtes	vous pûtes
ils finirent	ils perdirent	ils purent

venir	**tenir**
je vins	je tins
tu vins	tu tins
il vint	il tint
nous vînmes	nous tînmes
vous vîntes	vous tîntes
ils vinrent	ils tinrent

NOTE: **Venir** and **tenir** (and their compounds, such as **revenir, soutenir,** etc.) are the only verbs whose stem ends in a consonant for this tense. They nevertheless keep the accent over the **i**.

Following is a list of those irregular verbs studied to date which have irregular stems for the *passé simple*, together with the first person singular of this tense.

STEMS IN **i**

s'asseoir	**je m'assis**	naître	**je naquis**
dire	**je dis**	prendre	**je pris**
écrire	**j'écrivis**	produire	**je produisis**
faire	**je fis**	voir	**je vis**
mettre	**je mis**		

STEMS IN **u**

apercevoir	**j'aperçus**	lire	**je lus**
avoir	**j'eus**	mourir	**je mourus**
boire	**je bus**	plaire	**je plus**
connaître	**je connus**	pleuvoir	**il plut**
courir	**je courus**	recevoir	**je reçus**
croire	**je crus**	savoir	**je sus**
devoir	**je dus**	valoir	**je valus**
être	**je fus**	vivre	**je vécus**
falloir	**il fallut**	vouloir	**je voulus**

NOTE: **Falloir** and **pleuvoir** occur only in the third person singular.

A. Restate, using *passé composé* for *passé simple*.[1]

1. Les Normands *envahirent* l'Angleterre en 1066.[2]   2. Guillaume le Conquérant [3] *battit* le roi saxon Harold à Hastings.   3. Les Normands *apportèrent* le français aux Anglais.   4. Pendant quelque temps le français *fut* la seule langue permise à la cour.   5. Peu à peu cette langue *passa* de la noblesse dans le peuple.   6. Sans doute les Saxons *résistèrent* à la nouvelle langue.   7. Mais ils ne *purent* pas complètement en empêcher l'usage.   8. Il est vrai qu'avec le temps le français *disparut* comme langue officielle.   9. L'anglais *vint* le remplacer dans la cour aussi bien que parmi le peuple.   10. Pourtant, le français était resté pendant si longtemps la langue dominante qu'il *eut* une influence profonde sur le vocabulaire anglais.

90. *Depuis* and *depuis quand* with present and imperfect tenses

The present and imperfect tenses are used with **depuis** and **depuis quand** to indicate an action or situation begun in the past and still going on at the time of the verb.

Depuis quand *êtes*-vous ici?   How long *have* you *been* here?
Je *suis* ici depuis quinze jours.   I *have been* here two weeks.
Depuis quand *étiez*-vous ici lorsque je suis arrivé?   How long *had* you *been* here when I arrived?
J'*étais* ici depuis huit jours.[4]   I *had been* here a week.

Depuis quand pleut-il?   How long *has* it *been raining?*
Il pleut depuis une heure.   It *has been raining* for an hour.
Depuis quand pleuvait-il quand vous êtes venu?   How long *had* it *been raining* when you came?
Il pleuvait depuis un quart d'heure.   It *had been raining* for a quarter of an hour.

91. *Il y a* for *depuis*

Sometimes, when the duration rather than the action is stressed, **voilà . . . que** or **il y a . . . que** may be found instead of **depuis**. These can be used only at the beginning of a sentence.

Il y a quinze jours que je suis ici.   I have been here two whole weeks.[5]
Voilà une heure qu'il pleut.   It has been raining a solid hour.

---

[1] No drill is given on the *passé simple* since the student needs only to recognize its forms, not to use them orally.
[2] Read **mil soixante-six.**
[3] **Guillaume le Conquérant**   *William the Conqueror*
[4] Note that the French include the day from which the week is reckoned.
[5] Do not confuse with **il y a** meaning "ago," which is used only with past tenses.

This construction may also be used where confusion might result from the use of *depuis*, as in one of the examples in Section 90. I.e., **Il pleut depuis une heure** may mean not only "It has been raining for an hour," but also "It has been raining since one o'clock." **Il y a une heure qu'il pleut** can only mean the former. It is important to note that the use of **depuis** or its alternative expressions is limited to an action or situation begun in the past and still continuing at the time of the main verb. Where the action or situation is not brought up to a certain point (either past or present), but merely stands at an isolated point or in an isolated block of time in the past, **pendant** is used, or often no preposition at all. The tense in this case is *passé composé* or pluperfect. Contrast the following examples:

> **Le vieillard a cherché sa clef pendant un bon quart d'heure.** The old man looked for his key for a good quarter of an hour. (He is no longer looking for it.)
> **Le vieillard cherche sa clef depuis un bon quart d'heure.** The old man has been looking for his key a good quarter of an hour. (He is still looking.)
> **Il avait conduit (pendant) trois jours.** He had driven for three days. (He was no longer driving.)
> **Il conduisait depuis trois jours.** He had been driving for three days. (And was still driving.)

With future time, "for" is expressed by **pour** or is left unexpressed.

> **Je vais voyager pour deux semaines.** I am going to travel for two weeks.
> **Il restera (pour) un mois chez sa tante.** He will stay (for) a month at his aunt's.

B. Substitution Drill.

a. 1. Depuis quand êtes-*vous* ici? (*elle, tu, ils*)
2. *Je* suis ici depuis ce matin. (*Nous, Elle, Ils*)
3. Depuis combien de temps ¹ écrit-*elle?* (*vous, ils, tu*)
4. *Elle* écrit depuis une heure. (*Ils, Nous, Je*)
5. Depuis quand habitait-*on* cette maison? (*ils, vous, elle*)
6. *On* l'habitait depuis un an. (*Je, Nous, Elles*)

b. 1. Pendant combien de temps a-t-*on* joué du piano? (*ils, vous, tu*)
2. *Nous* avons joué pendant une heure. (*Ils, Je, On*)
3. Pour combien de temps resterez-*vous* dans le musée? (*on, tu, nous*)
4. *Nous* y resterons une demi-heure. (*Je, Il, Elles*)
5. *Nous* étions restés pendant deux heures. (*Il, Les garçons, Elles*)

---

¹ While **depuis quand?** can mean either "how long?" or "since when?" **depuis combien de temps?** can mean only "how long?"

LECTURE

Ce matin nous avons eu une leçon d'histoire. Je vais vous la résumer, et puisque dans les livres d'histoire presque tous les verbes sont au passé simple, je vais me servir de ce temps [1] partout où il est possible de l'employer.

Le professeur commença par dire que Charlemagne était un grand empereur [2] du neuvième [3] siècle qui fit la guerre pendant de longues années contre les Arabes dans le Midi, les Saxons dans le nord et d'autres ennemis à l'est. Il voulait que tout le monde soit chrétien.

Mais bien qu'il ait fait beaucoup de guerres, nous préférons nous souvenir de lui comme d'un monarque attiré par les arts de la paix, surtout parce qu'il s'est inté-ressé à l'éducation. Il appela à ses côtés des savants étrangers, comme Alcuin de York, Clément d'Irlande [4] et Diacre d'Italie. Ces hommes aidèrent les Français à créer des écoles pour le clergé,[5] qui à son tour ouvrit des écoles pour le peuple. Ces écoles qu'on venait de fonder étaient gratuites pour tout le monde. Malheureuse-ment ce système ne dura pas longtemps après l'époque de Charlemagne. Toutefois, il est fort probable que sans cette période où l'on s'occupa de l'instruction, l'Uni-versité de Paris, qui date du Moyen Age, n'aurait pas commencé si tôt.

Ensuite le professeur nous expliqua que la période entre Charlemagne et le Moyen Age proprement dit fut une période assez complexe. L'empire de Charle-magne fut divisé entre ses trois petits-fils. La partie occidentale,[6] qui revint [7] à Charles (dit « le Chauve »), devint la France; la partie orientale,[8] qui fut l'héritage de Louis (dit « le Germanique »), devint plus tard l'Allemagne. Quant à la partie que reçut Lothaire, le fils aîné,[9] et qui se trouvait prise [10] entre les deux autres, elle ne dura pas longtemps comme royaume séparé. En effet, même avant la mort de Lothaire, les deux autres frères jurèrent de s'unir contre lui, dans un document devenu fameux sous le nom de *Serment* [11] *de Strasbourg*, et avec le temps son royaume disparut. Mais le nom de Lothaire a survécu [12] jusqu'à nos jours dans le nom de Lorraine (autrefois Lotharingie), et ce pays a été, avec l'Alsace, la cause de bien des conflits [13] entre la France et l'Allemagne. On pourrait dire que Lothaire a pris sa revanche [14] contre ses deux frères. (Cette idée me plaît, car je conserve de la sympathie pour le pauvre frère aîné.) Selon notre professeur, le serment en langue romane fait à Strasbourg représente une étape importante dans le développement de la langue française.

---

[1] Here, **temps** means *tense.*
[2] **un empereur** *emperor*
[3] **neuvième** *ninth*
[4] **l'Irlande** *Ireland*
[5] **le clergé** *clergy*
[6] **occidental** *western*
[7] **revint** (from **revenir**) *came down*
[8] **oriental** *eastern*
[9] **aîné** *elder, eldest*
[10] **prise** (from **prendre**) *caught*
[11] **le serment** *oath*
[12] **survécu** (from **survivre**) *to survive*
[13] **le conflit** *conflict*
[14] **la revanche** *revenge*

Un événement capital pour la France eut lieu pendant le neuvième siècle: ce fut l'invasion de la France par les Normands. Arrivant du nord par la mer, ces hardis conquérants de race scandinave, qui attaquaient depuis quelque temps déjà les villes de la côte, commencèrent à remonter les fleuves et les rivières de la région au nord-ouest de Paris. Enfin, au siècle suivant, il devint inévitable de reconnaître leur puissance et de céder à leur chef, Rollon, un pays assez étendu, qui prit le nom de Normandie. Alors une chose curieuse arriva. C'est que ces gens si hardis oublièrent leur langue maternelle. Notre professeur nous raconta comment, un peu plus tard, leur nouveau chef, Guillaume le Conquérant, duc de Normandie, envahit l'Angleterre et battit le saxon Harold à la célèbre bataille de Hastings. Et la langue que les soldats de Guillaume apportèrent avec eux en Angleterre, ce fut le français.

A ce moment de son récit, le professeur s'arrêta. Je levai la main.

« Qu'est-ce qu'il y a, Maurice?

— Je voulais simplement exprimer mon admiration pour les Normands, monsieur.

— J'en suis content, mon garçon, mais pourquoi les admirez-vous tant? Je suppose que c'est parce qu'ils ont battu les Anglais.

— Ah non, monsieur. Moi, je trouve que l'exploit le plus remarquable c'est d'avoir appris le français en moins de deux siècles. »

Questions

In answering, use the *passé composé* when called for, rather than the *passé simple*.

1. Quand est-ce que Charlemagne a vécu? 2. Pourquoi a-t-il fait la guerre contre les Arabes, les Saxons et d'autres ennemis? 3. A quoi s'est-il surtout intéressé? 4. De quelle période date l'Université de Paris? 5. En combien de parties a-t-on divisé l'empire de Charlemagne? 6. Quels pays ont été les causes de bien des conflits entre la France et l'Allemagne? 7. Comment les Normands sont-ils arrivés en France? 8. Depuis quand les Normands attaquaient-ils les villes de la côte? 9. Quelle chose curieuse est arrivée aux Normands? 10. Quelle langue ont-ils apportée en Angleterre? 11. Qui a battu le roi saxon Harold? 12. Pourquoi Maurice admire-t-il tant les Normands?

VOCABULARY

à ses côtés to him, to his side	**en effet** = **en fait**
avec le temps in time, in due time	**peu à peu** little by little
avoir lieu to take place	**proprement dit** actual, properly so-called

attaquer to attack
la **bataille** battle
capital important
chauve bald
le **chef** chief, chieftain
chrétien Christian
conserver to preserve, maintain
la **cour** court
créer to create
une **demi-heure** half an hour
disparaître (**disparu**) to disappear
dit (*p.p. of* **dire**) called
le **duc** duke
durer to last, endure
un **effet** effect
un **ennemi** enemy
envahir to invade
une **époque** time, period
une **étape** step, stage (of development), stop (on journey)
étendu extensive
étranger, étrangère foreign
un **événement** event
exprimer to express
fameux, fameuse famous

fort strong, very
gratuit free
*****hardi** [1] bold, tough
jurer to swear
la **mort** death
la **noblesse** nobility
un **Normand** Norman
la **paix** peace
le **petit-fils** grandson
le **peuple** common people, masses
profond deep, profound
la **puissance** strength
le **récit** recitation, narrative
remonter to go up (a river)
la **rivière** river, tributary
le **roi** king
roman, romane Romance, Romanesque
le **royaume** kingdom
le **tour** turn, trick, tour; **à son tour** in (one's) turn
toutefois nevertheless
s'unir to unite, combine
un **usage** use, usage

PATTERN SENTENCE DRILL

1. Un vieillard demeurait dans un village canadien depuis son enfance.
   _____ travaillait _____.
   _____ la guerre.
   Des _____.
   _____ longtemps.

2. On peut dire que vous conduisez depuis longtemps.
   _____ elle _____.
   _____ peu de temps.
   _____ étudie _____.
   _____ tu _____.

---

[1] The asterisk before an **h** indicates that it is aspirate, permitting neither the dropping of a preceding vowel nor *liaison* with a preceding consonant.

3. Il y a plus de quarante ans que je conduis une machine.
   _____ habite cette ville.
   _____ dix _____.
   _____ nous _____.
   _____ moins _____.

4. Pendant trente ans j'avais voyagé en voiture à cheval.
   _____ il _____.
   _____ en auto.
   _____ la guerre _____.
   _____ nous _____.

5. J'ai acheté ma première voiture il y a trente-cinq ans.
   _____ un mois.
   _____ maison _____.
   Il _____.
   _____ deux jours.

6. J'en ai toujours une depuis ce temps-là.
   Elle _____.
   _____ son enfance.
   _____ souvent _____.
   _____ plusieurs _____.

17

Passive Voice

Substitutes for Passive

Même

Cardinal and Ordinal Numbers

PATTERN SENTENCES

1. Le musée du Louvre devrait être visité par tous les touristes.
2. On dit que c'est le musée le plus riche du monde.
3. Même si on allait au Louvre tous les jours pendant une quinzaine, on ne verrait pas tout.
4. La première impression qu'on a du musée c'est sa grandeur.
5. La seconde c'est sa richesse en chefs-d'œuvre.
6. Par exemple, on y trouve la Victoire de Samothrace, la Vénus de Milo et la Joconde.
7. La Victoire Ailée fut érigée au quatrième siècle av. J.-C.[1]

1. The Louvre museum should be visited by every tourist.
2. It is said to be the richest museum in the world.
3. Even if you went to the Louvre every day for two weeks you wouldn't see everything.
4. The first impression you get of the museum is its size.
5. The second is its wealth of master-pieces.
6. For example, you find there the Victory of Samothrace, the Venus de Milo, and the Mona Lisa.
7. The Winged Victory was erected in the fourth century B.C.

---

[1] Read **avant Jésus-Christ** [avɑ̃ ʒezykri].

8. La statue de Vénus est nommée d'après Milo, l'île où on l'a découverte.

8. The statue of Venus is named after Melos, the island where it was discovered.

9. Elle y a été trouvée il y a près de cent quarante ans.

9. It was found there nearly 140 years ago.

10. La Joconde a été achevée par Léonard de Vinci en quinze cent cinq environ.

10. The Mona Lisa was completed by Leonardo da Vinci around 1505.

11. D'autres œuvres de ce même artiste se trouvent aussi au Louvre.

11. Other works by this same artist are also found in the Louvre.

12. Même si l'art ne vous intéresse que médiocrement, vous serez frappé par ce vaste musée.

12. Even if you have but a moderate interest in art, you will be struck by this vast museum.

92. Passive voice

The passive voice is formed exactly as in English, by combining a form of the verb *to be* with the past participle of a verb. The past participle always agrees with the subject in gender and number.

Il est entouré.   He is surrounded.
Elle fut abandonnée par son ami.   She was abandoned by her friend.
Les livres perdus seront sans doute découverts demain.   The lost books will no doubt be found tomorrow.

NOTE: The tense of the passive is that of the auxiliary alone, the participle being disregarded. Thus, the first example above is present tense, even though the verb has two elements; the second is *passé simple*, and the third is simple future.

A. Change each of the following to the passive voice, making the present direct object the subject. Remember to make the participle agree where necessary. Keep the tense of the original.

Example: Les Normands ont envahi l'Angleterre en 1066.
L'Angleterre a été envahie par les Normands en 1066.

1. Robert de Sorbon fonda la Sorbonne.
2. Le gouvernement lui donnera un poste.
3. Le professeur pose quelques questions aux étudiants.
4. Les soldats peuvent traverser le fleuve.[1]
5. Les élèves mettent les chaises dans la salle de classe.

---

[1] The passive of an infinitive utilizes the infinitive **être** as auxiliary.

6. Les Parisiens avaient bâti cette magnifique cathédrale.
7. Les Gaulois ont construit ces murs-ci.
8. Les touristes visitent souvent le musée du Louvre.
9. Léonard de Vinci n'a pas fait cette peinture.
10. Est-ce que Louis XIV a commencé le palais de Versailles?

93. Substitutes for passive

The true passive is not too common in French. If no agent is actually mentioned, French prefers:

1. An active construction with **on** as subject.

> **On ferme ces portes à cinq heures.**   These doors are closed at five.
> **Ici on parle français.**   French is spoken here.

2. A reflexive construction.

> **Les portes du métro se ferment automatiquement.**   The doors on the subway are closed automatically.
> **Les billets pour le bal se vendaient partout.**   The tickets for the dance were being sold everywhere.

No hard and fast rule can be given as to when to use one or the other of these constructions, but undoubtedly the commoner is the active construction with **on**. Unless (as in the case of the subway doors) the action is performed by an impersonal agent, the student will rarely go wrong in using **on**. Conversely, many expressions with **on** are best rendered in English by a passive.

> **On donne des fleurs gratis tous les jours chez Laurent.**   Flowers are given away free every day at Lawrence's.
> **Quand nous allons chez Henri, on nous invite toujours à prendre un verre.**   When we go to Henry's, we are always invited to have a drink.

If the agent is mentioned, the passive may not usually be avoided. In this case, the preposition *by* is usually **par,** although if no action is involved, we sometimes find **de.**

> **Elle fut frappée par sa ressemblance avec son père.**   She was struck by his resemblance to her father.
> **Le roi était aimé de son peuple.**   The king was beloved by his people.

It is impossible in French to make a passive construction using as subject what would have been an indirect object in the active. For instance, "His grandfather gave him a watch" cannot be made passive with *him (he)* as subject, but only with *watch* as subject.

> **Son grand-père lui a donné une montre.**   His grandfather gave him a watch.
> **Une montre lui a été donnée par son grand-père.**   He was given a watch by his grandfather.

B. Express in French, using substitutes for the passive whenever possible.

1. That night the castle was attacked by the enemy. 2. The death of the king will be announced to the people immediately. 3. A prize is given to the student who writes the best poem. 4. The book will be found later, no doubt. 5. That language is not written as it is spoken.[1] 6. I was struck by the size of the palace. 7. When was the Venus de Milo discovered? 8. He was given a farm by his father. 9. That castle was begun a long time ago. 10. We were told to come back the next day. 11. The doors will be closed at nine o'clock sharp. 12. Paintings by da Vinci are found in many museums.

94. Uses of *même*

Même, some of whose meanings we have encountered already, may be either an adverb, in which case it is invariable, or an adjective, in which case it is variable. As an adverb it generally means *even*.

Même quand le soleil brillait, il faisait froid.   Even when the sun was shining, it was cold.
Tout le monde travaillait, même les enfants.   Everybody was working, even the children.
Il l'a fait tout de même (*or* **quand même**).   He did it anyhow (all the same, even so).

As an adjective, it means *same* when it precedes the noun, *very* or *self* when it follows. With a disjunctive pronoun, it always means *self*.

Les deux événements ont eu lieu le même jour.   The two events took place the same day.
Nous avons les mêmes questions que vous.   We have the same questions as you.
Le roi est mort le jour même.   The king died that very day.
L'ennemi est entré dans la ville même.   The enemy entered the very city (the city itself).
Il est venu lui-même.   He came himself. (Similarly, **elle-même, moi-même, eux-mêmes,** etc.)

95. *Even if*

In a sentence involving the expression *even if*, the most usual construction in French resembles English, the imperfect occurring in the "if clause," the conditional in the conclusion.

Même s'il venait, nous ne le verrions pas.   Even if he came, we would not see him.

---

[1] Use a reflexive.

This combination remains the same even when the English uses a "should" construction or a subjunctive.

> **Même s'il mourait, nous ne pleurerions pas.** Even if he should die, we would
> not weep.
> **Même s'il partait, je resterais.** Even if he were to leave, I would stay.

The student should learn to recognize a second method of handling a condition, which utilizes **que** for the conclusion, and omits the **même si** from the other clause. In this method, much less common than the other, the conditional is used in both parts of the sentence.

> **Il viendrait que nous ne le verrions pas.** Even if he came, we would not see him.
> **Il partirait tout de suite qu'il n'arriverait pas à temps.** Even if he left right
> away, he would not arrive in time.

> C. Read each of the following sentences, then reread adding **même, même**
> with a disjunctive pronoun, or an expression using **même** in a logical
> position, and give the English equivalent.
>
> *Example:* C'est le chapeau que vous portiez hier, n'est-ce pas?
> C'est le même chapeau que vous portiez hier, n'est-ce pas?
>
> 1. Dans la maison, il faisait froid.
> 2. Tous les deux ont raconté l'histoire.
> 3. Nous avons fait le travail.
> 4. Autrefois nous vivions dans les faubourgs mais maintenant nous
>   habitons la ville.
> 5. La secrétaire était malade, donc le patron a écrit la lettre.
> 6. Si vous étiez pauvre, je vous aimerais.
> 7. On parle français, allemand et italien en Suisse, mais on parle alle-
>   mand dans la capitale.
> 8. Qu'ils le fassent !
> 9. L'enfant est né le jour où la ville a été attaquée.
> 10. Le matin il pleuvait mais nous nous sommes mises en route.
> 11. Moi, je le trouve difficile à comprendre.
> 12. Elle a vendu ses bijoux, ses robes de soie, et enfin elle a vendu ses
>   beaux cheveux blonds.

96. Cardinal numbers from 51

Numbers beyond fifty continue on the same system as the lower numerals, except that **et** is not used beyond 71. Since there is no word in standard French for 70 or 90, numbers up to 19 are added to 60 and 80, respectively.

51	cinquante et un	82	quatre-vingt-deux
52	cinquante-deux	89	quatre-vingt-neuf
53	cinquante-trois	90	quatre-vingt-dix
60	soixante [1]	91	quatre-vingt-onze
61	soixante et un	92	quatre-vingt-douze
62	soixante-deux	99	quatre-vingt-dix-neuf
69	soixante-neuf	100	cent
70	soixante-dix	101	cent un
71	soixante et onze	102	cent deux
72	soixante-douze	200	deux cents
73	soixante-treize	201	deux cent un [3]
79	soixante-dix-neuf	202	deux cent deux
80	quatre-vingts	1000	mille
81	quatre-vingt-un [2]	2000	deux mille [4]

There is a noun **millier,** which is seldom used except in the plural, and only when no definite number of thousands is specified.

> **J'ai vu des milliers de fleurs dans le vaste jardin.** I saw thousands of flowers in the vast garden.
> **Plusieurs milliers de personnes sont venus.** Several thousand people came.

Otherwise, numbers less than a million are adjectives, modifying their noun directly. **Million,** however, and **milliard** (*billion*) are nouns like **millier,** requiring **de** before a succeeding noun.

deux cents hommes   **mille hommes**   **deux mille hommes**
BUT
un million d'hommes   **deux milliards d'hommes**

97. Dates

Dates of the years such as the following are usually read in hundreds:

> 1492 quatorze cent quatre-vingt-douze
> 1776 dix-sept cent soixante-seize
> 1812 dix-huit cent douze

However, in dates from 1001 to 1099, it is customary to use the term **mil** (rarely **mille**). For instance:

> 1066 mil soixante-six
> 1089 mil quatre-vingt-neuf

---

[1] The **x** is pronounced like **ss.**
[2] The **s** drops when numbers are added to **quatre vingts.**
[3] The **s** drops when numbers are added to **deux cents.**
[4] **Mille** never takes an **s.**

Some French speakers use **mil** in other dates, particularly for the nineteenth century and occasionally the twentieth century.

1802 mil huit cent deux
1830 mil huit cent trente
1914 mil neuf cent quatorze

It is rare to find **mil** used in other centuries, and inasmuch as the hundreds system is perfectly correct for all but the eleventh century, the student will do well to limit his use of **mil** to that period alone. The year 1000 itself is generally spelled in the conventional way: **l'an mille.** The terms B.C. and A.D. are expressed as follows:

B.C. **av. J.-C.** (avant Jésus-Christ)   A.D. **apr. J.-C.** (après Jésus-Christ)

98. Ordinals

Ordinal numbers (*third, fourth, tenth,* etc.) are made by adding **ième** to the cardinal number, after dropping the final **e** when there is one. **Cinq** inserts **u** before the ending, and **neuf** changes **f** to **v.**

deuxième	neuvième	vingt et unième
troisième	dixième	centième
quatrième	onzième	millième
cinquième	vingtième	

NOTE: The **x** of **deuxième, sixième,** and **dixième** is pronounced like **z.** The ordinals may be abbreviated, usually thus: **3ᵉ, 5ᵉ, 89ᵉ.** Roman numerals written as ordinals (**XVIIᵉ, XIXᵉ**) generally mean "centuries," and do not necessarily require the word **siècle.** Thus, **XVIIIᵉ** in a history book would normally mean "eighteenth century." The ordinal *first* is **premier** (abbreviated **1ᵉʳ**), which has a feminine **première** and corresponding plural forms. **Deuxième** has an alternative form **second,** which has regular feminine and plural forms. Ordinals are not used to distinguish monarchs except *the First:*

François Iᵉʳ (François Premier) Francis the First
BUT
François II (François Deux) Francis the Second
Charles IX (Charles Neuf) Charles the Ninth
Henri IV (Henri Quatre) Henry the Fourth

   D. Substitution Drill. (If written, write out numbers in full.)

   1. On a construit ces murs en *350* av. J.-C. (*200, 465, 570*)
   2. La bataille eut lieu en *1066*. (*999, 1325, 1482*)
   3. Je remarque sur la lettre la date *13/7/51*.[1] (*3/4/60, 2/6/59, 29/8/61*)

---

[1] In French the first number represents the day, the second the month.

4. J'ai entendu parler de Charles X, mais plus souvent de *Napoléon Ier*.
(*Henry IV, Louis XIV, Louis XV*)
5. J'ai ma *première* leçon aujourd'hui, et demain j'aurai ma seconde.
(*huitième, dixième, vingtième*)

LECTURE

Un jour notre professeur a invité un de ses amis à nous parler de l'architecture française. Ce monsieur, qui a pris sa tâche au sérieux, a apporté avec lui quantité[1] de projections, plusieurs gros livres d'illustrations, et un machin en bois qui m'intriguait par sa simplicité.

Après avoir posé tout cela sur le bureau, il a commencé sa conférence en disant qu'avant le onzième[2] siècle il n'y a pas de style d'architecture qu'on puisse appeler français. Certes, a-t-il dit, nous trouvons des monuments préhistoriques, comme les menhirs et les dolmens[3] de la Bretagne, et les restes romains, qui consistent principalement en arcs de triomphe, en temples, en arènes[4] et en bains. Ces derniers se trouvent surtout dans le Midi, mais on peut voir, à Paris même, des bains romains (appelés *thermes*) et un amphithéâtre qu'on appelle *les Arènes de Lutèce*. Quant aux constructions gauloises, elles étaient d'ordinaire en bois, et ont disparu avec le temps.

Avec la féodalité[5] sont venus les châteaux forts.[6] Ces citadelles formidables peuvent être considérées comme vraiment françaises. Leur construction fait preuve d'une ingéniosité considérable. Dans un des gros livres du professeur nous avons pu voir des photos de quelques grands châteaux forts, pour la plupart en ruines, comme le fameux Château Gaillard, bâti au XIIe par Richard Cœur de Lion[7] en Normandie; mais quelquefois intacts, comme le magnifique château de Pierrefonds près de Compiègne, qui a été restauré par Viollet-le-Duc en 1862. Il arrive même que des villages entiers ont été fortifiés de la même manière que les châteaux. Ces villages ont été appelés des *bourgs*, et leurs habitants des *bourgeois*.

Si c'est la nécessité de se protéger qui a produit les châteaux forts, c'est le désir de glorifier Dieu qui a produit les cathédrales. Commencées dans le Midi sur le

---

[1] See idioms in Vocabulary.
[2] Note that there is no *liaison* before **onze** and **onzième**.
[3] **Les menhirs et les dolmens**   Prehistoric stone monuments.   The menhir is a single upright stone, while the dolmen is in the form of a table.
[4] **Une arène** (often plural in French)   *arena*
[5] **la féodalité**   *feudalism*
[6] **le château fort**   *fortress castle*
[7] **Richard Cœur de Lion**   *Richard the Lion-Hearted*

PARIS

SEINE
BOIS DE VINCENNES
Porte de Pantin
Porte de Charenton
AV. JEAN-JAURÈS
RUE DE FLANDRE
Porte de la Nation
COURS DE VINCENNES
CIMETIÈRE DU PÈRE LACHAISE
PARC DES BUTTES CHAUMONT
BOUL. DE MÉNILMONTANT
DE LA VILLETTE
BOUL. DE BELLEVILLE
FAUBOURG ST. ANTOINE
BOUL. VOLTAIRE
Porte Daumesnil
DAUMESNIL
Gare de Lyon
BOUL. DE FLANDRE
Gare du Nord
Gare de l'Est
BOUL. MAGENTA
BOUL. ROCHECHOUART
BARBÈS
BOUL. DE CLICHY
Place de la Bastille
Gare de la Bastille
Musée Carnavalet
Pl. des Vosges
Archives Nationales
Hôtel de Ville
St. Gervais
Gare d'Austerlitz
SEINE
BOUL. DE L'HÔPITAL
BOUL. DE LA GARE
Pl. d'Italie
Porte d'Italie
AV. D'ITALIE
NEY
Sacré-Coeur
Église St. Pierre
CIMETIÈRE MONTMARTRE
Porte de St. Ouen
AV. DE ST. OUEN
RUE LAFAYETTE
BOUL. SEBASTOPOL
BOUL. RÉAUMUR
GRANDS BOULEVARDS
RUE DU 4 SEPTEMBRE
Bourse
Bibliothèque Nationale
Banque de France
Palais Royal
Arts et Métiers
Tour St. Jacques
Sainte-Chapelle
Notre-Dame
ÎLE DE LA CITÉ
Palais de Justice
Préfecture de Police
St. Séverin
Cluny
Sorbonne
Panthéon
Arènes
Mosquée
JARDIN DES PLANTES
RUE MONGE
Inst. du Radium
Val-de-Grâce
Gobelins
RUE ST. JACQUES
Observatoire
PARC MONTSOURIS
Opéra
BD. HAUSSMANN
RUE DE RIVOLI
Louvre
Théâtre Français
Palais des Tuileries
JARDIN DES TUILERIES
PL. DE LA CONCORDE
Orangerie
Gare d'Orsay
Institut
St. Germain-des-Prés
St. Sulpice
Odéon
Palais du Luxembourg
BOUL. ST. MICHEL
BOUL. ST. GERMAIN
BOUL. RASPAIL
SEINE
Madeleine
PL. VENDÔME
U.S. Embassy
Petit Palais
Grand Palais
Palais de l'Élysée
ROND POINT
AV. DES CHAMPS-ÉLYSÉES
Chambre des Députés
Palais de la Légion d'Honneur
Invalides
Gare des Invalides
AV. BOSQUET
École Militaire
Gare Montparnasse
CIMETIÈRE DU MONTPARNASSE
BOUL. MONTPARNASSE
AV. DU MAINE
RUE DE VAUGIRARD
Institut Pasteur
BOUL. DE COURCELLES
BD. DES BATIGNOLLES
Gare St. Lazare
PARC MONCEAU
AV. DE CLICHY
Porte de Clichy
Porte de St. Ouen
AV. DE FRIEDLAND
AV. DE LA GRANDE ARMÉE
PLACE DE L'ÉTOILE
Arc de Triomphe
AVENUE FOCH
AV. VICTOR-HUGO
AV. KLÉBER
Musée Galliera
Musée Guimet
Palais de Tokyo
Palais de Chaillot
Tour Eiffel
AV. DE NEUILLY
JARDIN DE RANELAGH
BOIS DE BOULOGNE
Porte de St. Cloud
BOUL. DE VERSAILLES
Porte de Versailles
PARC DES EXPOSITIONS
Porte d'Orléans
AV. D'ORLÉANS
SEINE

plan des anciennes basiliques [1] romaines, les premières cathédrales ont été caractérisées par des arcs arrondis en demi-cercle, des murs très épais et des fenêtres minuscules. Ce style d'architecture, appelé *style roman*, convenait au Midi, où l'on aimait les intérieurs frais et sombres. Dans le nord, au contraire, le besoin de la lumière explique ce qu'on appelle le *style français* (plus tard par erreur *style gothique*), caractérisé par l'ogive,[2] par de longs vitraux, par des murs moins épais et par des arcs-boutants.[3]

Pour comparer la solidité des arcs pointus et des arcs arrondis, le professeur a pris le machin qu'il avait apporté avec lui, et qui consistait simplement en deux planches attachées par un gond,[4] et l'a placé debout sur le bureau pour former un angle. Pour illustrer l'arc en demi-cercle, il a fixé l'angle à 90 degrés. Les planches sont tombées avec un grand bruit qui a réveillé plusieurs élèves sommeillants. Puis il a diminué l'angle à 60 degrés, et l'édifice est resté debout, sans glisser. Avec l'ogive on a pu, selon le professeur, ériger de très hauts bâtiments. Les grandes cathédrales telles que Chartres, Notre-Dame de Paris, Amiens et Reims sont restées jusqu'à nos jours comme témoins du génie du Moyen Age.

Après avoir parlé brièvement des vitraux, dont il nous a montré quelques reproductions, le professeur a continué en indiquant que le style des châteaux a changé au XVIe avec la Renaissance. Ce que je me rappelle surtout c'est que leur aspect est devenu de moins en moins militaire, et que les fenêtres se sont multipliées. Nous avons vu de belles projections des châteaux de la Loire tels que Blois, Amboise et Chenonceaux. Ce dernier, qui est très beau, a été bâti au-dessus d'une rivière. Après les châteaux, le professeur nous a fait voir quelques images des grands palais royaux de Chambord, Fontainebleau et Versailles et de leurs jardins magnifiques.

La dernière partie de l'heure a été consacrée a une brève description des mouvements plus récents, et pleine de termes comme baroque, rococo et néo-classique. Enfin le professeur a terminé par une projection d'une belle église moderne toute en ciment et en verre. A la fin de la conférence, il nous a demandé si nous avions des questions à poser. Levant la main, je lui ai demandé s'il pensait que nous pourrions retenir tout ce qu'il avait dit, puisqu'il avait traité près de neuf cents ans d'architecture en une heure.

« Franchement, non, a-t-il répondu.

— Alors, quel conseil nous donnez-vous, monsieur, pour fixer tout cela dans notre mémoire?

Sa réponse a été simple et positive:

— Suivez mon cours d'histoire de l'art. »

---

[1] **la basilique** *basilica*   [2] **ogive** *pointed or Gothic arch*   [3] **un arc-boutant** *flying buttress*   [4] **le gond** *hinge*

Questions

1. Qui a fait la conférence sur l'architecture? 2. Qu'est-ce que ce monsieur a apporté avec lui? 3. A quel siècle, selon le professeur, a commencé l'architecture vraiment française? 4. Dans quelle partie de la France trouve-t-on surtout les restes romains? 5. Pourquoi les constructions gauloises n'ont-elles pas duré? 6. Par qui Château Gaillard a-t-il été construit? 7. Comment s'appelait un village fortifié du Moyen Age? 8. Qu'est-ce qui a produit les cathédrales? 9. Par quoi les églises de style roman sont-elles caractérisées? 10. Pourquoi conviennent-elles au Midi? 11. Quelle est la différence entre les châteaux de la Renaissance et les châteaux forts?

VOCABULARY

entendre parler de   to hear about
faire preuve de   to show
par erreur   by mistake
pour la plupart   for the most part

prendre au sérieux   to take seriously
quantité de   a lot of, lots of
suivre un cours   to take a course
tous les deux   both, both of them

un **arc**   bow, arch
  arrondi   rounded
le **bain**   bath
le **bâtiment**   building
le **besoin**   need
le **bijou**   jewel
le **bourgeois**   (formerly, inhabitant of forti-
    fied village) middle-class citizen
  bref, brève   brief
  brièvement   briefly
le **cercle**   circle; **demi-cercle**   semi-circle
  certes   to be sure
le **ciment**   cement
la **conférence**   lecture
  consacrer   to devote
  convenir (convenu)   to be suitable,
    be appropriate
  debout   standing, upright
  Dieu   God
  diminuer   to diminish
une **église**   church
  entier, entière   whole, entire
  épais, épaisse   thick

le **faubourg**   outskirts, suburb
  gaulois   Gallic; un **Gaulois**   a Gaul
le **génie**   genius
  glisser   to slip, slide
une **ingéniosité**   ingenuity, ingeniousness
  intriguer   to intrigue, fascinate
le **machin**   thingamajig
le **patron**   boss
la **planche**   board
  pointu   pointed
  se protéger   to protect oneself
la **réponse**   answer, reply
  restaurer   to restore
le **reste**   relic; (*pl.*) remains
  retenir (retenu)   to keep, retain
  réveiller   to awaken
la **soie**   silk
  sommeillant   drowsy, drowsing
le **témoin**   evidence
  terminer   to end, finish
  traiter   to treat
le **vitrail** (*pl.* **vitraux**)   stained-glass win-
    dow

PATTERN SENTENCE DRILL

1. Le musée du Louvre devrait être visité par tous les touristes.
 ___ cathédrale de Notre-Dame _____.
 _____vue _____.
 _____ visiteurs.
 _____ peut _____.

2. On dit que c'est le musée le plus riche du monde.
 _____ splendide _____.
 _____ palais _____.
 ___ a remarqué_____.
 _____ les _____.

3. Même si on allait au Louvre tous les jours, on ne verrait pas tout.
 _____nous _____.
 _____comprendrions ___.
 _____ théâtre _____.
 _____vous _____.

4. La première impression qu'on a du musée c'est sa grandeur.
 _____ beauté.
 _____ Jeanne _____.
 _____ je _____.
 ___seule _____.

5. La Victoire Ailée a été érigée au quatrième siècle av. J.-C.
 ___grand monument_____.
 _____IX^e _____.
 _____ apr. J.-C.
 ___vieux murs _____.

6. Elle a été trouvée il y a près de cent quarante ans.
 Elles_____.
 _____ 200 _____.
 _____ perdues _____.
 _____ 3000 _____.

7. La Joconde a été achevée par Léonard de Vinci en quinze cent cinq.
 Ces tableaux _____.
 _____ finis _____.
 _____ cet artiste _____.
 _____ 1606.

8. D'autres œuvres de ce même artiste se trouvent au Louvre.

_____ statues _____.

_____ sculpteurs _____.

_____ dans cette galerie.

_____ s'achètent _____.

18

Demonstrative Pronouns

Possessive Pronouns

Verbs in *indre*

Compound Participle
and Infinitive

PATTERN SENTENCES

1. As-tu fini ta lettre? J'ai terminé la mienne.
2. La tienne est sans doute moins intéressante; celle-ci n'est pas finie.
3. Je plains ton pauvre ami.
4. Après avoir lu ton chef-d'œuvre, il va avoir mal à la tête.
5. Voilà! Toutes les deux sont finies. Allons les jeter à la boîte.
6. Je vais prendre mon vélo, prends-tu le tien?
7. Le mien est cassé, je prendrai celui de mon frère.
8. Le sien doit bien marcher. Il a l'air tout neuf.
9. Ayant décidé de sortir, si nous allions à la poste? J'ai un colis à envoyer.

1. Have you finished your letter? I have finished mine.
2. Yours is no doubt less interesting; this one is not done.
3. I pity your poor friend.
4. After reading your masterpiece, he is going to have a headache.
5. There! Both are finished. Let's go and mail them.
6. I'm going to take my bike. Are you taking yours?
7. Mine is broken. I'll take my brother's.
8. His must work well. It looks brand new.
9. Since we've decided to go out, how about going to the post office? I've got a package to send.

10. Mais c'est aujourd'hui un jour de fête. Crois-tu que la poste soit ouverte?

11. Non. Tu as raison. Tout de même, nous pourrons jeter les lettres.

12. Oui, et si nous faisions une promenade en vélo après, hein?

10. But today is a holiday. Do you think the post office will be open?

11. No. You're right. Even so, we can mail the letters.

12. Yes, and suppose we take a ride on our bikes afterwards, eh?

99. Demonstratives

The forms of the demonstrative adjective, treated in Lesson 5, are **ce** (**cet**), **cette, ces.** They are used before a noun, meaning *this, that, these, those.*

| **ce garçon** | **cet enfant** | **cet homme** | **cette femme** | **ces machines** |

To differentiate *this* from *that*, or *these* from *those*, **-ci** or **-là** may be added to the noun.

ce garçon-ci   this boy
ces hommes-ci   these men

cette femme-là   that woman
ces dames-là   those ladies

NOTE: The distinction is seldom necessary, and the **-ci** forms particularly are of relatively infrequent occurrence.

The demonstrative pronouns corresponding to these adjectives are **celui** (*m. sing.*), **celle** (*f. sing.*), **ceux** (*m. pl.*), and **celles** (*f. pl.*).   These never occur alone, but are accompanied usually by a clause or phrase.

celui en noir   the one in black
celle de M. Dupont   Mr. Dupont's (that of Mr. Dupont)
ceux que j'ai vus hier   the ones (those) I saw yesterday
celles qui m'ont frappé   the ones (those) which struck me

If no clause or phrase is present, **-ci** or **-là** must be added to the pronoun.

celui-ci, celle-ci   this one
celui-là, celle-là   that one

ceux-ci, celles-ci   these
ceux-là, celles-là   those

Unlike the nouns, the pronoun forms with both **-ci** and **-là** are of high frequency. Occasionally we find the **-ci** forms used to mean *the latter*, and the **-là** forms *the former*.

J'ai visité Châteaudun et Chenonceaux l'année passée.   Celui-ci est un château de la Renaissance, tandis que celui-là est un château fort.   I visited Châteaudun and Chenonceaux last year.   The latter is a Renaissance castle, while the former is a fortress castle.

A. Substitution Drill.

1. Il m'a donné *un livre*, mais je préfère celui que vous m'avez donné. (*une montre, des tomates, des cadeaux*)

2. J'ai acheté deux *robes;* celle-ci était très chère. (*mouchoirs, bouteilles de parfum, chapeaux*)

3. Connaissez-vous ces *dames*-là? Celle de droite vient de vous appeler. (*garçons, jeunes filles, messieurs*)

4. Toutes ces *peintures* sont bonnes, mais j'aime surtout celles de date récente. (*tableaux, voitures, meubles*)

5. Le *vélo* de Paul est plus neuf que celui de Georges. (*bicyclette, souliers, lunettes*)

6. On m'a montré un grand *appartement* et un petit. J'ai mieux aimé celui-ci que celui-là. (*maison, chien, voiture*)

100. Possessive pronouns

Once a noun has been mentioned, possession may be indicated by pronouns rather than adjectives. For instance, in "he has his bicycle, and I have mine," we know that *mine* means *my bicycle*. The usage is identical in French, except that the pronoun by its form shows the gender and number of the noun it replaces.

> **Il a son vélo, et j'ai *le mien*.** ⎫
> **Il a sa bicyclette, et j'ai *la mienne*.** ⎬ He has his bicycle, and I have *mine*.

The French for *mine* differs in the two sentences simply because of the difference in the gender of the nouns used for bicycle. Because of this sensitivity to gender and number, the French pronoun has four forms for each person.

le mien	la mienne	les miens	les miennes	mine
le tien	la tienne	les tiens	les tiennes	yours
le sien	la sienne	les siens	les siennes	his, hers, its
le nôtre	la nôtre	les nôtres	les nôtres	ours
le vôtre	la vôtre	les vôtres	les vôtres	yours
le leur	la leur	les leurs	les leurs	theirs

Note the circumflex which distinguishes the pronoun from the possessive adjective studied earlier. The gender and number of the possessive pronoun are determined solely by those of the noun it replaces, and bear no relation to the possessor.

> **Le garçon a son vélo, la jeune fille a aussi *le sien*.** The boy has his bike; the girl also has *hers*.
> **La jeune fille a sa bicyclette, le garçon a aussi *la sienne*.** The girl has her bicycle; the boy also has *his*.

The definite articles, which are an integral part of the possessive pronouns, combine with **à** and **de** in the usual way.

> **Il a ôté la sonnette de son vélo et l'a attachée *au mien*.** He took the bell off his bike and fastened it *to mine*.
> **Parlez-vous de mon vélo ou *du vôtre*?** Are you speaking of my bike or *yours?*

B. Substitution Drill.

1. Guy a donné son devoir, mais *Suzanne* a perdu le sien. (*nous, Robert, ses sœurs*)
2. Julie a fini sa tâche, mais *Jules* n'a pas fini la sienne. (*Diane, vous, ses frères*)
3. Voilà le *livre* de Jacques, mais où est le mien? (*cravate, parents, clefs*)
4. Voici mon vélo à moi, qu'avez-*vous* fait du vôtre? (*il, elle, tu*)
5. Je vous ferai une description de ma *maison*, et peut-être Marie vous fera-t-elle une description de la sienne. (*voyage, aventures, cadeaux*)
6. Louise soignait ses fleurs de temps en temps, mais *Paul* ne faisait pas attention aux siennes. (*Mme Laplanche, nous, les autres*)

101. Verbs in *indre*

Verbs in **indre** (like **craindre**) are all conjugated alike, showing a curious change of stem in the plural of the present tense and in all forms derived from this plural. The verbs all have a past participle in **int**.

craindre *to fear*

PRES. INDIC.	PRES. SUBJ.
je crains	je craigne
tu crains	tu craignes
il craint	il craigne
nous craignons	nous craignions
vous craignez	vous craigniez
ils craignent	ils craignent

PRES. PART.	IMPERF. TENSE	PAST PART.
craignant	**je craignais**	**craint**

NOTE: Like **craindre** are **joindre** (*to join*), **plaindre** (*to pity*), **atteindre** (*to reach*), **peindre** (*to paint*), **éteindre** (*to extinguish, put out the light*), and others in **indre**.

C. Substitution Drill.

1. *Je* crains les résultats de cet examen. (*Il, Nous, Vous, Ils*)
2. Enfin *elle* a atteint son but. (*je, Guy, nous, les soldats*)
3. Quand je suis entré, *Jean* éteignait la lumière. (*tu, vous, ils, on*)
4. *L'artiste* peindra un nouveau tableau. (*Ils, Nous, Je, Vous*)
5. Maman voudrait que *tu* la rejoignes pour le dîner. (*vous, Jean, les garçons, nous*)

102. Compound participle and infinitive

The compound form of the present participle is similar to English, except for agreement. It is formed by combining the present participle of **avoir** or **être** with the past participle of a verb.

ayant donné having given	**étant venu**(e)(s) having come
ayant fini having finished	**s'étant couché**(e)(s) having gone to bed

The past participle with **avoir** will be invariable except in the infrequent case of having a preceding direct object (**les ayant finis**), but with **être** its agreement will depend upon the subject of the sentence.

Étant arriv*ée* tard, *elle* **s'est couchée immédiatement.**   Having arrived late, she went to bed immediately.

The compound infinitive consists of the infinitive of **avoir** or **être** plus a past participle. Its principal use is with the preposition **après,** which requires it.

Après avoir parlé, il s'est assis.   After speaking (After having spoken), he sat down.
Après être tombée deux fois, elle décide de ne pas essayer de remonter.   After falling twice, she decides not to try to go up again.
Après s'être couchée, elle n'a pas pu s'endormir.   After going to bed, she could not fall asleep.

D. Express in French.

1. This boy is more intelligent than that one. 2. These hats are rather expensive; those aren't.[1] 3. Yesterday we saw Versailles and Blois. The latter [2] is much smaller than the former. 4. He borrowed *her* bicycle, and *I* borrowed Mary's. 5. Having seen her, I can understand everything. 6. After having listened to him, we went out. 7. Are the American roads better than those in [3] France? 8. By [4] my watch it is a quarter past ten; what time is it by yours? 9. By mine it is ten minutes past ten. 10. Having entered the house, we found nothing. 11. We fear what he can do. 12. Having heard the story, I pitied her. 13. After reaching his goal, he returned home. 14. After putting out the lights and locking the door, we went to bed. 15. He is painting his house, and they are painting theirs. 16. Having arrived early, she began to study.

---

[1] Insert **le** before the verb.
[2] Consider the genders as masculine.
[3] French says **de.**
[4] Use **à.**

LECTURE

Hier nous avons eu une révision en classe. Le professeur nous en avait avertis l'autre jour en recommandant que nous étudiions nos verbes à fond. Je ne savais pas très bien les miens ce matin-là, parce qu'un de mes amis m'avait invité la veille à l'accompagner au cinéma.

D'abord le professeur nous a dit d'écrire les temps primitifs de *savoir*. Je n'osais pas admettre que je n'avais pas étudié. Pensant le tromper, j'ai essayé de me faire donner des renseignements en faisant semblant de ne pas comprendre.

« Excusez-moi, dis-je d'un ton respectueux. Je n'ai pas bien compris. Vous avez dit . . . ?

— J'ai dit: Écrivez les temps primitifs de *savoir*, s'il vous plaît. Vous savez, les temps primitifs . . .

— Oh, oui, naturellement. Mais voulez-vous que je commence par le présent, comme en latin, ou préférez-vous le système — ah — plus — c'est-à-dire . . .

— Maurice, n'essayez pas de me tromper. Si vous continuez à hésiter, je commencerai à croire que vous n'avez pas étudié vos verbes. En français nous commençons les temps primitifs par l'infinitif.

— Bien sûr. L'infinitif de *savoir* est *savoir*. Ça, au moins, je le sais.[1] C'est ce qui suit l'infinitif qui m'embarrasse.

— Mais c'est bien simple, c'est le participe présent.

— Bien entendu: *savant*.

— Non, non, non! « Savant » est un nom [2] signifiant « homme érudit. » Le participe présent est *sachant*.

— Évidemment. *Sachant*. Voilà un bon commencement: *savoir, sachant*. Maintenant il s'agit de deviner le troisième.

— Franchement, Maurice, je crains fort que vous n'ayez même pas ouvert votre livre hier soir.

— Si, j'ai ouvert mon livre. Mais juste au moment où j'allais commencer à étudier, le téléphone a sonné. C'était mon ami Jules qui m'invitait à l'accompagner au cinéma. Naturellement je lui ai dit que j'avais des verbes à étudier, mais lorsqu'il m'a expliqué que c'était un film français . . . D'ailleurs, il a offert de m'aider à étudier les verbes plus tard.

— Et après?

---

[1] **Je le sais** *I know*. French feels the need for **le,** to refer to what has gone before: in this case **ça,** which in turn refers to the preceding sentence.

[2] Here, **nom** means *noun*.

— Après, je dois l'admettre, il était si tard, et mes yeux étaient si fatigués, les siens aussi . . .

— Je comprends. Heureusement pour vous, je sais bien que c'était un film français, car j'y ai assisté moi-même. Cette fois, je vous excuse. Et maintenant, les temps primitifs. Après le participe présent, on écrit le participe passé, en ce cas *su*.

— Merci, monsieur. A présent, nous avons *savoir*, *sachant*, *su*. Est-ce qu'il y a autre chose?

— Oui, après le participe passé, on écrit la première personne du singulier du présent, et puis la même personne du passé simple.

— Vous serez content d'apprendre, monsieur, que je connais ces deux formes: « je sais » et « je sus. »

— C'est exact. Maintenant il s'agit de faire la même chose avec *pouvoir*, *vouloir* et *devoir*.

— Monsieur, ne peut-on pas se passer de verbes? Je crois que si j'atteignais l'âge de Mathusalem,[1] je ne les saurais pas mieux. »

Questions

1. De quoi le professeur a-t-il averti la classe l'autre jour? 2. Qu'est-ce qu'il a recommandé? 3. Qui ne savait pas très bien les siens? 4. Pourquoi est-ce qu'il ne les avait pas étudiés? 5. Comment est-ce qu'il essaie de tromper le professeur? 6. Comment commence-t-on les temps primitifs en français? 7. Que veut dire le mot « savant »? 8. Qu'est-ce que le professeur craint fort, quand il entend les questions de Maurice? 9. Qu'est-ce qui est arrivé juste au moment où Maurice allait étudier? 10. Pourquoi n'a-t-il pas étudié plus tard? 11. Comment le professeur sait-il que c'était un film français? 12. De quoi est-ce que Maurice voudrait se passer?

VOCABULARY

à fond thoroughly
autre chose something else
bien sûr of course, why surely
d'un ton respectueux in a respectful tone
faire semblant de to pretend to

se faire donner des renseignements to get some information
se passer de to do without, get along without

---

[1] **Mathusalem** *Methuselah*

admettre (admis) to admit
assister à to be present (at), attend
avertir to warn
le **cas** case
deviner to guess, figure out
érudit learned, erudite
un **examen** examination
juste just, exact, right
les **lunettes** (*f.*) glasses

le **participe** participle
rejoindre (rejoint) to meet, join
le **résultat** result
la **révision** review
signifier to mean, signify
soigner to look after, care for
les **temps primitifs** principal parts
la **veille** eve, day (or night) before

PATTERN SENTENCE DRILL

1. As-tu fini ta lettre?   J'ai terminé la mienne.
   _____devoir?   _____.
   _ -il _____?   _____.
   _____ ?   Elle _____.
   _____devoirs?   _____.

2. La tienne est moins intéressante; celle-ci n'est pas finie.
   Le _____.
   _____ long _____.
   Les _____.
   _____ terminés.

3. Je plains ton pauvre ami.
   _____ son _____.
   Nous_____.
   _____ amie.
   Elle _____.

4. Après avoir lu ton chef-d'œuvre, il va avoir mal à la tête.
   _____ vu _____.
   _____ ils _____.
   _____ chefs-d'œuvre_____.
   _____ fini _____.

5. Toutes les deux sont finies.   Allons les jeter à la boîte.
   Tous _____.   _____.
   _____.   Allez _____.
   _____.   _____ mettre à la poste.
   _____ trois _____.   _____.

6. Je vais prendre mon vélo, prends-tu le tien?
   _____ livres _____?
   _____ -il _____?
   Nous _____?
   _____ -elles ___?

7. Le mien est cassé, je prendrai celui de mon frère.
   __ mienne _____.
   _____ sœur.
   _____nous_____.
   __ nôtres _____.

8. Ayant décidé de sortir, si nous allions à la poste?
   _____ théâtre?
   _____ nous amuser _____?
   _____ envie _____?
   _____ en ville?

9. Crois-tu que la poste soit ouverte?
   ____ -vous _____?
   _____ la banque _____?
   _____ fermée?
   _____ portes _____?

10. Si nous faisions une promenade en vélo après?
    _____ excursion _____?
    _____ auto ____?
    _____ voyage _____?
    _____ organisions _____?

19

Clause vs. Infinitive

Impersonal *il*

PATTERN SENTENCES

1. Avez-vous vu sortir le professeur?
2. Non; voulez-vous que je l'appelle?
3. Merci,[1] je ne veux pas que vous vous dérangiez pour moi.
4. Pourtant êtes-vous sûr qu'il est toujours là?
5. Je ne crois pas qu'il soit sorti. Il ne lui reste que cinq minutes avant sa classe.
6. D'ailleurs, il n'aurait pas pu quitter son cabinet sans que je le voie.
7. Est-ce que vous ne l'entendez pas feuilleter des papiers?
8. Si, je l'entends. Frappons à la porte.
9. Il faut que je lui fasse voir mon compte rendu aujourd'hui.
10. Je n'entends plus rien. Ouvrons la porte.

1. Have you seen the professor go out?
2. No; do you want me to call him?
3. No thank you, I don't want you to trouble yourself on my account.
4. Are you sure he is still there, though?
5. I don't think he has gone out. He has only five minutes left before his class.
6. Besides, he couldn't have left his office without my seeing him.
7. Can't you hear him leafing through papers?
8. Yes, I hear him. Let's knock on the door.
9. I've got to show him my report today.
10. I don't hear anything any more. Let's open the door.

---

[1] **Merci** may mean either *thank you* or *no thank you*, depending on the circumstances and on the tone of voice.

194

11. Personne! Ce doit être le vent qui faisait remuer les papiers.

11. Nobody! It must have been the wind that was moving the papers.

12. Ça par exemple! Cela prouve qu'il ne faut pas se fier à ses oreilles.

12. What do you know! That proves you mustn't trust your ears.

103. Clause vs. infinitive

In general, in sentences where one verb complements another, if the subject of the first verb is also the subject of the second, an infinitive complement is preferred, even though in English a clause may sometimes be used.

Il décide de revenir. He decides to return.
Je veux partir. I want to leave.
Ils craignent de ne pas pouvoir atteindre leur but. They are afraid they will not be able to achieve their goal.

On the other hand, if the subject changes, a clause, usually in the subjunctive, is the normal construction.

Elle voudrait l'acheter. She would like to buy it.
BUT
Elle voudrait que *vous* l'achetiez. She would like *you* to buy it.

Nous préférons descendre. We prefer to go down.
BUT
Nous préférons qu'*il* descende. We prefer to have *him* go down.

Nous voulons visiter le Château d'If *avant de* quitter Marseille. We want to visit the Château d'If before leaving Marseilles.
BUT
Nous voulons visiter le Château d'If *avant que* vous ne quittiez Marseille. We want to visit the Château d'If before you leave Marseilles.

Il l'a fait *sans* le savoir. He did it without knowing it.
BUT
Il l'a fait *sans que* nous le sachions. He did it without our knowing it.[1]

Important exceptions to this principle are the "communication" verbs (telling, ordering, asking) and **permettre,** which frequently take an infinitive construction even when the subject changes. Normally in this case the personal object is indirect, and the infinitive is preceded by **de.**

Je lui dis de fermer la fenêtre. I tell him to close the window.
Nous lui demandons de nous montrer ses films. We ask him to show us his movies.

---

[1] There are other pairs: **pour** (*in order to*) — **pour que** (*in order that*), **afin de** (*so as to*) — **afin que** (*so that*), etc.

L'officier commande à ses soldats de tirer sur l'ennemi. The officer commands his soldiers to fire on the enemy.

Ordonnez à ces messieurs de cesser leurs cris. Order those gentlemen to stop their shouting.

Permettez-moi de vous offrir ce cadeau. Permit me to offer you this present.

By exception, **prier** (*to pray, beg*) takes a direct object, but the infinitive construction remains the same.

J'ai prié les dames d'ôter leurs gants. I begged the ladies to take off their gloves.

Nous avons prié les gens de ne pas fumer. We requested the people not to smoke.

A. Read aloud, then change the infinitive to a clause, using the words in parentheses as subject and making any necessary changes in the sentence.

Example: Je veux partir. (il)

Je veux qu'il parte.

1. Elle désire quitter la maison. (vous, nous, Jean)
2. Nous craignons de ne pas pouvoir venir. (ils, elle, tu)
3. Elles aimeraient mieux savoir la vérité. (nous, Paul, vous)
4. Je voudrais le faire moi-même. (ils, vous, Georges)

B. Change from direct to indirect discourse by means of an infinitive construction.

Example: Il leur dit: « Entrez ! »

Il leur dit d'entrer.

1. Je lui ordonne: « Dites-moi la vérité ! »
2. Nous disons à l'enfant: « Ne pleure pas ! »
3. Il m'a demandé: « Montrez-moi votre cahier ! »
4. Le médecin a conseillé à la mère: « Envoyez l'enfant à la campagne. »
5. Elle a demandé au garçon: « Apportez-moi un verre d'eau ! »

104. Infinitive construction with *laisser, voir, entendre, faire*

Also permitting the infinitive construction with change of subject are the verbs **laisser, voir, entendre,** and **faire.**[1]

Laissez-moi payer l'addition. Let me pay the check.

On l'a laissé entrer sans rien payer. They let him enter without paying anything.

Elle a vu les oiseaux voler vers le sud. She saw the birds fly southward.

Entendez-vous le prisonnier marcher dans la chambre au-dessus? Do you hear the prisoner walking in the room above?

---

[1] And most verbs of perception (**écouter, regarder, observer,** etc.).

Frequently (always with **faire**) the infinitive follows the verb directly, its subject coming after. This is particularly true if the infinitive has no object or other complement.

> **Je fais monter le garçon.** I make the boy go up.
> **Nous allons faire travailler ces messieurs.** We are going to make those gentlemen work.
> **Avez-vous laissé sortir le chat?** Did you let the cat out?

Sometimes the infinitive has passive force, in which case it always follows the main verb directly.

> **J'ai vu construire cet édifice.** I saw that building being built.
> **Avez-vous vu battre l'enfant par cet homme?** Did you see the child being beaten by that man?
> **As-tu fait renouveler ta carte d'admission à la bibliothèque?** Have you had your library admittance card renewed?
> **Oui, je l'ai fait [1] renouveler hier par le bibliothécaire.** Yes, I had it renewed yesterday by the librarian.

If the infinitive itself has an object, it is customary to make the apparent object of **faire** indirect in form. If it is a noun, **par** often replaces **à** to prevent ambiguity.

> **Avez-vous fait écrire les phrases aux (par les) garçons?** Did you make the boys write the sentences?
> **Non, mais je leur ai fait réciter le poème.** No, but I made them recite the poem.

>> **C.** Read aloud, then reread substituting each of the following sentences as an infinitive construction in place of the italicized words.
>>
>> *Example:* Nous regardons *le peintre travailler*.
>> Le garçon joue.
>> Nous regardons le garçon jouer.
>>
>> 1. J'entends *parler le vieillard*.
>>   a. L'oiseau chante.
>>   b. Les enfants rient.
>>   c. L'auto démarre.
>>   d. La pluie tombe.
>> 2. Allez-vous laisser *votre fils conduire l'auto?*
>>   a. Ces demoiselles passent.
>>   b. Les étudiants partent de bonne heure.
>>   c. L'enfant va en ville tout seul.
>>   d. Le garçon récite son poème.

---

[1] The participle does not agree with **la (l')**, because the latter is only the apparent object of **faire**, being actually the object of the infinitive **renouveler**.

    3. Jeanne *m'a* vu *partir*.
       a. Nous arrivons.
       b. Ils descendent dans la rue.
       c. Vous montez sur la balustrade.
       d. Tu sors avec le colis.
    4. Nous avons fait *faire le devoir par l'élève*.
       a. Le garçon décrit la maison.
       b. Les étudiants finissent la leçon.
       c. La jeune fille raconte l'incident.
       d. L'enfant ramasse les morceaux de craie.
    5. On *lui* a fait *finir le devoir*.
       a. Nous descendons du premier étage.
       b. Je cède ma place au professeur.
       c. Elle met le chapeau sur la tête de l'enfant.
       d. Ils ouvrent leurs bagages.

105. *Il faut*

Il faut is generally followed by an infinitive when no subject is mentioned, otherwise by a clause in the subjunctive. Normally with the infinitive construction, the subject is assumed to be either the speaker or the person addressed, or else the ubiquitous **on.**

   Il faut étudier maintenant, je suppose. I must study now, I suppose.
   Il faut faire attention. You must pay attention.
   Pour être vraiment heureux, il faut travailler. To be really happy, one must
     work.
   BUT
   Il faut que ces gens s'en aillent. These people must go.
   Il fallait qu'elle descende vite. She had to go down quickly.

NOTE: The negative of **il faut, il ne faut pas,** usually means *you must not* or *one must not* rather than *it is not necessary,* particularly when used with a verb.

   Il ne faut pas négliger vos verbes. You must not neglect your verbs.
   Il ne faut pas jouer avec le feu. One must not play with fire.

   D. Read aloud, then change infinitive to clause with subjects in parentheses.
     Example: Il faut partir. (ils)
             Il faut qu'ils partent.
     1. Il faut aller en ville maintenant. (elle, vous)
     2. Il faudra céder à la force. (nous, ils)
     3. Il a fallu se lever tout de suite. (je, nous)
     4. Il fallait prendre ses repas dans la cuisine. (nous, les enfants)
     5. Il ne faut pas poser trop de questions. (vous, elles)

106. Impersonal *il*

We have met many uses of impersonal **il**, as in time and weather expressions, **il faut**, and the like. Less easily recognized, but very common, is the use of impersonal **il** where the real subject of the verb follows the verb.

Il ne lui restait que cent francs. He had only a hundred francs left.
Hier soir il lui est arrivé un accident. Last night he had an accident.
Tout à coup il m'est venu une idée. Suddenly an idea came to me.
Heureusement il existe des gens prêts à vous aider. Fortunately there exist people ready to help you.

E. Express in French.

1. He wants to leave now. 2. He wants them to leave now. 3. She is afraid she won't arrive in time. 4. She is afraid we won't arrive in time. 5. We would like to see the castle. 6. We would like to have them see the castle. 7. Let us visit the Sainte-Chapelle before we leave Paris. 8. Let us visit it before you leave Paris. 9. You must not leave the Louvre without seeing the Mona Lisa. 10. I told the boy to put the books on the table. 11. Let the gentleman pass. 12. I am making the students read the book. 13. They saw the children arrive in front of the museum. 14. I have only five days left. 15. When they have paid for their dinner, they will have only about twenty francs left. 16. She had the windows washed. 17. I have heard the story told. 18. Did you have that dress made?

LECTURE

Aujourd'hui le professeur nous a parlé de Paris. D'abord, il a demandé ce que nous savions de ses origines. Moi, qui suis toujours prêt à me risquer, j'ai répondu qu'il n'y avait aucun doute que la ville devait [1] son nom à Paris, ce héros troyen [2] devenu célèbre pour avoir tué Achille.

« Ah non, a dit le professeur. C'est plutôt de la tribu [3] dite Parisii, qui habitait l'Ile de la Cité il y a longtemps. L'Ile de la Cité est la partie la plus ancienne de Paris, située au milieu de la Seine comme vous le savez. A propos, quelle est la différence entre *cité* et *ville?*

— Il n'y a pas de différence, a répondu quelqu'un.

---

[1] Here **devoir** has its literal meaning of "owe."
[2] **troyen** *Trojan*
[3] **la tribu** *tribe*

— Si, a répliqué le professeur, dans des vieilles villes comme Londres ou Paris, la cité est la partie la plus ancienne, entourée autrefois par une enceinte [1] ou par un fossé. A Londres, c'est le quartier autour de la Tour de Londres. A Paris, c'est l'Ile de la Cité, où se trouvent la cathédrale de Notre-Dame, le Palais de Justice et la Sainte-Chapelle. Comme la Seine l'entoure, on n'avait pas besoin de fossé.

— Est-ce que le Palais de Justice est vraiment si ancien? a demandé un élève.

— Oh oui. Une partie au moins du bâtiment est ce qui reste de l'ancien palais de Louis IX, appelé plus tard Saint Louis. On sait qu'il a fait construire aussi la Sainte-Chapelle, au milieu du treizième siècle, pour abriter des reliques précieuses rapportées de Terre Sainte.

— Est-ce que c'est lui qui a fait bâtir le Louvre? ai-je demandé.

— Non, le Louvre avait été commencé sous Philippe Auguste un peu plus tôt. Philippe Auguste est le roi qui a fait une croisade [2] avec Richard Cœur de Lion et puis a conspiré contre lui avec Jean sans Terre.

— Mais je croyais que le Louvre était un musée.

— En effet, aujourd'hui. Cependant à l'origine c'était un palais royal, décoré et agrandi par plusieurs rois, depuis François Ier jusqu'à Louis XIV. Autrefois il était même plus grand qu'aujourd'hui, mais une partie en a été détruite à l'époque de la guerre franco-prussienne en 1870.

— N'y a-t-il pas de monuments modernes à Paris? a demandé mon ami Jacques.

— Si, a répondu le professeur. La Place de la Concorde avec ses beaux bâtiments et son obélisque date du dix-huitième siècle,[3] et le Panthéon a été construit vers la fin du même siècle. Celui-ci était d'abord une église, mais la Révolution, ayant rejeté toute forme de religion traditionnelle, l'a transformé en un temple de la déesse [4] Raison. Plus tard on en a fait un monument aux grands hommes de la patrie. Quelques-uns que vous connaissez, tels que Voltaire, Rousseau et Victor Hugo, y sont enterrés.

— Qu'est-ce que c'est que les Champs-Élysées, monsieur? a demandé une jeune fille à côté de moi.

— C'est une large avenue conduisant de la Place de la Concorde à l'Arc de Triomphe de l'Étoile, le grand monument commencé en 1806 par Napoléon Bonaparte.

— Pourquoi dit-on « de l'Étoile, » monsieur?

---

[1] **une enceinte** *enclosure, wall*
[2] **la croisade** *crusade*
[3] The obelisk itself was not brought from Egypt until the early 19th century.
[4] **la déesse** *goddess*

— L'Arc se trouve sur la Place de l'Étoile, ainsi appelée à cause de douze avenues qui en rayonnent dans toutes les directions. Cette partie de Paris a été dessinée par Pierre Charles l'Enfant, le même qui a fait le plan de Washington, D.C.

— Est-ce qu'il y a des gratte-ciel à Paris, monsieur? a demandé un garçon à cheveux roux derrière moi.

— Pas comme à New-York. Mais il y a toujours [1] les tours des grandes églises et les dômes des monuments comme le Panthéon et l'Hôtel des Invalides.[2] Ce dernier contient une chapelle érigée par Louis XIV pour honorer ses anciens soldats, et aussi le tombeau de Napoléon Ier. Et puis, il faut ajouter la Tour Eiffel, construite pour l'exposition de 1889. Pendant longtemps celle-ci n'a été dépassée en hauteur que par le Chrysler Building et l'Empire State Building à New-York.

— Peut-on y monter?

— Oui, il y a des ascenseurs, ou l'on peut y monter à pied si l'on a le courage et la force. Du sommet on peut voir beaucoup d'autres édifices que je n'ai pas encore cités, comme l'Opéra, le Sacré-Cœur, le Palais du Luxembourg, le Palais de Chaillot, et ainsi de suite.

— Monsieur, ai-je dit alors, il m'est venu une idée.

— Laquelle, Maurice?

— Si vous vouliez que je le fasse, je pourrais partir tout de suite pour la France. Et quand je reviendrais, je vous raconterais un tas de choses intéressantes sur Paris. »

Questions

1. Quelle est la différence entre *cité* et *ville?* 2. Qui a fait bâtir la Sainte-Chapelle? 3. Quel roi a conspiré avec Jean sans Terre contre Richard Cœur de Lion? 4. A quoi le Louvre sert-il aujourd'hui?[3] 5. Qu'est-ce que c'était autrefois? 6. Dans quelle guerre a-t-on détruit une partie du Louvre? 7. De quel siècle date la Place de la Concorde? 8. Par qui l'Arc de Triomphe a-t-il été commencé? 9. Où se trouve-t-il? 10. Quel est le Français qui a dessiné le plan de notre capitale? 11. Comment peut-on monter à la Tour Eiffel? 12. Si Maurice allait à Paris, que ferait-il quand il reviendrait?

---

[1] **toujours** *of course.* **Toujours** must not always be translated literally.
[2] **l'Hôtel des Invalides** *old soldiers' home.*   [3] Use **servir de.**

VOCABULARY

à quoi sert-il? what is it (used) for?

    abriter to shelter
    agrandir to enlarge
    ajouter to add
un **ascenseur** elevator
    cependant however
la **chapelle** chapel
    conseiller to advise
la **demoiselle** young lady
    dépasser to surpass
    détruire (détruit) to destroy
    enterrer to bury
    entourer to surround
une **étoile** star
le **fossé** ditch, moat
le **gratte-ciel** (*no change in pl.*) skyscraper
la ***hauteur** height
le ***héros** hero

aimer mieux = préférer

    ordonner to order
la **patrie** homeland, native land
    plutôt rather
    précieux precious
    prier to pray, beg, request
    rapporter to bring back
    rayonner to shine out, spread out
    répliquer to reply, retort
    se risquer to take a risk, venture
    roux, rousse red (of hair)
    sacré sacred
    saint holy, Saint (with a proper name)
la **terre** ground, dirt, earth; **Terre Sainte** Holy Land
le **tombeau** tomb
la **tour** tower
    tuer to kill

PATTERN SENTENCE DRILL

1. Avez-vous vu sortir le professeur?
    ____ -tu _____?
    _____ partir _____?
    _____ professeurs?
    ____ -on _____?

2. Je ne veux pas que vous vous dérangiez pour moi.
    _____ lui.
    Il _____.
    _____nous _____.
    ____ demande _____.

3. Je ne crois pas qu'il soit sorti.
    _____ entré.
    _____ elle _____.
    Il_____.
    ____ pense _____.

4. Il ne lui reste que cinq minutes avant sa classe.

_____ le concert.

_____ nous _____.

_____une heure _____.

_____ leur _____.

5. Il n'aurait pas pu quitter son cabinet sans que je le voie.
Elle _____.

_____ maison _____.

_____ nous _____.

Elles _____.

6. Est-ce que vous ne l'entendez pas feuilleter des papiers?

_____ livres?

_____ voyez _____?

_____ acheter _____?

_____ on _____?

7. Il faut que je lui fasse voir mon compte rendu.

_____chef-d'œuvre.

_____ nous _____.

_ faudra_____.

_____ leur _____.

8. Ce doit être le vent qui faisait remuer les papiers.

_____ tomber _____.

_____enfant _____.

_____ les journaux.

_____enfants _____.

9. Cela prouve qu'il ne faut pas se fier à ses oreilles.

_____ vous _____.

_____amis.

_____ nous _____.

_____battre _____.

20

Fractions

Approximate Numbers

Imperfect and
Pluperfect Subjunctive

PATTERN SENTENCES

1. Un demi plus¹ un tiers font cinq sixièmes, n'est-ce pas?

2. Puisque vous me le dites, je le crois. Autrement je ne l'aurais pas cru.

3. Vous me flattez. D'ordinaire vous ne croyez pas la moitié de ce que je vous dis.

4. Dites! Combien de personnes ont assisté au concert hier soir?

5. Une centaine, je suppose. Mais les trois quarts de l'assistance ont failli s'endormir avant la fin.

6. On me dit que vous partez dans une quinzaine pour la France.

7. Même plus tôt que cela. Je m'en vais de demain en huit.

8. Combien de temps vous faudra-t-il pour y arriver?

---

1. One-half and one-third make five-sixths, don't they?

2. Since you tell me so, I believe it. Otherwise I would not have believed it.

3. You flatter me. Usually you don't believe half of what I tell you.

4. Say! How many people attended the concert last night?

5. About a hundred, I guess. But three quarters of the audience nearly fell asleep before the end.

6. They tell me you are leaving in a couple of weeks for France.

7. Even sooner than that. I leave a week from tomorrow.

8. How long will it take you to get there?

---

¹ Pronounce [plys].

9. Une dizaine de jours. Comme Georges et Henri, je fais la traversée par un paquebot assez lent.

9. Ten days or so. Like George and Henry, I am making the crossing in a rather slow boat.

10. Ah oui. A propos, Georges m'a écrit: « Je n'ai jamais été si content qu'un voyage fût terminé. »

10. Oh yes. By the way, George wrote me: "I have never been so glad that a trip was over."

11. Vraiment? Henri me dit dans une lettre: « J'aurais voulu que le voyage prît plus de temps. »

11. Really? Henry tells me in a letter: "I would have liked the trip to take longer."

12. Eh bien, bon voyage! J'espère vous revoir dans deux mois.

12. Well, bon voyage! I hope to see you again in a couple of months.

NOTE: **Dans** with a time expression means *in* in the sense of *at the end of*, while **en** means *in* in the sense of *during*. *He can do this job in two months* could be either:

Il peut faire ce travail en deux mois. (i.e., in the course of two months)

OR

Il peut faire ce travail dans deux mois. (i.e., he can get to it at the end of two months)

107. Fractions

Fractions differ from ordinals only through "one-fourth," being identical with them from "one-fifth."

one-half **un demi (une moitié)**	one-quarter **un quart**
one-third **un tiers**	three-fourths **trois quarts**
two-thirds **deux tiers**	
BUT	
one-fifth **un cinquième**	four-sevenths **quatre septièmes**
nine-tenths **neuf dixièmes**	five twenty-firsts **cinq vingt-et-unièmes**

Demi has a feminine **demie**, seldom seen except in time expressions: **une heure et demie, deux heures et demie; la demie sonne** (*it is striking half past*). Otherwise, it is usually attached to a noun by a hyphen, preceding the noun and remaining invariable: **une demi-heure, une demi-tasse.** **Moitié** can be used only as a noun and must have an article. If there is a plural complement, the verb agrees with the complement rather than with **moitié.**

La moitié des gens étaient déjà partis. Half of the people had already left.
Il ne reste pas beaucoup de bonbons. Jeannot en a mangé plus de la moitié.
There aren't many candies left. Johnny has eaten more than half of them.

In a definite context French generally uses the definite article with fractions, where English prefers the indefinite.

Je n'ai vu que le quart de la collection. I saw only a quarter of the collection.

108. Approximate numbers

An approximation of certain numbers is obtained by adding **aine** to the cardinal number, dropping the final **e** if there is one, and in the cases of **dix** changing **x** to **z**. In actual practice this occurs only with 8, 10, 12, 15, 20, even tens to 60, and 100.

Millier, already discussed, serves as the approximation of **mille.**

une huitaine	about eight days, a week	**une quinzaine**	about fifteen, a fortnight
une dizaine	about ten, ten or so	**une vingtaine**	about twenty, a score
une douzaine	about twelve, a dozen	**une trentaine**	about thirty
une quarantaine	**une cinquantaine**	**une soixantaine**	**une centaine**

Trentaine, quarantaine, cinquantaine, and **soixantaine** often refer to approximate age.

> **Elle ne doit pas être loin de la cinquantaine.** She can't be far from fifty.

Quarantaine also has the special meaning of *quarantine*, being the forty days or so that ships suspected of carrying the plague were formerly required to stand offshore before landing.

> **A.** Express in French.
>
> 1. I'm going to spend about a week at Jim's. 2. There are a dozen apples in this box. 3. She has been here a fortnight. 4. $\frac{3}{4} + \frac{1}{8} = \frac{7}{8}$. 5. $\frac{1}{3} + \frac{1}{5} = \frac{8}{15}$. 6. A score of people were waiting for the king.

109. Imperfect and pluperfect subjunctive

The imperfect subjunctive is a purely literary tense. The beginning student need study it only for purposes of identification. Its stem is found in the *passé simple* by simply dropping the last letter of the first person singular.

> **je donna** i   **je fini** s   **je perdi** s   **j'eu** s   **je fu** s   **je pri** s   **je vin** s

The endings, which are the same for all verbs, are like those of the present subjunctive with an **ss** prefixed, except for an odd third person singular form: **sse, sses, ^t, ssions, ssiez, ssent.**

je donnasse	je finisse	je perdisse
tu donnasses	tu finisses	tu perdisse
il donnât	il finît	il perdît
nous donnassions	nous finissions	nous perdissions
vous donnassiez	vous finissiez	vous perdissiez
ils donnassent	ils finissent	ils perdissent

NOTE: Since CONJUGATION II already has **ss** as part of the stem in the present, the present and imperfect subjunctive are alike except for the third person singular.

Combining the imperfect subjunctive of **avoir** or **être** with a past participle produces the pluperfect subjunctive.

dire	**aller**
j'eusse dit	je fusse allé
tu eusses dit	tu fusses allé
il eût dit	il fût allé
nous eussions dit	nous fussions allés
vous eussiez dit	vous fussiez allé(s)
ils eussent dit	ils fussent allés

110. Uses of imperfect and pluperfect subjunctive

The imperfect and pluperfect subjunctives occur only in literature, and only when the main verb is past (or, rarely, conditional). In speech or informal writing, the two are replaced normally by the present and past subjunctive, respectively. Here are examples showing formal and informal versions of the same sentence:

The king asked the nobles to do their duty.
FORMAL: **Le roi demanda que les nobles *fissent* leur devoir.**
INFORMAL: **Le roi a demandé que les nobles *fassent* leur devoir.**

The girl was sorry her mother had left.
FORMAL: **La jeune fille regrettait que sa mère *fût partie*.**
INFORMAL: **La jeune fille regrettait que sa mère *soit partie*.**

In literature, the pluperfect subjunctive often replaces the conditional perfect.

A le voir, on *eût dit* qu'il était fou. To see him, you *would have said* he was crazy. (replaces **aurait dit**)

B. Make the following statements informal by changing the verbs.

1. Le général commanda que ses officiers entrassent dans la forêt.
2. Paul regrettait que Madeleine fût arrivée si tard.
3. On ne crut pas qu'un seul homme pût faire cela.
4. Le patron fut content que M. Laforgue eût accompli sa tâche.
5. Pierre aurait voulu que les devoirs fussent moins longs.
6. Il eût même voulu que quelqu'un les fît pour lui.
7. Il était tout à fait possible que son amie fût déjà partie.
8. Nous fûmes fâchés que le concert eût été si court.
9. J'entrai dans la maison pour que mes amis ne me crussent pas timide.
10. Paul sortit sans que Louise l'eût entendu.

LECTURE

Cette leçon est la vingtième: le professeur nous a avertis que c'est la dernière, ce qui me rend un peu triste. Au début de ce cours, je m'attendais à ne pas aimer le français, mais à présent que le cours touche à sa fin, je dois avouer que, tout compte fait, je me suis bien amusé, et qu'en même temps j'ai beaucoup appris.

Aujourd'hui le professeur nous a parlé de quelques différences entre les usages français et anglais. Par exemple, il nous a expliqué qu'on emploie la virgule pour les décimales et le point pour les mille ($\pi = 3,1416$; la maison a coûté 50.000 francs). En français, huit jours (ou une huitaine) veut dire une semaine, et quinze jours (ou une quinzaine), deux semaines. Il nous a rappelé qu'en France la semaine commence le lundi, et il nous a expliqué les expressions « d'aujourd'hui en huit » et « d'aujourd'hui en quinze. »

Alors quelqu'un a demandé si l'on mesurait et comptait de la même façon en France qu'en Amérique.

« Ah non, dit le professeur. C'est-à-dire, on compte à peu près de la même façon, avec le système métrique. Par exemple, quand il s'agit d'argent, on compte en francs, chaque franc se divisant en cent centimes.

— Combien vaut le franc actuellement?

— A l'heure qu'il est, je ne suis pas certain. Mais pendant mon dernier séjour en France, il n'y a pas longtemps, le change officiel était de quatre à cinq pour un dollar. Un franc d'aujourd'hui, vous savez, représente cent francs d'après-guerre. En effet, le franc actuel n'est pas loin de sa valeur traditionnelle, au moins par rapport au dollar.

— Est-ce qu'on mesure les poids en « livres » comme en anglais?

— Non, en grammes; [1] c'est encore le système métrique. Il y a mille grammes dans un kilogramme, qui pèse un peu plus de deux livres anglaises. Et à propos de livres anglaises, savez-vous d'où vient le système monétaire [2] anglais, et les abréviations £/s/d?

— Je crois que l'*s* représente « shilling, » n'est-ce pas? dit une étudiante.

— Pas précisément, répond le professeur. C'est-à-dire, c'est le shilling aujourd'hui, mais réellement le système est l'ancien système français, et ces abréviations représentent « Livres/sous/deniers. » Le denier était autrefois la douzième partie d'un sou, et le sou la vingtième partie d'une livre. En fait, on a gardé le terme

---

[1] Colloquially, as at the grocer's, the term **livre** is still commonly used for weight.
[2] **monétaire** *monetary*

« sou » en France dans quelques expressions comme « il n'a pas le sou, » c'est-à-dire, « il n'a pas d'argent. »

Enfin nous avons abordé le sujet de la température.

« Est-ce qu'on se sert du thermomètre Fahrenheit en France, monsieur?

— Non, on emploie le système centigrade.

— Quelle est la différence entre les deux, monsieur?

— Mais vous avez dû apprendre cela dans vos classes de sciences. Dans le thermomètre centigrade, ou « de Celsius » comme on l'appelle parfois d'après son inventeur, il n'y a que cent degrés entre les points de congélation [1] et d'ébullition [2] de l'eau.

— Vous voulez dire que l'eau gèle à zéro et bout à cent degrés?

— Parfaitement, tandis que dans notre système l'eau gèle à 32 degrés et bout à 212 degrés.

— Est-ce qu'il y a d'autres systèmes pour mesurer la température, monsieur?

— Oui, il y a le système Réaumur. Les degrés sont encore plus grands que ceux du système centigrade.

— Est-ce que le thermomètre Réaumur s'emploie beaucoup en France?

— Non, il est beaucoup moins employé que le thermomètre centigrade. Néanmoins, il y a à Paris une rue importante appelée « rue Réaumur » en l'honneur de l'inventeur du système.

— Monsieur, dis-je alors, puis-je vous demander quelque chose?

— Mais bien entendu, mon garçon, qu'est-ce que c'est?

— Vous vous rappelez ce zéro que vous m'avez donné il y a quelque temps?

— Oui, Maurice, je m'en souviens bien.

— Alors, dites, monsieur: est-ce que c'était un zéro Fahrenheit, centigrade ou Réaumur? »

Questions

1. Quels étaient les sentiments de Maurice au début du cours de français? 2. Qu'est-ce qu'il doit avouer maintenant? 3. Combien de centimes y a-t-il dans un franc? Combien de sous? 4. Combien vaut le franc actuellement? 5. Combien de grammes y a-t-il dans un kilogramme? 6. Que représentent les abréviations £/s/d? 7. Est-ce qu'un kilogramme est plus ou moins lourd qu'une livre anglaise?

---

[1] **la congélation** *freezing*
[2] **l'ébullition** *boiling*

8. Est-ce qu'on se sert du thermomètre Fahrenheit en France? 9. Qui est Celsius? 10. A quel degré est-ce que l'eau gèle dans le système centigrade? 11. Comment a-t-on honoré l'inventeur du système Réaumur? 12. Dans quel système les degrés sont-ils les plus grands? les moins grands?

VOCABULARY

à l'heure qu'il est   at the present time
à présent que   now that
à propos de   speaking of
d'aujourd'hui en huit (quinze)   a week (two weeks) from today
de la même façon   in the same way

en même temps   at the same time
par rapport à   in comparison to
toucher à sa fin   to be nearing its end
tout compte fait   everything considered, all in all

aborder   to take up (a subject)
actuel, actuelle   present
s'attendre à   to expect to
avouer   to admit, confess
bouillir (*3rd sing.* bout)   to boil
le change   exchange
compter   to count
coûter   to cost
d'après-guerre   post-war
le début   beginning
la forêt   forest
geler   to freeze
le gramme   gram

la livre   pound
mesurer   to measure
néanmoins   nevertheless
parfaitement   exactly, precisely
peser   to weigh
le poids   weight
le point   point, period (*punct.*)
réellement   actually
le séjour   stay
triste   sad
la valeur   value
la virgule   comma

Selections for Memorization[1]

Psaume 23 *Psaume de David*

> L'Éternel est mon berger; je n'aurai point de disette.
> Il me fait reposer dans de verts pâturages;
> Il me mène le long des eaux tranquilles.
> Il restaure mon âme;
> Il me conduit dans des sentiers unis,   5
> Pour l'amour de son nom.
>
> Même quand je marcherais dans la vallée de l'ombre de la mort,
> Je ne craindrais aucun mal ! Car tu es avec moi:
> C'est ton bâton et ta houlette qui me consolent.
> Tu dresses la table devant moi,   10
> A la vue de ceux qui me persécutent.
> Tu oins ma tête d'huile; ma coupe déborde.
>
> Oui, le bonheur et la grâce m'accompagneront
> Tous les jours de ma vie,
> Et je passerai de longs jours dans la maison de l'Éternel.   15

Ariette

Paul Verlaine

> Il pleure dans mon cœur
> Comme il pleut sur la ville.
> Quelle est cette langueur
> Qui pénètre mon cœur?
>
> O bruit doux de la pluie,   5
> Par terre et sur les toits!
> Pour un cœur qui s'ennuie,
> O le chant de la pluie!
>
> Il pleure sans raison
> Dans ce cœur qui s'écœure ! 10
> Quoi ! nulle trahison?
> Ce deuil est sans raison.
>
> C'est bien la pire peine
> De ne savoir pourquoi,
> Sans amour et sans haine,   15
> Mon cœur a tant de peine.

---

[1] A special vocabulary for these poems appears on page 214.

Le Corbeau et le Renard

Jean de la Fontaine

Maître corbeau, sur un arbre perché,
    Tenait en son bec un fromage.
Maître renard, par l'odeur alléché,
    Lui tint à peu près ce langage:
    « Hé ! Bonjour, monsieur du corbeau,   5
Que vous êtes joli ! que vous me semblez beau !
    Sans mentir, si votre ramage
    Se rapporte à votre plumage,
Vous êtes le phénix des hôtes de ces bois.»
A ces mots le corbeau ne se sent pas de joie;   10
    Et, pour montrer sa belle voix,
Il ouvre un large bec, laisse tomber sa proie.
Le renard s'en saisit, et dit: « Mon bon monsieur,
    Apprenez que tout flatteur
    Vit aux dépens de celui qui l'écoute: 15
Cette leçon vaut bien un fromage, sans doute.»
    Le corbeau, honteux et confus,
Jura, mais un peu tard, qu'on ne l'y prendrait plus.

Correspondances

Charles Baudelaire

La Nature est un temple où de vivants piliers
Laissent parfois sortir de confuses paroles;
L'homme y passe à travers des forêts de symboles
Qui l'observent avec des regards familiers.

Comme de longs échos qui de loin se confondent   5
Dans une ténébreuse et profonde unité,
Vaste comme la nuit et comme la clarté,
Les parfums, les couleurs et les sons se répondent.

Il est des parfums frais comme des chairs d'enfants,
Doux comme les hautbois, verts comme les prairies,   10
— Et d'autres, corrompus, riches et triomphants,

Ayant l'expansion des choses infinies,
Comme l'ambre, le musc, le benjoin et l'encens,
Qui chantent les transports de l'esprit et des sens.

A quoi bon entendre?

Victor Hugo

A quoi bon entendre
Les oiseaux des bois?
L'oiseau le plus tendre
Chante dans ta voix.

Que Dieu montre ou voile 5
Les astres des cieux !
La plus pure étoile
Brille dans tes yeux.

Qu'avril renouvelle
Le jardin en fleur !   10
La fleur la plus belle
Fleurit dans ton cœur.

Cet oiseau de flamme,
Cet astre du jour,
Cette fleur de l'âme,   15
S'appelle l'amour.

Au Lecteur

Alfred de Musset

Ce livre est toute ma jeunesse;
Je l'ai fait sans presque y songer.
Il y paraît, je le confesse,
Et j'aurais pu le corriger.

Mais quand l'homme change sans cesse, 5
Au passé pourquoi rien changer?
Va-t'en, pauvre oiseau passager;
Que Dieu te mène à ton adresse !

Qui que tu sois, qui me liras,
Lis-en le plus que tu pourras,   10
Et ne me condamne qu'en somme.

Mes premiers vers sont d'un enfant,
Les seconds d'un adolescent,
Les derniers à peine d'un homme.

Ici-bas

Sully Prudhomme

Ici-bas tous les lilas meurent,
Tous les chants des oiseaux sont courts;
Je rêve aux étés qui demeurent
    Toujours . . .

Ici-bas les lèvres effleurent   5
Sans rien laisser de leur velours;
Je rêve aux baisers qui demeurent
    Toujours . . .

Ici-bas tous les hommes pleurent
Leurs amitiés ou leurs amours;   10
Je rêve aux couples qui demeurent
    Toujours . . .

Vocabulary for Poems

Psaume 23

amour love, sake
bâton stick, rod
bonheur happiness, goodness
consoler to console, comfort
coupe cup, bowl
déborder to run over
disette famine, want
dresser to set up, prepare
Éternel Eternal, Lord
grâce grace, mercy
houlette shepherd's staff
huile oil
le long de along
oindre to anoint
ombre shadow, shade
pâturage pasture
persécuter to persecute
psaume psalm
(se) reposer to rest, lie down
sentier path
uni smooth, level
vallée valley
vue sight, view

Ariette

deuil grief
haine hatred
s'écœurer to become sick
trahison betrayal

Le Corbeau et le Renard

alléché attracted
à peu près about, approximately

aux dépens de at the expense of
bec beak
confus embarrassed
corbeau crow
flatteur flatterer
honteux ashamed
hôte denizen
langage discourse
maître master
ne se sent pas de joie is beside himself with joy
odeur odor
phénix paragon
proie prey
ramage voice
renard fox
saisir to seize
sans mentir no fooling
se rapporter à to match

Correspondances

ambre ambergris
à travers through
benjoin benzoin
chair flesh
clarté daylight
corrompu corrupt
encens incense
hautbois oboe
Il est There are
pilier pillar
son sound
ténébreux shadowy
unité unity

A quoi bon entendre?

à quoi bon what's the use of
astre star
cieux skies
flamme flame
fleurir to bloom
renouveler to renew
voiler to hide

Au Lecteur

adresse destination
condamner to condemn
en somme as a whole
jeunesse youth
oiseau passager bird of passage
paraître to appear
qui que tu sois whoever you may be
sans cesse ceaselessly
songer to think
vers verses

Ici-bas

amitié friendship
baiser kiss
effleurer to touch lightly
ici-bas here on earth
lèvre lip
lilas lilac
velours velvet

Appendix

Complete Conjugation of Regular Verbs

	I **donner**	II **finir**	III **perdre**
PRESENT INDICATIVE	je donne tu donnes il donne nous donnons vous donnez ils donnent	je finis tu finis il finit nous finissons vous finissez ils finissent	je perds tu perds il perd [1] nous perdons vous perdez ils perdent
IMPERFECT INDICATIVE	je donnais tu donnais il donnait nous donnions vous donniez ils donnaient	je finissais tu finissais il finissait nous finissions vous finissiez ils finissaient	je perdais tu perdais il perdait nous perdions vous perdiez ils perdaient
PASSÉ SIMPLE	je donnai tu donnas il donna nous donnâmes vous donnâtes ils donnèrent	je finis tu finis il finit nous finîmes vous finîtes ils finirent	je perdis tu perdis il perdit nous perdîmes vous perdîtes ils perdirent
FUTURE	je donnerai tu donneras il donnera nous donnerons vous donnerez ils donneront	je finirai tu finiras il finira nous finirons vous finirez ils finiront	je perdrai tu perdras il perdra nous perdrons vous perdrez ils perdront
CONDITIONAL	je donnerais tu donnerais il donnerait nous donnerions vous donneriez ils donneraient	je finirais tu finirais il finirait nous finirions vous finiriez ils finiraient	je perdrais tu perdrais il perdrait nous perdrions vous perdriez ils perdraient
IMPERATIVE	Donne! Donnons! Donnez!	Finis! Finissons! Finissez!	Perds! Perdons! Perdez!

[1] Verbs of the third conjugation whose stem does not end in **c** or **d** add a **t** in the third person singular. **romp[re] il rompt.**

PRESENT SUBJUNCTIVE	je donne	je finisse	je perde
	tu donnes	tu finisses	tu perdes
	il donne	il finisse	il perde
	nous donnions	nous finissions	nous perdions
	vous donniez	vous finissiez	vous perdiez
	ils donnent	ils finissent	ils perdent

IMPERFECT SUBJUNCTIVE	je donnasse	je finisse	je perdisse
	tu donnasses	tu finisses	tu perdisses
	il donnât	il finît	il perdît
	nous donnassions	nous finissions	nous perdissions
	vous donnassiez	vous finissiez	vous perdissiez
	ils donnassent	ils finissent	ils perdissent

PRESENT PARTICIPLE	donnant	finissant	perdant

COMPOUND PARTICIPLE	ayant donné	ayant fini	ayant perdu

COMPOUND INFINITIVE	avoir donné	avoir fini	avoir perdu

PASSÉ COMPOSÉ	j'ai donné [1]	nous avons donné
	tu as donné	vous avez donné
	il a donné	ils ont donné

PLUPERFECT INDICATIVE	j'avais donné	nous avions donné
	tu avais donné	vous aviez donné
	il avait donné	ils avaient donné

PAST ANTERIOR	j'eus donné	nous eûmes donné
	tu eus donné	vous eûtes donné
	il eut donné	ils eurent donné

FUTURE PERFECT	j'aurai donné	nous aurons donné
	tu auras donné	vous aurez donné
	il aura donné	ils auront donné

CONDITIONAL PAST	j'aurais donné	nous aurions donné
	tu aurais donné	vous auriez donné
	il aurait donné	ils auraient donné

---

[1] Here and below the conjugation of **donner** alone is given. These tenses of **finir** and **perdre** are conjugated in the same way as **donner,** by adding the past participle of the verb, **fini** and **perdu,** to the form of **avoir** that is shown.

PAST SUBJUNCTIVE	j'aie donné	nous ayons donné
	tu aies donné	vous ayez donné
	il ait donné	ils aient donné
PLUPERFECT SUBJUNCTIVE	j'eusse donné	nous eussions donné
	tu eusses donné	vous eussiez donné
	il eût donné	ils eussent donné

Complete Conjugation of *Avoir* and *Être*

	avoir *to have*		**être** *to be*	
PRESENT INDICATIVE	j'ai	nous avons	je suis	nous sommes
	tu as	vous avez	tu es	vous êtes
	il a	ils ont	il est	ils sont
IMPERFECT INDICATIVE	j'avais	nous avions	j'étais	nous étions
	tu avais	vous aviez	tu étais	vous étiez
	il avait	ils avaient	il était	ils étaient
PASSÉ SIMPLE	j'eus	nous eûmes	je fus	nous fûmes
	tu eus	vous eûtes	tu fus	vous fûtes
	il eut	ils eurent	il fut	ils furent
FUTURE	j'aurai	nous aurons	je serai	nous serons
	tu auras	vous aurez	tu seras	vous serez
	il aura	ils auront	il sera	ils seront
CONDITIONAL	j'aurais	nous aurions	je serais	nous serions
	tu aurais	vous auriez	tu serais	vous seriez
	il aurait	ils auraient	il serait	ils seraient
PRESENT SUBJUNCTIVE	j'aie	nous ayons	je sois	nous soyons
	tu aies	vous ayez	tu sois	vous soyez
	il ait	ils aient	il soit	ils soient
IMPERFECT SUBJUNCTIVE	j'eusse	nous eussions	je fusse	nous fussions
	tu eusses	vous eussiez	tu fusses	vous fussiez
	il eût	ils eussent	il fût	ils fussent
IMPERATIVE	Aie! Ayons! Ayez!		Sois! Soyons! Soyez!	

Compound tenses are formed as for regular verbs: **j'ai eu (été), j'avais eu (été)**, etc. For complete patterns, see regular verbs above.

PRESENT PARTICIPLE	ayant	étant
COMPOUND PARTICIPLE	ayant eu	ayant été
COMPOUND INFINITIVE	avoir eu	avoir été

Conjugation of a Reflexive Verb: *Se Coucher*

PRESENT INDICATIVE	je me couche tu te couches il se couche	nous nous couchons vous vous couchez ils se couchent
IMPERFECT INDICATIVE	je me couchais tu te couchais il se couchait	nous nous couchions vous vous couchiez ils se couchaient

Other simple tenses are conjugated as for regular verbs, with the addition of the reflexive object as above.

PASSÉ COMPOSÉ	je me suis couché(e) tu t'es couché(e) il s'est couché elle s'est couchée	nous nous sommes couché(e)s vous vous êtes couché(e)(s) ils se sont couchés elles se sont couchées

Other compound tenses are conjugated similarly, using **être** as auxiliary and making the past participle agree with the reflexive object if it is direct.

IMPERATIVE	Couche-toi! Couchons-nous! Couchez-vous!
PRESENT PARTICIPLE	se couchant
COMPOUND PARTICIPLE	s'étant couché(e)(s)
COMPOUND INFINITIVE	s'être couché(e)(s)

NOTE: The reflexive object will vary with the subject of the sentence, and the agreement of the participle will be with this object if it is direct.

Verbs with Spelling Peculiarities

E-stem verbs (**lever, mener,** etc.) generally add a grave accent to the **e** of the stem whenever the following syllable contains a silent **e: je lève, je mène, ils lèvent,** etc. **Jeter** and its compounds double the **t** instead of using a grave accent, and **appeler** and its compounds double the **l: je jette, j'appelle.** These changes will occur in the present tense (indicative and subjunctive), in the future, and in the conditional; also in the imperative singular.

False e-stem verbs (**céder, préférer**) change the acute accent to grave in the two present tenses, but not in the future or conditional: **je cède, je préfère,** but **je céderai, je préférerai, je céderais.**

Verbs in yer (**employer, essuyer**) change **y** to **i** before a silent **e: j'emploie, j'essuie, ils emploient.** Those in **ayer** may be written with either **y** or **i: j'essaye** or **j'essaie; je payerais** or **je paierais.**

Verbs in cer take a cedilla under the **c** before **a** or **o: nous commençons.**

Verbs in ger retain the **e** after the **g** under similar circumstances: **nous mangeons, il mangeait.**

Summary of Common Irregular Verbs (other than *Avoir* and *Être*)

(Principal parts will be listed at left, tenses at right; future stem will be given only when irregular; tenses will be given in full only when irregular.)

---

aller *to go*

INFINITIVE **aller** (FUT. STEM **ir–**) FUT. **irai** COND. **irais**
PRES. PART. **allant** IMPF. INDIC. **allais** PRES. SUBJ. **aille, ailles, aille, allions, alliez, aillent**
PAST PART. **allé** (all compound tenses with **être**)
PRES. INDIC. **vais, vas, va, allons, allez, vont** IMPERATIVE **va, allons, allez**
PASSÉ SIMPLE **allai** IMPF. SUBJ. **allasse**

---

asseoir *to seat*

NOTE: This verb, generally used reflexively (*to sit*), retains much of the confusion of forms that characterized French verbs in the Middle Ages.

INFINITIVE **asseoir** (FUT. STEM **assiér–** *or* **assoir–**) FUT. **assiérai** *or* **assoirai** COND. **assiérais** *or* **assoirais**
PRES. PART. **asseyant** *or* **assoyant** IMPF. INDIC. **asseyais** *or* **assoyais** PRES. SUBJ. **asseye, asseyes, asseye, asseyions, asseyiez, asseyent** *or* **assoie, assoies, assoie, assoyions, assoyiez, assoient**

PAST PART. **assis** (compound tenses with **avoir** when nonreflexive, with **être** when reflexive)

PRES. INDIC. **assieds, assieds, assied, asseyons, asseyez, asseyent** *or* **assois, assois, assoit, assoyons, assoyez, assoient** IMPERATIVE **assieds, asseyons, asseyez** *or* **assois, assoyons, assoyez**

PASSÉ SIMPLE **assis** IMPF. SUBJ. **assisse**

---

battre *to beat*

NOTE: Irregular only in omitting a **t** in the singular of the present indicative: **bats, bats, bat**

---

boire *to drink*

INFINITIVE **boire** FUT. **boirai** COND. **boirais**

PRES. PART. **buvant** IMPF. INDIC. **buvais** PRES. SUBJ. **boive, boives, boive, buvions, buviez, boivent**

PAST PART. **bu** (all compound tenses with **avoir**)

PRES. INDIC. **bois, bois, boit, buvons, buvez, boivent** IMPERATIVE **bois, buvons, buvez**

PASSÉ SIMPLE **bus** IMPF. SUBJ. **busse**

---

connaître *to know*

NOTE: *Like* **connaître: reconnaître, paraître, apparaître, disparaître**

INFINITIVE **connaître** FUT. **connaîtrai** COND. **connaîtrais**

PRES. PART. **connaissant** IMPF. INDIC. **connaissais** PRES. SUBJ. **connaisse**

PAST PART. **connu** (all compound tenses with **avoir**)

PRES. INDIC. **connais, connais, connaît, connaissons, connaissez, connaissent** IMPERATIVE **connais, connaissons, connaissez**

PASSÉ SIMPLE **connus** IMPF. SUBJ. **connusse**

---

courir *to run*

NOTE: *Like* **courir: parcourir**

INFINITIVE **courir** (FUT. STEM **courr–**) FUT. **courrai** COND. **courrais**

PRES. PART. **courant** IMPF. INDIC. **courais** PRES. SUBJ. **coure**

PAST PART. **couru** (all compound tenses with **avoir**)

PRES. INDIC. **cours, cours, court, courons, courez, courent** IMPERATIVE **cours, courons, courez**

PASSÉ SIMPLE **courus** IMPF. SUBJ. **courusse**

---

craindre *to fear*

NOTE: *Like* **craindre: peindre, joindre, atteindre, plaindre**

INFINITIVE **craindre** FUT. **craindrai** COND. **craindrais**

PRES. PART. **craignant** IMPF. INDIC. **craignais** PRES. SUBJ. **craigne**

PAST PART. **craint** (all compound tenses with **avoir**)

PRES. INDIC. **crains, crains, craint, craignons, craignez, craignent** IMPERATIVE **crains, craignons, craignez**

PASSÉ SIMPLE **craignis** IMPF. SUBJ. **craignisse**

---

croire *to believe*

INFINITIVE **croire** FUT. **croirai** COND. **croirais**
PRES. PART. **croyant** IMPF. INDIC. **croyais** PRES. SUBJ. **croie, croies, croie, croyions, croyiez, croient**
PAST PART. **cru** (all compound tenses with **avoir**)
PRES. INDIC. **crois, crois, croit, croyons, croyez, croient** IMPERATIVE **crois, croyons, croyez**
PASSÉ SIMPLE **crus** IMPF. SUBJ. **crusse**

---

devoir *to owe, ought, must*

NOTE: *Like* **devoir: apercevoir, recevoir** (**c** becomes **ç** before **o** and **u: aperçois, reçu**)

INFINITIVE **devoir** (FUT. STEM **devr–**) FUT. **devrai** COND. **devrais**
PRES. PART. **devant** IMPF. INDIC. **devais** PRES. SUBJ. **doive, doives, doive, devions, deviez, doivent**
PAST PART. **dû** (all compound tenses with **avoir**)
PRES. INDIC. **dois, dois, doit, devons, devez, doivent** IMPERATIVE (lacking)
PASSÉ SIMPLE **dus** IMPF. SUBJ. **dusse**

---

dire *to say*

INFINITIVE **dire** FUT. **dirai** COND. **dirais**
PRES. PART. **disant** IMPF. INDIC. **disais** PRES. SUBJ. **dise**
PAST PART. **dit** (all compound tenses with **avoir**)
PRES. INDIC. **dis, dis, dit, disons, dites, disent** IMPERATIVE **dis, disons, dites**
PASSÉ SIMPLE **dis** IMPF. SUBJ. **disse**

---

dormir *to sleep*

NOTE: *Like* **dormir: s'endormir, partir, sentir, servir, sortir**. **S'endormir, partir, sortir** are compounded with **être**.

INFINITIVE **dormir** FUT. **dormirai** COND. **dormirais**
PRES. PART. **dormant** IMPF. INDIC. **dormais** PRES. SUBJ. **dorme**
PAST PART. **dormi** (all compound tenses with **avoir**)
PRES. INDIC. **dors, dors, dort, dormons, dormez, dorment** IMPERATIVE **dors, dormons, dormez**
PASSÉ SIMPLE **dormis** IMPF. SUBJ. **dormisse**

écrire *to write*

NOTE: *Like* **écrire: décrire**

INFINITIVE **écrire** FUT. **écrirai** COND. **écrirais**
PRES. PART. **écrivant** IMPF. INDIC. **écrivais** PRES. SUBJ. **écrive**
PAST PART. **écrit** (all compound tenses with **avoir**)
PRES. INDIC. **écris, écris, écrit, écrivons, écrivez, écrivent** IMPERATIVE **écris, écrivons, écrivez**
PASSÉ SIMPLE **écrivis** IMPF. SUBJ. **écrivisse**

---

envoyer   *to send*

INFINITIVE **envoyer**   (FUT. STEM **enverr–**)   FUT. **enverrai**   COND. **enverrais**
PRES. PART. **envoyant**   IMPF. INDIC. **envoyais**   PRES. SUBJ. **envoie, envoies, envoie, envoyions, envoyiez, envoient**
PAST PART. **envoyé**   (all compound tenses with **avoir**)
PRES. INDIC. **envoie, envoies, envoie, envoyons, envoyez, envoient**   IMPERATIVE **envoie, envoyons, envoyez**
PASSÉ SIMPLE **envoyai**   IMPF. SUBJ. **envoyasse**

---

faire   *to do, make*

INFINITIVE **faire**   (FUT. STEM **fer–**)   FUT. **ferai**   COND. **ferais**
PRES. PART. **faisant**   IMPF. INDIC. **faisais**   PRES. SUBJ. **fasse, fasses, fasse, fassions, fassiez, fassent**
PAST PART. **fait**   (all compound tenses with **avoir**)
PRES. INDIC. **fais, fais, fait, faisons, faites, font**   IMPERATIVE **fais, faisons, faites**
PASSÉ SIMPLE **fis**   IMPF. SUBJ. **fisse**

---

falloir   *to be necessary*

NOTE: Used only in the third person singular.

INFINITIVE **falloir**   (FUT. STEM **faudr–**)   FUT. **faudra**   COND. **faudrait**
PRES. PART. (lacking)   IMPF. INDIC. **fallait**   PRES. SUBJ. **faille**
PAST PART. **fallu**   (all compound tenses with **avoir**)
PRES. INDIC. **faut**   IMPERATIVE (lacking)
PASSÉ SIMPLE **fallut**   IMPF. SUBJ. **fallût**

---

lire   *to read*

INFINITIVE **lire**   FUT. **lirai**   COND. **lirais**
PRES. PART. **lisant**   IMPF. INDIC. **lisais**   PRES. SUBJ. **lise**
PAST PART. **lu**   (all compound tenses with **avoir**)
PRES. INDIC. **lis, lis, lit, lisons, lisez, lisent**   IMPERATIVE **lis, lisons, lisez**
PASSÉ SIMPLE **lus**   IMPF. SUBJ. **lusse**

---

mettre   *to put*

NOTE: *Like* **mettre: admettre, omettre, permettre, promettre, remettre, soumettre**

INFINITIVE **mettre**   FUT. **mettrai**   COND. **mettrais**
PRES. PART. **mettant**   IMPF. INDIC. **mettais**   PRES. SUBJ. **mette**
PAST PART. **mis**   (all compound tenses with **avoir**)
PRES. INDIC. **mets, mets, met, mettons, mettez, mettent**   IMPERATIVE **mets, mettons, mettez**
PASSÉ SIMPLE **mis**   IMPF. SUBJ. **misse**

mourir *to die*

INFINITIVE **mourir** (FUT. STEM **mourr–**) FUT. **mourrai** COND. **mourrais**
PRES. PART. **mourant** IMPF. INDIC. **mourais** PRES. SUBJ. **meure, meures, meure, mourions, mouriez, meurent**
PAST PART. **mort** (all compound tenses with **être**)
PRES. INDIC. **meurs, meurs, meurt, mourons, mourez, meurent** IMPERATIVE **meurs, mourons, mourez**
PASSÉ SIMPLE **mourus** IMPF. SUBJ. **mourusse**

naître *to be born*

INFINITIVE **naître** FUT. **naîtrai** COND. **naîtrais**
PRES. PART. **naissant** IMPF. INDIC. **naissais** PRES. SUBJ. **naisse**
PAST PART. **né** (all compound tenses with **être**)
PRES. INDIC. **nais, nais, naît, naissons, naissez, naissent** IMPERATIVE **nais, naissons, naissez**
PASSÉ SIMPLE **naquis** IMPF. SUBJ. **naquisse**

ouvrir *to open*

NOTE: *Like* **ouvrir: offrir, couvrir, souffrir, découvrir**

INFINITIVE **ouvrir** FUT. **ouvrirai** COND. **ouvrirais**
PRES. PART. **ouvrant** IMPF. INDIC. **ouvrais** PRES. SUBJ. **ouvre**
PAST PART. **ouvert** (all compound tenses with **avoir**)
PRES. INDIC. **ouvre, ouvres, ouvre, ouvrons, ouvrez, ouvrent** IMPERATIVE **ouvre, ouvrons, ouvrez**
PASSÉ SIMPLE **ouvris** IMPF. SUBJ. **ouvrisse**

plaire *to please*

INFINITIVE **plaire** FUT. **plairai** COND. **plairais**
PRES. PART. **plaisant** IMPF. INDIC. **plaisais** PRES. SUBJ. **plaise**
PAST PART. **plu** (all compound tenses with **avoir**)
PRES. INDIC. **plais, plais, plaît, plaisons, plaisez, plaisent** IMPERATIVE **plais, plaisons, plaisez**
PASSÉ SIMPLE **plus** IMPF. SUBJ. **plusse**

pleuvoir *to rain*

NOTE: Used in third person singular only.

INFINITIVE **pleuvoir** (FUT. STEM **pleuvr–**) FUT. **pleuvra** COND. **pleuvrait**
PRES. PART. **pleuvant** IMPF. INDIC. **pleuvait** PRES. SUBJ. **pleuve**
PAST PART. **plu** (all compound tenses with **avoir**)
PRES. INDIC. **pleut** IMPERATIVE (lacking)
PASSÉ SIMPLE **plut** IMPF. SUBJ. **plût**

pouvoir   *to be able*

NOTE: In the first person singular, **puis** must be used in a question: **Puis-je?** Otherwise either form may be used.

INFINITIVE **pouvoir**   (FUT. STEM **pourr–**)   FUT. **pourrai**   COND. **pourrais**

PRES. PART. **pouvant**   IMPF. INDIC. **pouvais**   PRES. SUBJ. **puisse, puisses, puisse, puissions, puissiez, puissent**

PAST PART. **pu**   (all compound tenses with **avoir**)

PRES. INDIC. **peux** *or* **puis, peux, peut, pouvons, pouvez, peuvent**   IMPERATIVE (lacking)

PASSÉ SIMPLE **pus**   IMPF. SUBJ. **pusse**

---

prendre   *to take*

NOTE: *Like* **prendre: apprendre, comprendre, surprendre**

INFINITIVE **prendre**   FUT. **prendrai**   COND. **prendrais**

PRES. PART. **prenant**   IMPF. INDIC. **prenais**   PRES. SUBJ. **prenne, prennes, prenne, prenions, preniez, prennent**

PAST PART. **pris**   (all compound tenses with **avoir**)

PRES. INDIC. **prends, prends, prend, prenons, prenez, prennent**   IMPERATIVE **prends, prenons, prenez**

PASSÉ SIMPLE **pris**   IMPF. SUBJ. **prisse**

---

produire   *to produce*

NOTE: *Like* **produire: conduire, traduire, réduire, construire**

INFINITIVE **produire**   FUT. **produirai**   COND. **produirais**

PRES. PART. **produisant**   IMPF. INDIC. **produisais**   PRES. SUBJ. **produise**

PAST PART. **produit**   (all compound tenses with **avoir**)

PRES. INDIC. **produis, produis, produit, produisons, produisez, produisent**   IMPERATIVE **produis, produisons, produisez**

PASSÉ SIMPLE **produisis**   IMPF. SUBJ. **produisisse**

---

rire   *to laugh*

INFINITIVE **rire**   FUT. **rirai**   COND. **rirais**

PRES. PART. **riant**   IMPF. INDIC. **riais**   PRES. SUBJ. **rie, ries, rie, riions, riiez, rient**

PAST PART. **ri**   (all compound tenses with **avoir**)

PRES. INDIC. **ris, ris, rit, rions, riez, rient**   IMPERATIVE **ris, rions, riez**

PASSÉ SIMPLE **ris**   IMPF. SUBJ. **risse**

---

savoir   *to know*

INFINITIVE **savoir**   (FUT. STEM **saur–**)   FUT. **saurai**   COND. **saurais**

PRES. PART. **sachant**   IMPF. INDIC. **savais**   PRES. SUBJ. **sache, saches, sache, sachions, sachiez, sachent**

PAST PART. **su**   (all compound tenses with **avoir**)

PRES. INDIC. **sais, sais, sait, savons, savez, savent**   IMPERATIVE **sache, sachons, sachez**

PASSÉ SIMPLE **sus**   IMPF. SUBJ. **susse**

---

suivre   *to follow*

INFINITIVE **suivre**   FUT. **suivrai**   COND. **suivrais**
PRES. PART. **suivant**   IMPF. INDIC. **suivais**   PRES. SUBJ. **suive**
PAST PART. **suivi**   (all compound tenses with **avoir**)
PRES. INDIC. **suis, suis, suit, suivons, suivez, suivent**   IMPERATIVE **suis, suivons, suivez**
PASSÉ SIMPLE **suivis**   IMPF. SUBJ. **suivisse**

---

tenir   *to hold*

NOTE: *Like* **tenir**: **obtenir, venir, devenir, se souvenir,** and others ending in **tenir** and **venir**.   **Venir, devenir, se souvenir** are compounded with **être**.

INFINITIVE **tenir**   (FUT. STEM **tiendr–**)   FUT. **tiendrai**   COND. **tiendrais**
PRES. PART. **tenant**   IMPF. INDIC. **tenais**   PRES. SUBJ. **tienne, tiennes, tienne, tenions, teniez, tiennent**
PAST PART. **tenu**   (all compound tenses with **avoir**)
PRES. INDIC. **tiens, tiens, tient, tenons, tenez, tiennent**   IMPERATIVE **tiens, tenons, tenez**
PASSÉ SIMPLE **tins, tins, tint, tînmes, tîntes, tinrent**   IMPF. SUBJ. **tinsse, tinsses, tînt, tinssions, tinssiez, tinssent**

---

valoir   *to be worth*

INFINITIVE **valoir**   (FUT. STEM **vaudr–**)   FUT. **vaudrai**   COND. **vaudrais**
PRES. PART. **valant**   IMPF. INDIC. **valais**   PRES. SUBJ. **vaille, vailles, vaille, valions, valiez, vaillent**
PAST PART. **valu**   (all compound tenses with **avoir**)
PRES. INDIC. **vaux, vaux, vaut, valons, valez, valent**   IMPERATIVE **vaux, valons, valez**
PASSÉ SIMPLE **valus**   IMPF. SUBJ. **valusse**

---

vivre   *to live*

NOTE: *Like* **vivre**: **survivre**

INFINITIVE **vivre**   FUT. **vivrai**   COND. **vivrais**
PRES. PART. **vivant**   IMPF. INDIC. **vivais**   PRES. SUBJ. **vive**
PAST PART. **vécu**   (all compound tenses with **avoir**)
PRES. INDIC. **vis, vis, vit, vivons, vivez, vivent**   IMPERATIVE **vis, vivons, vivez**
PASSÉ SIMPLE **vécus**   IMPF. SUBJ. **vécusse**

---

voir   *to see*

NOTE: *Like* **voir**: **revoir**

INFINITIVE **voir**   (FUT. STEM **verr–**)   FUT. **verrai**   COND. **verrais**
PRES. PART. **voyant**   IMPF. INDIC. **voyais**   PRES. SUBJ. **voie, voies, voie, voyions, voyiez, voient**
PAST PART. **vu**   (all compound tenses with **avoir**)
PRES. INDIC. **vois, vois, voit, voyons, voyez, voient**   IMPERATIVE **vois, voyons, voyez**
PASSÉ SIMPLE **vis**   IMPF. SUBJ. **visse**

---

vouloir *to wish, want*

NOTE: The regular imperative is rare. The special form **veuillez** (followed by an infinitive) is fairly common, meaning "please."

INFINITIVE **vouloir** (FUT. STEM **voudr–**) FUT. **voudrai** COND. **voudrais**

PRES. PART. **voulant** IMPF. INDIC. **voulais** PRES. SUBJ. **veuille, veuilles, veuille, voulions, vouliez, veuillent**

PAST PART. **voulu** (all compound tenses with **avoir**)

PRES. INDIC. **veux, veux, veut, voulons, voulez, veulent** (IMPERATIVE **veuille** [rare], **veuillons** [rare], **veuillez**)

PASSÉ SIMPLE **voulus** IMPF. SUBJ. **voulusse**

Irregular verbs listed under other verbs.

admettre *see* **mettre**	**joindre** *see* **craindre**	**remettre** *see* **mettre**
apercevoir *see* **devoir**	**obtenir** *see* **tenir**	**revenir** *see* **tenir**
apparaître *see* **connaître**	**offrir** *see* **ouvrir**	**revoir** *see* **voir**
apprendre *see* **prendre**	**omettre** *see* **mettre**	**sentir** *see* **dormir**
atteindre *see* **craindre**	**paraître** *see* **connaître**	**servir** *see* **dormir**
comprendre *see* **prendre**	**parcourir** *see* **courir**	**sortir** *see* **dormir**
conduire *see* **produire**	**partir** *see* **dormir**	**souffrir** *see* **ouvrir**
construire *see* **produire**	**peindre** *see* **craindre**	**soumettre** *see* **mettre**
couvrir *see* **ouvrir**	**permettre** *see* **mettre**	**se souvenir** *see* **tenir**
découvrir *see* **ouvrir**	**plaindre** *see* **craindre**	**surprendre** *see* **prendre**
décrire *see* **écrire**	**promettre** *see* **mettre**	**survivre** *see* **vivre**
devenir *see* **tenir**	**recevoir** *see* **devoir**	**traduire** *see* **produire**
disparaître *see* **connaître**	**reconnaître** *see* **connaître**	**venir** *see* **tenir**
s'endormir *see* **dormir**	**réduire** *see* **produire**	

French Terms Used in English

The English language is rich in terms of French origin, because of the Norman conquest and centuries of relations between France and England. It would be utterly impossible, within limited scope, to compound anything like a complete list of such terms. However, a certain number of expressions, though not new to English, still retain a certain Gallic flavor which adds zest and piquancy to English writing and speech. In addition, various French culinary, military, and diplomatic terms have become so widely accepted as peculiarly apropos that no cultured person of our day should be ignorant of their meaning. The student who pretends to genuine *savoir faire* should be familiar with at least the following expressions. Terms used in the lessons have been omitted.

Culinary or restaurant terms

au gratin (from **gratter,** scrape) with a browned crust of bread crumbs, often mixed with butter and cheese

au jus (in the juice) served in thin gravy from the meat itself

bisque rich cream soup thickened with a puree, usually tomato

croûtons [1] (from **croûte,** crust) small pieces of bread fried or toasted, used in soups or with a puree

demitasse (half cup) small cup of or for black coffee

entrée [2] meat dish not classed as a roast, or a main dish served in place of meat

julienne (from Julien, French caterer of Boston) cut into thin strips (usually vegetables)

lyonnaise (from the city of Lyon) with flaked or sliced fried onions

macédoine mixture of vegetables or fruits, often diced

maître d'hôtel major-domo, head waiter; sauce of melted butter, chopped parsley, salt, pepper, and lemon juice or vinegar

pièce de résistance most substantial dish of a meal

petits fours (little ovens) small ornamentally iced cakes or meringues

ragoût (from **ragoûter,** to restore the taste) stew of meat and vegetables, highly seasoned

table d'hôte (host's table) meal for which one pays a fixed price regardless of what one orders

Military or diplomatic terms

aide de camp (camp assistant) officer attached to a general or other high-ranking officer

attaché (attached) member of diplomatic staff of ambassador or minister

chargé d'affaires (in charge of affairs) diplomatic representative temporarily authorized to deal with another country's minister of foreign affairs

coup de grâce (mercy stroke) blow or action taken to finish off an individual or group

coup d'état (stroke of state) sudden political move bringing about a change of government

esprit de corps (corps spirit) sense of

unity and pride that binds members of an outfit together

hors de combat (out of fighting) wounded or otherwise rendered incapable of fighting

liaison (linking) system of organized relationship between branches of the service

matériel (material) military equipment

reconnaissance (getting to know) obtaining of advance information on terrain or on position of enemy

saboteur (person with wooden shoes, referring to old custom of trampling property) person responsible for destroying or putting out of commission enemy installations

---

[1] The accents are sometimes omitted on French terms in English usage.

[2] In France, **entrée** generally applies to the course preceding the main course of a formal dinner and following the **hors-d'œuvre.**

General terms

affaire de cœur love affair

arrière pensée (rear thought) hidden motive or thought behind an action

au courant (in the current) well-informed, up-to-date

bête noire (black beast) person or object of aversion or detestation; bugaboo

blasé (blunted) insensible to enjoyment because of overindulgence in pleasures; indifferent

bon vivant man-about-town, person who spends his time in the best restaurants, theaters, etc.

carte blanche (blank card) permission granted to a person to do as he likes

C'est la vie! expression of resignation or acceptance of life as it is

chaise longue (long chair) combination of chair and footstool for reclining

cliché (stereotyped plate) hackneyed or worn expression

coup de théâtre dramatic development, unexpected turn of events

cul de sac (bottom of sack) dead end, impasse

de rigueur required or obligatory for good form

en famille at home, among the family, privately

en masse in a mass, as a whole

entre nous just between ourselves

fait accompli completed action, rendering discussion academic

faux pas (false step) blunder, usually social

gauche (left-handed) awkward, gawky, clumsy

je ne sais quoi (I don't know what, the ancient *nescio quid* of Latin times) an inexpressible something, an element that defies description

joie de vivre (joy of living) general sense of its "being good to be alive"; keen enjoyment of the pleasures of life

laissez faire (probably from famous phrase of Gournay, 18th-century French economist: "laissez faire, laissez passer") policy of noninterference in business by government, application of the same principle in other spheres

mal de mer seasickness

mise en scène (putting on stage) stage setting, arrangement of scenery and players for a scene

noblesse oblige (nobility obliges) the notion that one's rank or station brings with it the responsibility to act accordingly

nom de plume pen name

nouveau riche a person with a newly acquired fortune (the term is slightly scornful)

papier mâché (chewed paper) mastic of paper and glue molded into imitations of other materials

par excellence pre-eminently, above all

pince-nez (pinch-nose) glasses without ear supports

protégé (protected) person under the wing of another, a star pupil or favorite understudy

qui vive (who lives) watchfulness (used in the expression *on the qui vive*, meaning "on the alert")

raconteur (teller) good story teller, person with a ready stock of amusing anecdotes

raison d'être reason for the existence of something

sang-froid (cold-blood) composure, coolness under trying circumstances

savoir faire knowledge or ability to "get around" in society with grace and ease

tête-à-tête (head-to-head) intimate conversation

tour de force (trick of force) feat of strength or skill seemingly beyond credibility

Faux Amis

Because of the historical relationship between French and English, a host of parallel terms exists in the two languages. In the course of time, however, changes of meaning as well as form have taken place in both languages, so that it is often impossible to interchange terms even when their origin was the same. Expressions of common appearance but whose meanings are far apart are termed **faux amis** (false friends), because their similarity of form may lead to false guesses as to meaning. From the vast list of **faux amis,** we have chosen a modest selection, presented in pairs for contrast. In each case, the correct modern translation is given in the other language.

ability **pouvoir** *m.*
habileté *f.* know-how, cleverness

achieve **réussir**
achever terminate

actual **réel, véritable**
actuel present

advertisement **réclame** *f.*
advertising **publicité** *f.*
avertissement *m.* warning

appeal (a decision) **faire appel de;** (to someone) **plaire (à quelqu'un)**
appeler (de loin, au téléphone) call; **(donner un nom)** name

argument **discussion** *f.*, **dispute** *f.*
argument *m.* reason, fact, evidence

assist (someone to do something) **aider (quelqu'un à faire quelque chose)**
assister à attend (a meeting, etc.)

attend (a meeting, etc.) **assister à (une réunion,** etc.)
attendre wait, wait for

balance (of object, body) **équilibre** *m.*; (of account) **solde** *m.*
balance *f.* **(pour peser)** scale (for weighing)

band (of thieves) **bande** *f.* **(de voleurs);** (jazz) **orchestre** *m.*; (military) **musique** *f.*; (hat) **ruban** *m.*
bande *f.* **(de voleurs)** band (of thieves); **(pour pansements)** bandage (for dressing of wounds)

boss **patron** *m.*
bosse *f.* bump, protuberance

candid **franc**
candide inexperienced, easily fooled

car **auto** *f.*, **voiture** *f.*
car *m.* excursion bus
car for, because

change (from something to another) **changement** *m.*; (for 1,000 francs) **monnaie** *f.* **(de 1.000 fr.)**
change *m.* rate of exchange

character (in play) **personnage** *m.*
caractère *m.* temper (of a person)

conductor (orchestra) **chef** *(m.)* **d'orchestre;** (train) **contrôleur** *m.*
conducteur *m.* driver, motorman

command **ordre** *m.*
commande *f.* order (purchase)

conference (meeting) **réunion** *f.*; (interview) **entrevue** *f.*
conférence *f.* lecture, diplomatic meeting

confused **troublé**
confus (person) ashamed; (thing) unclear

convention **congrès** *m.*
convention *f.* agreement

correct **exact**
correct (**manières**) proper (manners)

course (school) **cours** *m.*; (golf) **terrain** *m.*; (meal) **plat** *m.*
course *f.* (**de chevaux**) race; (**dans les magasins**) errands, shopping

court (of king) **cour** *f.*; (justice) **cour** *f.*; (tennis) **court** *m.*
court *m.* (**de tennis**) court
court short

dancing **danse** *f.*
dancing *m.* dance hall

date (with someone) **rendez-vous** *m.*; (fruit) **datte** *f.*
date *f.* date (day of month)

demand **exiger**
demander ask, ask for

deserve **mériter**
desservir (**compagnie de chemin de fer, aérienne,** etc.) serve; (**la table**) clear (after a meal)

design (a house) **faire les plans de;** (scheme, plan) **avoir l'intention**
désigner designate

design (on paper) **dessin** *m.*; (intention) **dessein** *m.*, **projet** *m.*
dessin *m.* (**art**) drawing; (**d'une machine**) design

dress (someone) **habiller;** (oneself) **s'habiller;** (a wound) **panser**
dresser (**une liste**) draw up; (**une tente**) put up (a tent); (**un animal**) train

editor **rédacteur** *m.*
éditeur *m.* publisher

eventually **finalement**
éventuellement possibly, perhaps

evidence (of witness) **témoignage** *m.*; (pieces of evidence) **faits** *m. pl.*
évidence *f.* an obvious fact or idea

famous **célèbre**
fameux delicious, excellent; famous

figure (of person) **silhouette** *f.*; (number) **chiffre** *m.*; (of speech or style) **figure** *f.*
figure *f.* (**visage**) face; (**style**) figure

file (records) **dossier** *m.*; (tool) **lime** *f.*
file *f.* (**de gens, autos**) line (of people, cars)

formal **de cérémonie;** (of dress) **de soirée**
formel (**beauté**) pertaining to form, of form; (**ordre**) strict

formally **officiellement**
formellement strictly (e.g., **formellement interdit,** strictly forbidden)

furniture (of room) **mobilier** *m.*; (general) **meubles** *m. pl.*
fourniture *f.* providing, supplying

genial **sociable**
génial characterized by genius

grief **chagrin** *m.*
grief *m.* complaint

habit **habitude** *f.*

habit *m.* man's formal suit; **habits** *m. pl.* garments

inhabited **habité**
inhabité uninhabited

injure **blesser**
injurier insult

issue **problème** *m.,* **question** *f.*
issue *f.* exit, way out

labor (work) **main** (*f.*) **d'œuvre, travail** *m.*; (as opposed to management) **ouvriers** *m. pl.*
labeur *m.* hard work
labour *m.* ploughing, ploughed field

large **grand**
large wide

lecture **conférence** *f.*
lecture *f.* reading

library **bibliothèque** *f.*
librairie *f.* bookstore, publishing house

mass (quantity) **masse** *f.*; (in Catholic service) **messe** *f.*
masse *f.* large quantity

mess **gâchis** *m.,* **désordre** *m.*
messe *f.* (Catholic) mass

move (vehicle as subject) **marcher, bouger, se déplacer**; (from a house) **déménager**; (into a house) **emménager**; (an object from one place to another) **déplacer**; (someone emotionally) **émouvoir**; (make a motion in a meeting) **proposer**
mouvoir (rare substitute for **déplacer**); se mouvoir (rare substitute for **se déplacer**)

name (give a name) **appeler, nommer**; (quote) **citer**
nommer give a name to, appoint

noted **célèbre**
noté put on record; **bien noté** appreciated by superiors

office (doctor, lawyer) **cabinet** *m.,* **bureau** *m.*; (political) **situation** *f.*
office *m.* (**dans la maison**) pantry; (**organisation**) agency; (**religieux**) ceremony

opportunity **occasion** *f.*
opportunité *f.* opportuneness, quality of happening at the right time

paper (material) **papier** *m.*; (newspaper) **journal** *m.*; (written assignment) **devoir** *m.,* **composition** *f.*; (for a journal) **article** *m.*
papier *m.* paper (material), newspaper article

part (portion) **partie** *f.*; (of actor) **rôle** *m.*; (of hair) **raie** *f.*; parts (of car, etc.) **pièces** (*f.*) **détachées**
part *f.* share, portion; **de la part de** from, on behalf of

party (political) **parti** *m.*; (gathering) **réunion** *f.*; (group of people) **groupe** *m.*
parti *m.* political party; **prendre un parti** make a decision

patron (of establishment) **client** *m.*; (of restaurant) **habitué** *m.*; (of the arts) **protecteur** *m.*
patron *m.* (**d'une affaire, organisation**) boss; (**d'une robe**) pattern (of a dress)

physician **médecin** *m.*
physicien *m.* physicist

place (location) **endroit** *m.*, **lieu** *m.*;
(rank) **place** *f.*

place *f.* (**dans une ville**) square; (**dans
le train, cinéma,** etc.) seat; (**situation**)
job; (**abstrait**) room, space

port (harbor) **port** *m.*; (side of ship)
babord *m.*; (wine) **porto** *m.*

port *m.* (**de mer**) port, harbor; (**d'une
personne**) carriage, bearing; (**d'une
lettre ou d'un paquet**) postage, shipment

post (stake) **poteau** *m.*; (position)
poste *m.*

poste *m.* job, position; **poste émetteur de
radio, de T.V.** sending station; **poste
récepteur** receiver, set

poste *f.* post office

rapport (between people) **relations** *f. pl.*,
rapports *m. pl.*

rapport *m.* (**entre choses, idées**) relation;
(**document**) report; (**d'une valeur**)
income (of security)

report (document) **rapport;** (newspaper)
reportage *m.*; (of gun) **détonation** *f.*

report *m.* carry-over

relations (relatives) **parents** *m. pl.*; (relationship) **parenté** *f.*

relation *f.* person you know; (**d'un
événement**) report, account

rent **loyer** *m.*

rente *f.* (**d'une valeur**) income

resume **reprendre, recommencer**

résumer summarize, sum up

Roman **romain**

roman *m.* novel

roman (*adj.*) Romanic, Romanesque

romance **histoire** (*f.*) **d'amour**

romance *f.* melody

sensible **raisonnable, sensé**

sensible sensitive

servant **serviteur** *m.*, **servante** *f.*,
domestique *m.* or *f.*; (civil service)
fonctionnaire *m.*

servant (present participle of **servir**)

smoking **fumer;** no smoking **défense de
fumer**

smoking *m.* tuxedo, dinner clothes

suit (law) **procès** *m.*; (garment) **costume**
m., **complet** *m.*, (lady's) **tailleur** (*m.*) **de
dame**; (cards) **couleur** *f.*

suite (of rooms) **appartement** *m.*

suite *f.* sequence; (**d'un roi**) retinue;
les suites the consequences

support (one's family) **faire vivre;** (an
opinion) **soutenir**

supporter bear, endure

tenant **locataire** *m.*

tenant *m.* holder (of title, etc.)

theater (legitimate) **théâtre** *m.*; (movie)
cinéma *m.*

théâtre *m.* theater (legitimate only)

ticket (rail, ship) **billet** *m.*; (subway, bus)
ticket *m.*; (political) **liste** *f.*; (traffic
violation) **le procès verbal** (referred
to as **le P.V.**)

ticket *m.* (**métro, autobus**) ticket; (**ra-
tionnement**) coupon

trouble **gêner, déranger**

troubler disturb, upset; (**eau**) roil, stir
up

use **utiliser, employer, se servir de**

user wear out

vest **gilet** *m.*

veste *f.* jacket, suit coat

Elements of English Grammar

I. Parts of Speech

A. Nouns name a person, place, or object. They can be singular (*bicycle, rug, man, sheep*) or plural (*bicycles, rugs, men, sheep*); masculine (*boy, man, brother*), feminine (*girl, woman, sister*), or neuter (*horse,*[1] *book, river, beauty, distance*).

Nouns function in the following ways.

SUBJECT OF VERB: The *house* is on Main Street.
PREDICATE NOUN: The house is a *mansion*.
DIRECT OBJECT OF VERB OR VERBAL: He wanted to see the *professor*.
INDIRECT OBJECT OF VERB OR VERBAL: He wanted to give the *professor* a book.
SUBJECT OF INFINITIVE: He wanted the *professor* to see the book.
OBJECT OF PREPOSITION: Give this to the *student*.
OBJECTIVE COMPLEMENT: They elected him *president*.
APPOSITIVE: John, *King* of England, was compelled to sign the Magna Charta.
NOMINATIVE OF ADDRESS: *Officer*, can you help us?

B. Pronouns stand in place of nouns and are classified as follows:

PERSONAL: I, you, he, she, it, we, they
Personal pronouns are commonly classified by person, number, and in the third person singular, gender.

	Singular	**Plural**
First Person	I, my, mine, me	we, our, ours, us
Second Person	you, your, yours	you, your, yours
Third Person	he, his, him, she, her, hers, it, its	they, their, theirs, them

RELATIVE: who, whoever, which, that, what, whatever (The boy *whom* I saw has gone.)
DEMONSTRATIVE: this, that, these, those (*That* book is more interesting than *these*.)
INDEFINITE: each, some, someone, everyone, any, anyone, no one, few, all (Does *anyone* ever know *everything?*)
INTERROGATIVE: who, which, what (*Who* told you that?)
POSSESSIVE: mine, yours, his, hers, its, ours, theirs (*Yours* was the best suggestion made.)
RECIPROCAL: each other, one another (They helped *each other*.)

---

[1] Animals may be referred to as "he" or "she," but grammatically they are usually treated as neuter ("it").

REFLEXIVE: myself, yourself, himself, ourselves   (He helped *himself.*)
INTENSIVE: myself, yourself, himself, ourselves   (I *myself* will attend to it.)

C. Verbs assert action, condition, or state of being.

The horse *galloped.*   The book *is* on the table.   They *seem* industrious.

D. Adjectives modify (describe or limit) nouns and pronouns.

DESCRIPTIVE: a *good* dinner, a *beautiful* song, *cold* days
LIMITING: *my* [1] pencil, *your, his, our, their* house (**possessive**); *that, this* automobile (**demonstrative**);   *whose, which, what* questions (**interrogative**);   *any* choice, *neither* plan (**indefinite**);   *the* idea, *a* boy, *an* ostrich (**articles, definite and indefinite**);   the man *whose* daughter married (**relative**);   *one* example, *third* man (**numerical**)

E. Adverbs modify (qualify or limit) verbs, adjectives, other adverbs, or entire sentences.

Naturally we shall attend the meeting.
MANNER: He walked *slowly.*
TIME: *Now* she believes you; *then* she didn't.
LOCATION: *Outside,* a large crowd gathered.
DEGREE: They talked *very* briefly.

F. Prepositions indicate the relationship between nouns and pronouns and some other word in the sentence. The following words are among those which are often or always used as prepositions: *in, at, by, of, from, with, for, off, above, after, between, behind, except, until, in front of, on account of, in place of.*

They continued the search *despite* the heat.
The dog emerged *from* the doghouse.
Their business is conducted *with* the utmost formality.

G. Conjunctions connect words, phrases, and clauses. They are either co-ordinating (*and, or, nor, but, either . . . or, yet*) or subordinating (*if, although, unless, since, because, so that, that, as, where, when*).

George *and* Paula had expected to stay abroad, *but* they returned today.
Neither John *nor* Peter won the tournament, *although* both tried hard.

H. Interjections express strong or sudden feeling and have no grammatical connection with any other part of the sentence.

Oh! why did you say that?   *Good heavens!* they've done it again.

---

[1] *My, your, his, her, its, our, their* are also often thought of as the "possessive case" of pronouns rather than as possessive adjectives.

II. Comparison

Descriptive adjectives and adverbs may usually be compared in one of two ways: *fast, faster, fastest;* or *slowly, more slowly, most slowly.* The degrees are called positive, comparative, superlative.

III. Verbals

Verbals are verb forms which are used as nouns, adjectives, and sometimes adverbs.

GERUND (present or perfect participle used as noun): *Skating* is less dangerous than *skiing.*

PARTICIPLE (verbal used as adjective): *Having completed* his aria, the *puffing* basso left the stage. The book was left *unfinished.*

INFINITIVE (verbal used as noun, adjective, or adverb): He promised *to come* early. She left me a book *to read.* We did not wait *to see* him. The pitcher appeared *to have been emptied.*

IV. Cases

Cases indicate the relation of nouns and pronouns to other words in a sentence. In English the three cases are as follows.

NOMINATIVE (subject of verb, except infinitive or gerund): *He* came. *We* all left. (predicate nominative): This is *she.*

POSSESSIVE (to show ownership or relationship): *my brother's* wife (subject of gerund): I left without *his* knowing it.

OBJECTIVE (direct object): She called *him.* (indirect object): She told *him* the truth. (object of preposition): She left without *him.* (subject of infinitive): She wants *him* to go. (complement of infinitive): She thought it to be *him.*

V. Tenses

Tenses are changes in verb forms that indicate the time an action takes place. In English there are six tenses: present, past, future, present perfect, past perfect, future perfect. A conjugation is a grouping of verb forms by tense, voice (active or passive), person, number, and/or mood (indicative, imperative, or subjunctive).

Most verbs have a **progressive** form in addition to the **simple** forms here shown: *I am striking, I was striking, I shall be striking, etc.* The **present** and **past** tenses also commonly have **emphatic** forms (regularly used for the simple negative and interrogative): *I do strike, I did strike, Do I strike?*, etc.

Conjugation of the verb *to strike*

PRINCIPAL PARTS: strike, struck, struck or stricken, striking

INDICATIVE MOOD

ACTIVE VOICE		PASSIVE VOICE	

Present Tense

Singular	Plural	Singular	Plural
I strike	we strike	I am struck	we are struck
you strike	you strike	you are struck	you are struck
he (she, it) strikes	they strike	he (she, it) is struck	they are struck

Simple form: I strike   *Progressive form:* I am striking   *Emphatic form:* I do strike

Past Tense

I struck	we struck	I was struck	we were struck
you struck	you struck	you were struck	you were struck
he struck	they struck	he was struck	they were struck

Future Tense

I shall strike	we shall strike	I shall be struck	we shall be struck
you will strike	you will strike	you will be struck	you will be struck
he will strike	they will strike	he will be struck	they will be struck

Present Perfect Tense

Singular	Plural	Singular	Plural
I have struck	we have struck	I have been struck	we have been struck
you have struck	you have struck	you have been struck	you have been struck
he has struck	they have struck	he has been struck	they have been struck

Past Perfect Tense

I had struck	we had struck	I had been struck	we had been struck
you had struck	you had struck	you had been struck	you had been struck
he had struck	they had struck	he had been struck	they had been struck

Future Perfect Tense

I shall have struck	we shall have struck	I shall have been struck	we shall have been struck
you will have struck	you will have struck	you will have been struck	you will have been struck
he will have struck	they will have struck	he will have been struck	they will have been struck

NOTE: There are no formal tenses in English corresponding to the French conditional tense (*I would strike*) and conditional perfect tense (*I would have struck*). In English *would* is referred to as a modal auxiliary.

IMPERATIVE MOOD

strike   be struck

SUBJUNCTIVE MOOD [1]

Present Tense

SINGULAR: (if) I, you, he strike

PLURAL: (if) we, you, they strike

(if) I, you, he be struck

(if) we, you, they be struck

Past Tense

SINGULAR: (if) I, you, he struck (*or* were to strike)

PLURAL: (if) we, you, they struck (*or* were to strike)

(if) I, you, he were struck

(if) we, you, they were struck

VI. Agreement

Every verb should agree in number with its subject, and every pronoun should agree in number with its antecedent.

The *damage* to the ships *was* restricted to the port side.

The *repairs were* made in drydock.

Each person *was* thanked for *his* contribution.

VII. Clauses

A clause is a group of words which contains a verb and its subject. There are two kinds of clauses: **main** (independent, principal) and **subordinate** (dependent).

A main clause can stand alone as a simple sentence since it has a subject and a verb and is not introduced by a subordinating conjunction.

When the bell rings, *the class is over.*   or   The class is over.

As soon as you finish, *we can leave.*   or   We can leave.

A subordinate clause cannot stand alone. It is usually introduced by a subordinating conjunction (*after, although, because, since, while, unless*) or a relative pronoun (*who, which, that, what*).

When the bell rings, the class is over.

I will call you Tuesday *while I am in town.*

He introduced me to Mr. Thomas, *who had just arrived.*

---

[1] Except for the verb *to be* (*if I were you*), the subjunctive form of the verb differs from the indicative only in the third person singular. It is used less frequently in English than in French.

French-English Vocabulary

NOTE: The key to the phonetic transcriptions within the brackets is to be found in the Introduction, pages xii–xx.

à [a]   in, to, at, with

abandonner [abɑ̃dɔne]   to abandon

abondant [abɔ̃dɑ̃]   abundant

abord [abɔːr]: **d'—**   first

aborder [abɔrde]   to take up (a subject)

abréviation [abrevjasjɔ̃]*f.*   abbreviation

abriter [abrite]   to shelter

accepter [aksɛpte]   to accept

accident [aksidɑ̃] *m.*   accident

accompagner [akɔ̃paɲe]   to go with, accompany

accomplir [akɔ̃pliːr]   to accomplish, finish, fulfill

accord [akɔːr]: **D'—!**   Right! Agreed!

acheter [aʃte]   to buy

achever [aʃve]   to complete, finish

Achille [aʃil]   Achilles

acteur [aktœːr], **actrice** [aktris]   actor, actress

actif, active [aktif, aktiːv]   active

actuel, –le [aktɥɛl]   present

actuellement [aktɥɛlmɑ̃]   now, today

addition [adisjɔ̃]*f.*   bill, check

admettre [admɛtr]   to admit

admiration [admirasjɔ̃]*f.*   admiration

admirer [admire]   to admire

admission [admisjɔ̃]*f.*   admission

adroit [adrwa]   clever

afin [afɛ̃]: **— de**   so as to; **— que**   so that, in order that

affiche [afiʃ]*f.*   poster

Afrique [afrik]*f.*   Africa

âge [ɑːʒ] *m.*   age

âgé [ɑʒe]   old

agir [aʒiːr]   to act; **s'— de**   to be about, be concerned with

agrandir [agrɑ̃diːr]   to enlarge

agréable [agreabl]   pleasant

aider [ɛde]   to help

ailé [ɛle]   winged

ailleurs [ajœːr]: **d'—**   besides

aimer [ɛme]   to like; **— mieux**   to prefer

aîné [ɛne]   elder, eldest

ainsi [ɛ̃si]   thus, in this way; **— que**   as well as, in the same manner as

air [ɛːr] *m.*   air; **avoir l'—**   to seem; **en plein —**   outdoors

ajouter [aʒute]   to add

Allemagne [almaɲ]*f.*   Germany

allemand [almɑ̃]   German

allemand [almɑ̃] *m.*   German (*language*)

Allemand [almɑ̃] *m.*   German (*person*)

aller [ale]   to go; **— à**   to suit; **s'en —** to go away; **Allez-y!**   Go to it! **Comment allez-vous aujourd'hui?**   How are you today? **Elle ne te va pas bien.**   It doesn't suit you.

allié [alje] *m.*   ally

allier [alje]   to ally; **s'—**   to ally oneself

allusion [alyzjɔ̃]*f.*: **faire —**   to allude

alors [alɔːr]   then; **Zut —!**   Darn!

Alpes [alp]*f. pl.*   Alps

ambassadeur [ɑ̃basadœːr] *m.*   ambassador

ambiance [ɑ̃bjɑ̃ːs]*f.*   surroundings, atmosphere

âme [ɑːm]*f.*   soul

américain [amerikɛ̃]   American

Américain [amerikɛ̃] *m.*   American (*person*)

Amérique [amerik]*f.*   America

ami(e) [ami] *m., f.*   friend

amphithéâtre [ɑ̃fiteɑːtr] *m.*   amphitheater

amuser [amyze] to amuse; **s'—** to have a good time

an [ɑ̃] *m.* year; **l'— mille** the year 1000

ancien, –ne [ɑ̃sjɛ̃, ɑ̃sjɛn] old, former

anglais [ɑ̃glɛ] English

anglais [ɑ̃glɛ] *m.* English (*language*)

Anglais [ɑ̃glɛ] *m.* Englishman

angle [ɑ̃ɪgl] *m.* angle

Angleterre [ɑ̃glətɛɪr]*f.* England

animal [animal] *m.* animal

année [ane]*f.* year; **l'— passée** last year

anniversaire [anivɛrsɛɪr] *m.* birthday, anniversary

annoncer [anɔ̃se] to announce

antique [ɑ̃tik] antique, old-fashioned

antiquité [ɑ̃tikite]*f.* antique

août [u] *m.* August

apercevoir [apɛrsəvwaɪr] to notice

apéritif [aperitif] *m.* apéritif, appetizer (drink)

appartement [apartəmɑ̃] *m.* apartment

appeler [aple] to call; **s'—** to be named, be called

appétissant [apetisɑ̃] tasty, appetizing

appliquer [aplike] to apply

apporter [apɔrte] to bring

apprendre [aprɑ̃ɪdr] to learn

approcher [aprɔʃe]: **s'— (de)** to approach

après [aprɛ] after, afterward; **— avoir . . .** (after) having . . .; **— tout** after all; **d'—** according to; **d'après-guerre** post-war

apr. J.-C. = après Jésus-Christ [aprɛ ʒezykri] A.D.

après-midi [aprɛmidi] *m.* afternoon; **l'—** in the afternoon

Arabe [arab] *m.* Arab

arbre [arbr] *m.* tree

arc [ark] *m.* bow, arch; **arc-boutant** [arbutɑ̃] flying buttress

architecture [arʃitɛktyɪr] *f.* architecture

argent [arʒɑ̃] *m.* money, silver

argenterie [arʒɑ̃tri]*f.* silverware

armoire [armwaɪr]*f.* clothes closet, wardrobe

arrêter [arɛte]: **s'—** to stop

arriver [arive] to arrive, happen

arrondi [arɔ̃di] rounded

art [ar] *m.* art

article [artikl] *m.* article

artiste [artist] *m.* or *f.* artist

ascenseur [asɑ̃sœɪr] *m.* elevator

Asie [azi]*f.* Asia

aspect [aspɛ] *m.* aspect

assemblage [asɑ̃blaɪʒ] *m.* collection

asseoir [aswaɪr] to seat; **s'—** to sit down

assez [ase] enough, rather, quite

assiette [asjɛt]*f.* plate

assistance [asistɑ̃ɪs]*f.* audience

assister [asiste] **à** to be present (at), attend

assurance [asyrɑ̃ɪs]*f.* assurance

assurer [asyre] to assure

Atlantique [atlɑ̃tik] *m.* Atlantic Ocean

attacher [ataʃe] to attach

attaquer [atake] to attack

atteindre [atɛ̃ɪdr] **(à)** to attain, reach

attendre [atɑ̃ɪdr] to wait for, wait; **s'— à** to expect to

attention [atɑ̃sjɔ̃]*f.* attention; **faire —** to pay attention; **Attention!** Look out! Careful!

attirer [atire] to attract; **s'—** to attract each other

auberge [obɛrʒ]*f.* inn

aucun [okœ̃] no, not any

au-dessus de [odsy də] above, over

Auguste [ogyst] Augustus

aujourd'hui [oʒurdɥi] today; **d'— en huit (quinze)** a week (two weeks) from today

auquel [okɛl] to which (one)

aussi [osi] also, and so; **— bien que** as well as; **— . . . que** as . . . as; **tout — . . . que** just as . . . as; **nous —** so do we

aussitôt que [osito kə] as soon as

Australie [ostrali]*f.* Australia

autant [otɑ̃] as many, as much

auteur [otœɪr] *m.* author

auto [oto]*f.* car; **— d'occasion** used car; **en —** by car

automatiquement [otomatikmɑ̃] automatically

automne [otɔn] *m.* fall, autumn
autour de [otur də] around
autre [oːtr] other; — **chose** something else
autrefois [otrəfwa] formerly, once
autrement [otrəmɑ̃] otherwise
avant [avɑ̃] before, (*with neg.*) until; — **de**, — **que** before
av. J.-C. = avant Jésus-Christ [avɑ̃ ʒezykri] B.C.
avec [avɛk] with
avenir [avniːr] *m.* future
aventure [avɑ̃tyːr]*f.* adventure
avenue [avny]*f.* avenue
avertir [avɛrtiːr] to warn
avion [avjɔ̃] *m.* airplane
avis [avi] *m.* notice, warning, opinion; **à mon** — in my opinion
avoir [avwaːr] to have; — **à** to have to, must; — **faim** to be hungry; — **peur** to be afraid; — **raison** to be right; — **sommeil** to be sleepy
avouer [avwe] to admit, confess
avril [avril] *m.* April

bagage [bagaːʒ] *m.* baggage
bain [bɛ̃] *m.* bath
baisser [bɛse]: **se** — to bend down
bal [bal] *m.* ball, dance
balle [bal]*f.* ball
balustrade [balystrad]*f.* railing
banque [bɑ̃ːk]*f.* bank
barbe [barb]*f.* beard
bas, –se [ba, baːs] low
bataille [bataːj]*f.* battle
bateau [bato] *m.* boat, ship
bâtiment [batimɑ̃] *m.* building
bâtir [batiːr] to build
batterie (*f.*) **de cuisine** [batri d kɥizin] kitchen utensils
battre [batr] to beat; **se** — to fight
bavarder [bavarde] to gossip, chat
beau, bel, belle [bo, bɛl, bɛl] beautiful, handsome; **la belle** the beauty (woman); **faire beau** to be nice (weather); **des plus belles** one of the most beautiful
beaucoup [boku] much, many

beauté [bote]*f.* beauty
Belgique [bɛlʒik]*f.* Belgium
berger [bɛrʒe] *m.* shepherd
besoin [bəzwɛ̃] *m.* need; **avoir** — **de** to need
beurre [bœːr] *m.* butter
bibliothécaire [biblɔtekɛːr] *m.* librarian
bibliothèque [biblɔtɛk]*f.* library
bicyclette [bisiklɛt]*f.* bicycle
bien [bjɛ̃] well, quite; — **des** many, lots of; — **entendu** of course; — **installé** comfortable; — **que** although; — **sûr** of course, why surely; **Eh** —, ... Well, ...
bientôt [bjɛ̃to] shortly, soon; **A** — I'll be seeing you
bifteck [biftɛk] *m.* (beef)steak
bijou [biʒu] *m.* jewel
billet [bijɛ] *m.* ticket, note
biographique [biɔgrafik] biographical
bizarre [bizaːr] bizarre
blanc, blanche [blɑ̃, blɑ̃ːʃ] white
blessure [blɛsyːr]*f.* wound
bleu [bløِ] blue
blond [blɔ̃] blond
boire [bwaːr] to drink
bois [bwa] *m.* wood
boîte [bwat]*f.* box, can
bon, –ne [bɔ̃, bɔn] good, kind, fine; **le** — the good man; **Ah** —! How nice!
Bonjour [bɔ̃ʒuːr] Good morning, hello
Bonsoir [bɔ̃swaːr] Good evening
bouche [buʃ]*f.* mouth
bouillir [bujiːr] to boil
bourg [buːr] *m.* burg, fortified village
bourgeois [burʒwa] *m.* middle-class citizen (*formerly, inhabitant of fortified village*)
bouteille [butɛːj]*f.* bottle
boutique [butik]*f.* shop
bras [bra] *m.* arm
brave [braːv] brave, worthy
bref, brève [brɛf, brɛːv] brief
Bretagne [brətaɲ]*f.* Brittany
brièvement [briɛvmɑ̃] briefly
briller [brije] to shine
brique [brik]*f.* brick
brosser [brɔse] to brush

brouillard [brujaːr] *m.* fog
bruit [brɥi] *m.* noise
brusquement [bryskəmã] abruptly
Bruxelles [brysɛl] *f.* Brussels
buffet [byfɛ] *m.* buffet, sideboard
bureau [byro] *m.* desk, office
but [by, byt] *m.* goal, aim

ça (**cela**) [sa, s(ə)la] that; **Comment ça va?** How are you? How are things?
cabinet [kabinɛ] *m.* office
cacher [kaʃe] to hide
cadeau [kado] *m.* gift, present
café [kafe] *m.* coffee, café; — **au lait** coffee with milk
cahier [kaje] *m.* notebook
calendrier [kalãdrje] *m.* calendar
camion [kamjɔ̃] *m.* truck
campagne [kãpaɲ] *f.* country; **à la —** in (to) the country
canadien, –ne [kanadjɛ̃, kanadjɛn] Canadian
canal [kanal] *m.* canal
capital [kapital] important
capitale [kapital] *f.* capital
car [kaːr] for
caractériser [karakterize] to characterize
caractéristique [karakteristik] typical
carré [kare] square
carte [kart] *f.* map, card, menu; **à la —** from the menu
cas [kɑ] *m.* case; **en tout —** anyhow
casser [kɑse] to break
casserole [kasrɔl] *f.* saucepan
cathédral [katedral] *f.* cathedral
cauchemar [koʃmar] *m.* nightmare
cause [koːz] *f.* cause; **à — de** because of
causer [koze] to chat
cave [kaːv] *f.* cellar
ce [sə], **cet, cette** [sɛt] this, that; *pl.* **ces** [se] these, those
ce [sə] it, this, that; **C'est ça** That's it; **c'est-à-dire** that is, that is to say; **c'est que** it's that, it's just that; **— que** what (*obj.*); **— qui** what (*subj.*)
ceci [səsi] this
céder [sede] to give up, yield

cela (**ça**) [s(ə)la, sa] that
célèbre [selɛːbr] famous
celui, celle [səlɥi, sɛl] the one (that); **celui-ci** this one, the latter; **celui-là** that one, the former; *pl.* **ceux, celles** [sø, sɛl] the ones (those)
cent [sã] one hundred
centaine [sãtɛn] *f.* about a hundred
centigrade [sãtigrad] centigrade
centime [sãtim] *m.* *1/100 of a franc*
centre [sãːtr] *m.* center
cependant [s(ə)pãdã] however
cercle [sɛrkl] *m.* club, circle; **demi-cercle** semi-circle
cérémonie [seremɔni] *f.* ceremony
certain [sɛrtɛ̃] certain
certes [sɛrt] to be sure
cesser [sese] to stop, cease
chacun [ʃakœ̃] each one
chaise [ʃɛːz] *f.* chair
chambre [ʃãːbr] *f.* room, bedroom; **— à coucher** bedroom
champ [ʃã] *m.* field
change [ʃãːʒ] *m.* exchange
changer [ʃãʒe] to change
chant [ʃã] *m.* singing, melody
chanter [ʃãte] to sing
chapeau [ʃapo] *m.* hat
chapelle [ʃapɛl] *f.* chapel
chaque [ʃak] each
chat [ʃa] *m.* cat
château [ʃato] *m.* castle; **— fort** fortress castle
chaud [ʃo] hot, warm
chauve [ʃoːv] bald
chef [ʃɛf] *m.* chief, chieftain; **chef-d'œuvre** [ʃɛdœːvr] masterpiece
chemin [ʃ(ə)mɛ̃] *m.* road; **le bon —** the right road
cheminée [ʃ(ə)mine] *f.* chimney, fireplace
cher, chère [ʃɛːr] dear, expensive
chercher [ʃɛrʃe] to look for, seek
cheval [ʃ(ə)val] *m.* horse
cheveux [ʃ(ə)vø] *m. pl.* hair
chez [ʃe]: **— des amis** at the home of friends; **— Jacques** at, to Jim's; **je vais chez moi** I am going home

chic [ʃik] nice, swell
chien [ʃjɛ̃] *m.* dog
chimie [ʃimi] *f.* chemistry
chimiste [ʃimist] *m.* chemist
chocolat [ʃɔkɔla] *m.* chocolate, hot chocolate
choisir [ʃwaziːr] to choose
choix [ʃwa] *m.* choice; **au —** at your choice
chose [ʃoːz] *f.* thing
chrétien [kretjɛ̃] Christian
christianisme [kristjanism] *m.* Christianity
ciment [simɑ̃] *m.* cement
cinéma [sinema] *m.* movies
cinq [sɛ̃k, sɛ̃] five
cinquante [sɛ̃kɑ̃ːt] fifty
citadelle [sitadɛl] *f.* citadel
cité [site] *f.* old city
citer [site] to name, cite, quote
clair [klɛːr] clear, bright
clarinette [klarinɛt] *f.* clarinet
classe [klɑːs] *f.* class
classique [klasik] classical
clef [kle] *f.* key (*often written* **clé**)
clergé [klɛrʒe] *m.* clergy
client [kliɑ̃] *m.* client
climat [klima] *m.* climate
cloche [klɔʃ] *f.* bell
cœur [kœːr] *m.* heart
coin [kwɛ̃] *m.* corner
colis [kɔli] *m.* package
collection [kɔlɛksjɔ̃] *f.* collection
collège [kɔlɛːʒ] *m.* *secondary school*
combien [kɔ̃bjɛ̃] how much
commander [kɔmɑ̃de] to order, command
comme [kɔm] like, as; **— je serais heureux!** how happy I would be!
commencement [kɔmɑ̃smɑ̃] *m.* beginning
commencer [kɔmɑ̃se] to begin
comment [kɔmɑ̃] how; **Comment!** What! What's that!
commenter [kɔmɑ̃te] to comment on, explain
commun [kɔmœ̃]: **en —** in common
comparer [kɔ̃pare] to compare
complet [kɔ̃plɛ] *m.* suit
complètement [kɔ̃plɛtmɑ̃] completely

complexe [kɔ̃plɛks] complex
compliqué [kɔ̃plike] complicated
comprendre [kɔ̃prɑ̃ːdr] to understand
compte [kɔ̃t]: **le — rendu** report, account; **tout — fait** everything considered, all in all
compter [kɔ̃te] to expect to, count
concierge [kɔ̃sjɛrʒ] *m.* superintendent, caretaker
condition [kɔ̃disjɔ̃] *f.* condition
conditionnel [kɔ̃disjɔnɛl] conditional; **— passé** conditional perfect
conduire [kɔ̃dɥiːr] to drive, lead
conduite [kɔ̃dɥit] *f.* behavior; **— intérieure** sedan
conférence [kɔ̃ferɑ̃ːs] *f.* lecture
confier [kɔ̃fje] to entrust
conflit [kɔ̃fli] *m.* conflict
confondre [kɔ̃fɔ̃ːdr] to confuse
congélation [kɔ̃ʒelasjɔ̃] *f.* freezing
conjuguer [kɔ̃ʒyge] to conjugate
connaissance [kɔnɛsɑ̃ːs] *f.* knowledge, acquaintance; *pl.* knowledge
connaître [kɔnɛːtr] to know, be acquainted with
conquérant [kɔ̃kerɑ̃] *m.* conqueror
consacrer [kɔ̃sakre] to devote
conseil [kɔ̃sɛːj] *m.* advice
conseiller [kɔ̃sɛje] to advise
conséquent [kɔ̃sekɑ̃]: **par —** consequently
conservation [kɔ̃sɛrvasjɔ̃] *f.* conservation
conserver [kɔ̃sɛrve] to preserve, maintain
considérable [kɔ̃siderabl] considerable
considérer [kɔ̃sidere] to consider
consister [kɔ̃siste] to consist
conspirer [kɔ̃spire] to conspire
constitution [kɔ̃stitysjɔ̃] *f.* constitution
construction [kɔ̃stryksjɔ̃] *f.* construction
construire [kɔ̃strɥiːr] to build, construct
contagieux [kɔ̃taʒjø] contagious
contemporain [kɔ̃tɑ̃pɔrɛ̃] contemporary
contenir [kɔ̃tniːr] to contain
content [kɔ̃tɑ̃] glad
continuer [kɔ̃tinɥe] to continue
contraire [kɔ̃trɛːr] contrary, opposite; **au —** on the contrary
contre [kɔ̃ːtr] against

convenir [kɔ̃vniːr]   to be suitable, be appropriate
conversation [kɔ̃vɛrsasjɔ̃] *f.*   conversation
corriger [kɔriʒe]   to correct
côte [koːt] *f.*   coast
côté [kote] *m.*   side;   **à** — **de** beside, by; **à ses** —**s** to him, to his side;   **de l'autre** — on the other side, on the other hand;   **d'un** — on one side, on the one hand
coucher [kuʃe]   to put to bed;   **se** — to go to bed, lie down
coucher [kuʃe] *m.*:   — **du soleil** sunset
couler [kule]   to flow
couleur [kulœːr] *f.*   color
couloir [kulwaːr] *m.*   corridor
coupable [kupabl]   guilty
couper [kupe]   to cut
cour [kuːr] *f.*   court, yard
courage [kuraːʒ] *m.*   courage
couramment [kuramã]   currently
courant [kurã] *m.*   current
courir [kuriːr]   to run
courrier [kurje] *m.*   mail
cours [kuːr] *m.*   course;   **faire un** — to give a lecture
court [kuːr]   short
cousin [kuzɛ̃] *m.*   cousin
couteau [kuto] *m.*   knife
coûter [kute]   to cost
couvert [kuvɛːr] *m.*   table setting;   **mettre le** — to set the table
couverture [kuvɛrtyːr] *f.*   cover
couvrir [kuvriːr]   to cover
craie [krɛ] *f.*   chalk
craindre [krɛ̃ːdr]   to fear
cravate [kravat] *f.*   necktie
crayon [krɛjɔ̃] *m.*   pencil
créer [kree]   to create
creux, creuse [krø, krøːz]   hollow
cri [kri] *m.*   cry
critique [kritik] *m.*   critic
croire [krwaːr]   to believe;   **je crois que oui** I believe so
croisade [krwazad] *f.*   crusade
croissant [krwasã] *m.*   breakfast roll
cruel, –le [krɥɛl]   cruel
cuiller [kɥijɛːr] *f.*   spoon

cuire [kɥiːr]   to cook;   **bien cuit** well done
cuisine [kɥizin] *f.*   cooking, kitchen;   **faire la** — to cook
cuisinière [kɥizinjɛːr] *f.*   stove, cook
cultiver [kyltive]   to cultivate
curieux, curieuse [kyrjø, kyrjøːz]   curious

dame [dam] *f.*   lady
dans [dã]   in, into;   *(time expressions)* at the end of
danseur, danseuse [dãsœːr, dãsøːz]   dancer
date [dat] *f.*   date
dater [date]   to date
davantage [davãtaːʒ]   more
de [də]   of, from;   **de ... en ...** from ... to ..., from one ... to another
debout [dəbu]   standing, upright
début [deby] *m.*   beginning
décembre [desãːbr] *m.*   December
décider [deside]   to decide
décimale [desimal] *f.*   decimal
décor [dekɔːr] *m.*   décor
décorer [dekɔre]   to decorate
découverte [dekuvɛrt] *f.*   discovery
découvrir [dekuvriːr]   to discover
décrire [dekriːr]   to describe
déesse [deɛs] *f.*   goddess
défaire [defɛːr]:   **se** — **de** to get rid of
défilé [defile] *m.*   parade
degré [dəgre] *m.*   degree
dehors [dəɔːr]   outside, outdoors
déjà [deʒa]   already
déjeuner [deʒœne]   to have lunch
déjeuner [deʒœne] *m.*   lunch;   **petit** — breakfast
délicieux [delisjø]   delicious
demain [dəmɛ̃]   tomorrow;   **A** —! See you tomorrow!   — **soir** tomorrow night;   **de** — **en huit** a week from tomorrow
demande [d(ə)mãːd] *f.*   request
demander [d(ə)mãde]   to ask, ask for;   **se** — to wonder
démarrer [demare]   to start *(vehicle)*
demeurer [dəmœre]   to live, reside
demi, –e [dəmi]   half;   **une demi-heure** half an hour;   **... et demi(e)** half past ...

demoiselle [dəmwazɛl]*f.* young lady

dent [dɑ̃]*f.* tooth

dentelle [dɑ̃tɛl]*f.* lace

département [departmɑ̃] *m.* *political division in France*

dépasser [depɑse] to surpass

dépêcher [depɛʃe]: **se —** to hurry

depuis [dəpɥi] since; **— combien de temps?** how long? **— quand?** how long? since when?

déranger [derɑ̃ʒe]: **se —** to trouble oneself

dernier, dernière [dɛrnje, dɛrnjɛr] last

derrière [dɛrjɛr] behind; **par —** in the back

dès [dɛ] since; **— que** as soon as

désagréable [dezagreabl] unpleasant, disagreeable

descendant [desɑ̃dɑ̃] *m.* descendant

descendre [desɑ̃dr] to go down

description [dɛskripsjɔ̃]*f.* description

désigner [deziɲe] to designate

désir [deziːr] *m.* desire

désirer [dezire] to wish, desire

désordre [dezɔrdr] *m.* confusion

dessert [desɛːr] *m.* dessert

dessiner [desine] to draw

dessus [dəsy] on it, on top

détaché [detaʃe] detached, separate

détail [detaːj] *m.* detail; **en —** in detail

déterminer [detɛrmine] to determine

détruire [detrɥiːr] to destroy

deux [dø] two

devancer [dəvɑ̃se] to anticipate

devant [dəvɑ̃] in front of

développement [devlɔpmɑ̃] *m.* development

devenir [dəvniːr] to become

deviner [dəvine] to guess, figure out

devoir [dəvwaːr] to owe, ought

devoir [dəvwaːr] *m.* assignment, homework

dictée [dikte]*f.* dictation

dictionnaire [diksjɔnɛːr] *m.* dictionary

Dieu [djø] *m.* God

différence [diferɑ̃ːs]*f.* difference

difficile [difisil] hard, difficult

difficulté [difikylte]*f.* trouble, difficulty

diligent [diliʒɑ̃] diligent

dimanche [dimɑ̃ːʃ] *m.* Sunday; **le —** Sundays

diminuer [diminɥe] to diminish

dîner [dine] to have dinner, dine

dîner [dine] *m.* dinner

dire [diːr] to say, tell; **Dis donc!** Say!

direction [dirɛksjɔ̃]*f.* direction

disparaître [disparɛːtr] to disappear

disque [disk] *m.* record

distraction [distraksjɔ̃]*f.* amusement, recreation

distraitement [distrɛtmɑ̃] absent-mindedly

distribuer [distribɥe] to distribute

dit [di] called

divan [divɑ̃] *m.* sofa

divers [divɛːr] diverse, varied

diviser [divize] to divide; **se —** to be divided

dix [dis, di, diːz] ten

dix-huit [dizɥit, dizɥi] eighteen

dix-neuf [diznœf] nineteen

dix-sept [disɛt] seventeen

dizaine [dizɛn]*f.* about ten

document [dɔkymɑ̃] *m.* document

doigt [dwa] *m.* finger

dollar [dɔlaːr] *m.* dollar

dôme [doːm] *m.* dome

dominant [dɔminɑ̃] dominant

dommage [dɔmaːʒ] too bad, a pity

donc [dɔ̃k] then, therefore

donner [dɔne] to give; **— sur** to open on, look out on; **se — du mal** to take trouble

dont [dɔ̃] of whom, of which, whose

dormir [dɔrmiːr] to sleep

doute [dut] *m.* doubt; **sans —** no doubt, doubtless

douter [dute] to doubt

doux, douce [du, dus] sweet, mild

douzaine [duzɛn]*f.* about twelve, a dozen

douze [duːz] twelve

droit [drwa] right, straight

duc [dyk] *m.* duke

duquel [dykɛl] of which

dur [dyːr] hard

durer [dyre] to last, endure

eau [o]*f.* water; — **courante** running water

ébullition [ebylisjɔ̃]*f.* boiling

écho [eko] *m.* echo

éclairer [eklɛre] to light, illuminate

école [ekɔl]*f.* school; **à l'—** at (to, in) school

écouter [ekute] to listen

écrire [ekriːr] to write

édifice [edifis] *m.* edifice

éducation [edykasjɔ̃]*f.* education

effet [ɛfɛ] *m.* effect; **en —** in fact

égal [egal] equal; **ça m'est égal** I don't care, it's all the same to me

église [egliːz]*f.* church

électricité [elɛktrisite]*f.* electricity

électrique [elɛktrik] electric

élégant [elegɑ̃] elegant

élève [elɛːv] *m. or f.* pupil, student

embarrasser [ɑ̃barase] to embarrass

embrasser [ɑ̃brase] to kiss, embrace

empêcher [ɑ̃peʃe] to prevent

empereur [ɑ̃prœːr] *m.* emperor

empire [ɑ̃piːr]*f.* empire

employer [ɑ̃plwaje] to use

emprunter [ɑ̃prœ̃te] to borrow

en [ɑ̃] in, to, while

en [ɑ̃] some, any, of it, of them, from it (them), away

enceinte [ɑ̃sɛ̃ːt]*f.* enclosure, wall

encore [ɑ̃kɔːr] yet, still, again; — **un(e)** another; — **plus fort** all the more, all the stronger; — **une fois** once more

encre [ɑ̃ːkr]*f.* ink

endormir [ɑ̃dɔrmiːr]: **s'—** to fall asleep

endroit [ɑ̃drwa] *m.* place, spot

énergie [enɛrʒi]*f.* energy

enfance [ɑ̃fɑ̃ːs]*f.* childhood

enfant [ɑ̃fɑ̃] *m. or f.* child

enfin [ɑ̃fɛ̃] finally, at last

engager [ɑ̃gaʒe] to engage, use

ennemi [ɛnmi] *m.* enemy

ennuyer [ɑ̃nɥije] to bore, annoy; **s'—** to be bored, become weary

enseigner [ɑ̃seɲe] to teach

ensemble [ɑ̃sɑ̃ːbl] together

ensemble [ɑ̃sɑ̃ːbl] *m.* ensemble, total

ensuite [ɑ̃sɥit] then, next

entendre [ɑ̃tɑ̃ːdr] to hear; **s'—** to agree; — **dire que** to hear that; — **parler de** to hear about

enterrer [ɑ̃tere] to bury

entier, entière [ɑ̃tje, ɑ̃tjɛːr] whole, entire

entourer [ɑ̃ture] to surround

entre [ɑ̃ːtr] between, among

entrée [ɑ̃tre]*f.* entrance; **porte d'—** front door

entrer [ɑ̃tre] to enter

envahir [ɑ̃vaiːr] to invade

envers [ɑ̃vɛːr] *m.* reverse; **à l'—** upside down

envie [ɑ̃vi]: **avoir — de** to feel like, want to

environ [ɑ̃virɔ̃] around

envoyer [ɑ̃vwaje] to send

épais, –se [epɛ, epɛs] thick

époque [epɔk]*f.* time, period

ériger [eriʒe] to erect

erreur [ɛrœːr]: **par —** by mistake

érudit [erydi] learned, erudite

escalier [ɛskalje] *m.* stairway

Espagne [ɛspaɲ]*f.* Spain

espèce [ɛspɛs]*f.* kind, type

espérer [ɛspere] to hope

esprit [ɛspri] *m.* mind, spirit, wit

essai [ɛsɛ] *m.* try

essayer [ɛsɛje] to try, try on

essuyer [ɛsɥije] to wipe, erase

est [ɛst] *m.* east

et [e] and

établissement [etablismɑ̃] *m.* place, establishment

étage [etaːʒ] *m.* floor, story

étape [etap]*f.* step, stage (*of development*), stop (*on journey*)

état [eta] *m.* state

États-Unis [etazyni] *m. pl.* United States

été [ete] *m.* summer; **en —** in the summer

éteindre [etɛ̃ːdr] to put out the light

étendu [etɑ̃dy] extensive

étoile [etwal]*f.* star

étonner [etɔne] to astonish, astound

étranger, étrangère [etrɑ̃ʒe, etrɑ̃ʒɛːr] foreign

étranger [etrãʒe] *m.* stranger, foreigner

être [ɛːtr] to be; — **à** to belong to; **Soit!** [swat] All right, O.K.

étude [etyd] *f.* study; **faire des —s** to study, go to school

étudiant, –e [etydjã, etydjãːt] student

étudier [etydje] to study

Europe [œrɔp] *f.* Europe

événement [evɛnmã] *m.* event

évidemment [evidamã] evidently

évident [evidã] evident

évier [evje] *m.* sink

éviter [evite] to avoid

exact [ɛgzakt] correct

exactement [ɛgzaktəmã] exactly

examen [ɛgzamɛ̃] *m.* examination

examiner [ɛgzamine] to examine

excellent [ɛksɛlã] excellent

excursion [ɛkskyrsjɔ̃] *f.* trip, excursion

excuser [ɛkskyze] to excuse; **s'—** to apologize

exemplaire [ɛgzãmplɛːr] *m.* copy, volume

exemple [ɛgzãːpl] *m.* example; **Ça par —!** What do you know! **par —** for example

exercice [ɛgzɛrsis] *m.* exercise

exister [ɛgziste] to exist

exorbitant [ɛgzɔrbitã] exorbitant

expliquer [ɛksplike] to explain

exploit [ɛksplwa] *m.* exploit

exposition [ɛkspozisjɔ̃] *f.* exposition

expression [ɛksprɛsjɔ̃] *f.* expression

exprimer [ɛksprime] to express

extérieur [ɛksterjœːr] *m.* exterior, outside

extraordinaire [ɛkstraɔrdinɛːr] extraordinary

extrême [ɛkstrɛːm] extreme

extrêmement [ɛkstrɛmmã] extremely

fâché [faʃe] angry, sorry

facile [fasil] easy

facilement [fasilmã] easily

façon [fasɔ̃] *f.* way; **de la même —** in the same way; **sans —** informal, free and easy

faillir [fajiːr] to narrowly miss, come near (doing something)

faire [fɛːr] to do, make; (*of weather*) — **du brouillard, (très) chaud, frais, (bien) froid, mauvais, du soleil, sombre, du vent** to be foggy, (very) hot, cool, (quite) cold, bad, sunny, dark, windy; **ça ne fait rien** that makes no difference; **Ça ne vous fait rien?** Do you mind?

fait [fɛ] *m.* fact; **au —** by the way, that reminds me; **en —** in fact

falloir [falwaːr] to be necessary; **il faut** it is necessary, one must; **comme il faut** proper, properly

fameux, fameuse [famø, famøːz] famous; **Fameux!** Wonderful!

familier, familière [familje, familjɛːr] familiar

famille [famiːj] *f.* family

fatigué [fatige] tired

faubourg [fobuːr] *m.* outskirts, suburb

faute [fot] *f.* mistake

fauteuil [fotœːj] *m.* armchair, easy chair

faux, fausse [fo, fos] false, wrong

femme [fam] *f.* woman, wife

fenêtre [fənɛːtr] *f.* window

féodalité [feɔdalite] *f.* feudalism

fer [fɛːr] *m.* iron

ferme [fɛrm] *f.* farm

fermer [fɛrme] to close, shut; **— à clef** to lock

fête [fɛːt] *f.* feast, holiday

feu [fø] *m.* fire

feuilleter [fœjte] to leaf through

février [fevrje] *m.* February

fier [fje]: **se — à** to trust

fil [fil] *m.* wire, thread

fille [fiːj] *f.* daughter, girl; **jeune —** young lady, girl

film [film] *m.* movie, film

fils [fis] *m.* son

fin [fɛ̃] *f.* end

finir [finiːr] to finish; **— par** to end up (by); **je n'en finirais pas** I would never finish

fixé [fikse] fixed, stuck

fixer [fikse] to fix, attach

flatter [flate] to flatter

fleur [flœːr] *f.* flower

fleuve [flœːv] *m.* river

foi [fwa]: **Ma —!** My goodness!

fois [fwa] *f.* time; **encore une —** once more, again; **une — pour toutes** once and for all

fond [fɔ̃] *m.* back, bottom, end; **à —** thoroughly

fondateur [fɔ̃datœːr] *m.* founder

fondement [fɔ̃dmã] *m.* foundation, base

fonder [fɔ̃de] to found

force [fɔrs] *f.* force

forêt [fɔrɛ] *f.* forest

forme [fɔrm] *f.* form

former [fɔrme] to form

formidable [fɔrmidabl] formidable

fort [fɔːr] strong, very

fortement [fɔrtmã] strongly

fortifié [fɔrtifje] fortified

fossé [fɔse] *m.* ditch, moat

fou, folle [fu, fɔl] mad

fourchette [furʃɛt] *f.* fork

fourneau [furno] *m.* stove

fournir [furniːr] to provide, furnish

frais, fraîche [frɛ, frɛːʃ] cool, fresh

franc, franche [frã, frãːʃ] frank

franc [frã] *m.* franc

français [frãsɛ] French; **à la française** in the French manner, French style

français [frãsɛ] *m.* French (*language*)

Français, -e [frãsɛ, frãsɛːz] Frenchman, Frenchwoman

franchement [frãʃmã] frankly

franco-prussien [frãkoprysjɛ̃] Franco-Prussian

frapper [frape] to strike, impress, knock

frère [frɛːr] *m.* brother

frigidaire [friʒidɛːr] *m.* refrigerator

frire [friːr] to fry

froid [frwa] cold

fromage [frɔmaːʒ] *m.* cheese

fruit [frɥi] *m.* fruit

fumer [fyme] to smoke

futur [fytyːr] *m.* future

galerie [galri] *f.* gallery

gant [gã] *m.* glove

garçon [garsɔ̃] *m.* boy

garder [garde] to keep, guard

gare [gaːr] *f.* station

gâteau [gato] *m.* cake

gauche [goːʃ] left

gaulois [golwa] Gallic

Gaulois [golwa] *m.* Gaul (*person*)

gaz [gaz] *m.* gas

geler [ʒəle] to freeze

général [ʒeneral] *m.* general; **en —** in general

génie [ʒeni] *m.* genius

gens [ʒã] *m. pl.* people

gentil, –le [ʒãti, ʒãtiːj] nice

géographie [ʒeɔgrafi] *f.* geography

germanique [ʒɛrmanik] Germanic

glace [glas] *f.* mirror

glisser [glise] to slip, slide

glorifier [glɔrifje] to glorify

gond [gɔ̃] *m.* hinge

gothique [gɔtik] Gothic

gouvernement [guvɛrnəmã] *m.* government

grain [grɛ̃] *m.* grain

grammaire [grammɛːr] *f.* grammar

gramme [gram] *m.* gram

grand [grã] large, tall; **le —** the tall fellow

grandeur [grãdœːr] *f.* size

grand-mère [grãmɛːr] *f.* grandmother

grand-père [grãpɛːr] *m.* grandfather

gratis [gratis] gratis

gratte-ciel [gratsjɛl] *m.* skyscraper

gratuit [gratɥi] free

gris [gri] gray

gros, –se [gro, groːs] fat, big, bulky

guerre [gɛːr] *f.* war; **— mondiale** world war

guimbarde [gɛ̃bard] *f.* jalopy

habiller [abije] to clothe, dress; **s'—** to get dressed, dress

habiter [abite] to dwell, live

habitant [abitã] *m.* resident, inhabitant

habitude [abityːd] *f.* habit; **d'—** usually

*****hardi** [ardi] bold, tough

*****haricot** [ariko] *m.* bean; **—s verts** string beans

harmonie [armɔni] *f.* harmony
*hasard [azaɪr] *m.*: par — by chance
*haut [o] high
*hauteur [otœɪr] *f.* height
*Haye: la — [la ɛ] The Hague
hein? [ɛ̃] eh?
herbe [ɛrb] *f.* grass
héritage [eritaɪʒ] *m.* heritage
*héros [ero] *m.* hero
hésiter [ezite] to hesitate
heure [œɪr] *f.* hour, o'clock; à l'— on time; à l'— qu'il est at the present time; de bonne — early; Quelle — est-il? What time is it?
heureusement [œrøzmɑ̃] fortunately
heureux, heureuse [œrø, œrøɪz] happy
*heurter [œrte]: se — to bump oneself
hier [jɛɪr] yesterday; — soir last night
histoire [istwaɪr] *f.* history, story
historien [istɔrjɛ̃] *m.* historian
hiver [ivɛɪr] *m.* winter
homme [ɔm] *m.* man
honneur [ɔnœɪr] *m.* honor
honorer [ɔnɔre] to honor
hôpital [opital] *m.* hospital
*hors de [ɔr də] outside, outside of
*hors-d'œuvre [ɔrdœɪvr] *m.* appetizer
hôtel [otɛl] *m.* hotel
*huit [ɥit, ɥi] eight; — jours a week
*huitaine [ɥitɛn] *f.* about eight days, a week
humain [ymɛ̃] human

ici [isi] here; par — this way
idéal [ideal] ideal
idée [ide] *f.* idea
ignorance [iɲɔrɑ̃ɪs] *f.* ignorance
île [iɪl] *f.* island
illustration [illystrasjɔ̃] *f.* illustration, picture
illustre [illystr] famous, illustrious
illustrer [illystre] to illustrate
image [imaɪʒ] *f.* picture
imaginer [imaʒine]: s'— to imagine
immédiatement [immedjatmɑ̃] immediately

immeuble [immœɪbl] *m.* house, building, property
imparfait [ɛ̃parfɛ] imperfect
impatient [ɛ̃pasjɑ̃] impatient
importance [ɛ̃pɔrtɑ̃ɪs] *f.* importance
important [ɛ̃pɔrtɑ̃] important
impossible [ɛ̃pɔsibl] impossible
impression [ɛ̃prɛsjɔ̃] *f.* impression
impressionnisme [ɛ̃prɛsjɔnizm] *m.* impressionism
impressionniste [ɛ̃prɛsjɔnist] *m.* impressionist
inachevé [inaʃve] unfinished
incident [ɛ̃sidɑ̃] *m.* incident
Indien [ɛ̃djɛ̃] *m.* Indian
indiquer [ɛ̃dike] to indicate
individuellement [ɛ̃dividɥɛlmɑ̃] individually
inévitable [inevitabl] inevitable
infanterie [ɛ̃fɑ̃tri] *f.* infantry
infini [ɛ̃fini] infinite
infinitif [ɛ̃finitif] *m.* infinitive
influence [ɛ̃flɥɑ̃ɪs] *f.* influence
ingéniosité [ɛ̃ʒenjɔzite] *f.* ingenuity
inquiétude [ɛ̃kjetyd] *f.* worry
insister [ɛ̃siste] to insist
instruction [ɛ̃stryksjɔ̃] *f.* instruction, education
intact [ɛ̃takt] intact
intensité [ɛ̃tɑ̃site] *f.* intensity
intention [ɛ̃tɑ̃sjɔ̃]: avoir l'— de to mean to, intend to
intéressant [ɛ̃terɛsɑ̃] interesting
intéresser [ɛ̃terɛse] to interest; s'— à to be interested in
intérêt [ɛ̃terɛ] *m.* interest
intérieur [ɛ̃terjœɪr] *m.* interior
interroger [ɛ̃terɔʒe] to question
intriguer [ɛ̃trige] to intrigue, fascinate
inutile [inytil] useless
invasion [ɛ̃vazjɔ̃] *f.* invasion
inventeur [ɛ̃vɑ̃tœɪr] *m.* inventor
invitation [ɛ̃vitasjɔ̃] *f.* invitation
inviter [ɛ̃vite] to invite
Irlande [irlɑ̃ɪd] *f.* Ireland
Italie [itali] *f.* Italy
italien, −ne [italjɛ̃, italjɛn] Italian

jamais [ʒamɛ] never

jambe [ʒãːb]*f.* leg

jambon [ʒãbɔ̃]*m.* ham

janvier [ʒãvje]*m.* January

Japon [ʒapɔ̃]*m.* Japan

jardin [ʒardɛ̃]*m.* garden; — **potager** vegetable garden

jeter [ʒəte, ʒte] to throw; **se —** to empty (*of river*); — **un coup d'œil** to glance

jeudi [ʒØdi]*m.* Thursday

jeune [ʒœn] young

Joconde [ʒɔkɔ̃ːd]*f.* Mona Lisa

joindre [ʒwɛ̃dr] to join

joli [ʒɔli] pretty

jouer [ʒwe] to play

jour [ʒuːr]*m.* day; **un —** some day, one day

journal [ʒurnal]*m.* newspaper

journée [ʒurne]*f.* day (*duration stressed*)

joyeux, joyeuse [ʒwajØ, ʒwajØːz] merry

juge [ʒyːʒ]*m.* judge

juillet [ʒɥijɛ]*m.* July

juin [ʒɥɛ̃]*m.* June

Jules César [ʒyl sezaːr] Julius Caesar

jurer [ʒyre] to swear

jusqu'à [ʒyska] up to, until; — **ce que** until

juste [ʒyst] just, exact, right

justice [ʒystis]*f.* justice

kilogramme [kilɔgram]*m.* kilogram

là [la] there; **là-bas** over there, down there

laisser [lɛse] to let, allow, leave; — **tomber** to drop

lait [lɛ]*m.* milk

laitue [lɛty]*f.* lettuce

lampe [lãːp]*f.* lamp

langue [lãːg]*f.* tongue, language

langueur [lãgœːr]*f.* listlessness

large [larʒ] wide, broad

Larousse [larus]*m.* *French dictionary*

latin [latɛ̃]*m.* Latin (*language*)

laver [lave] to wash; **se —** to wash oneself, wash up; **se — les mains** to wash one's hands

leçon [ləsɔ̃]*f.* lesson

lecture [lɛktyːr]*f.* reading

légume [legym]*m.* vegetable

lendemain [lãdmɛ̃]*m.* next day

lent [lã] slow

lequel, laquelle, lesquels, lesquelles [ləkɛl, lakɛl, lekɛl, lekɛl] which, which one(s)

lettre [lɛtr]*f.* letter

lever [ləve] to lift, raise; **se —** to get up

lever [ləve]*m.*: — **de soleil** sunrise

liaison [ljezɔ̃]*f.* linking, joining

libre [libr] free

lierre [ljɛːr]*m.* ivy

lieu [ljØ]*m.* place; **au — de** instead of; **avoir —** to take place

linge [lɛ̃ːʒ]*m.* linen

lire [liːr] to read

Lisbonne [lizbɔn]*f.* Lisbon

liste [list]*f.* list

lit [li]*m.* bed

littérature [literatyːr]*f.* literature

livre [liːvr]*m.* book

livre [liːvr]*f.* pound

livrer [livre] to deliver

loi [lwa]*f.* law

loin [lwɛ̃] far

Londres [lɔ̃ːdr]*m.* London

long, longue [lɔ̃, lɔ̃ːg] long; **de — en large** up and down

longtemps [lɔ̃tã] a long time

longuement [lɔ̃gmã] at length

lorsque [lɔrsk(ə)] when

louer [lwe, lue] to rent, hire

lourd [luːr] heavy

Louvre [luːvr]*m.* *Paris museum*

lumière [lymjɛːr]*f.* light

lundi [lœdi]*m.* Monday

lunettes [lynɛt]*f. pl.* glasses

lustre [lystr]*m.* chandelier

lycée [lise]*m.* *secondary school*

Lyon [ljɔ̃]*m.* Lyons

machin [maʃɛ̃]*m.* gadget, thingamajig

machine [maʃin]*f.* machine, car; — **à écrire** typewriter; — **à laver** washing machine

madame [madam]*f.* Mrs. *(abbr.* **Mme;** *pl.* **mesdames)**

mademoiselle [madmwazɛl]*f.* Miss *(abbr.* **Mlle;** *pl.* **mesdemoiselles)**

magasin [magazɛ̃] *m.* store

magnifique [maɲifik] magnificent

mai [mɛ] *m.* May

main [mɛ̃]*f.* hand; **à la —** in one's hand

maintenant [mɛ̃tnɑ̃] now

mais [mɛ] but

maison [mɛzɔ̃]*f.* house, home

mal [mal] *m.* harm, evil; **avoir — à la tête** to have a headache; **se faire —** to hurt oneself

mal [mal] badly, poorly; **— comprendre, — entendre** to misunderstand

malade [malad] sick, ill

maladie [maladi]*f.* illness, disease

malgré [malgre] in spite of

malheureux, malheureuse [malœr∅, malœr∅ːz] unhappy, unfortunate

maman [mamɑ̃]*f.* Mom, mother

Manche: la — [la mɑ̃ːʃ] English Channel

manger [mɑ̃ʒe] to eat; **— au prix fixe** to order a set meal

manière [manjɛːr]*f.* manner

manquer [mɑ̃ke] to miss; **— de** to fail to

marchand [marʃɑ̃] *m.* dealer, salesman

marche [marʃ]*f.* step *(of stair)*

marché [marʃe] *m.* market; **bon —** low-priced, reasonable; **faire le —** to shop

marcher [marʃe] to walk, work *(of mechanisms)*

mardi [mardi] *m.* Tuesday

mars [mars] *m.* March

Marseille [marsɛːj]*f.* Marseilles

masseur, masseuse [masœːr, mas∅ːz] *m.,f.* masseur, masseuse

maternel, –le [matɛrnɛl] maternal

mathématicien [matematisjɛ̃] *m.* mathematician

Mathusalem [matyzalɛm] *m.* Methuselah

matière [matjɛːr]*f.* matter, subject

matin [matɛ̃] *m.* morning; **le —** in the morning; **du —** A.M.

mauvais [mɔvɛ] bad, wrong

méchant [meʃɑ̃] naughty, wicked

médecin [medsɛ̃] *m.* doctor

médecine [medsin]*f.* medicine

médiéval [medjeval] medieval

médiocrement [medjɔkrəmɑ̃] moderately

meilleur [mɛjœːr] better; **le —** best

membre [mɑ̃ːbr] *m.* member

même [mɛːm] same, even; **-même** -self

mémoire [memwaːr]*f.* memory

mener [məne] to lead

menu [məny] *m.* menu

mer [mɛːr]*f.* sea; **au bord de la —** at the seashore

merci [mɛrsi] thank you

mercredi [mɛrkrədi] *m.* Wednesday

mère [mɛːr]*f.* mother

mesure [məzyːr]*f.* measure; **à — que** as, in proportion as

mesurer [məzyre] to measure

méthode [metɔd]*f.* method

métrique [metrik] metric

métro [metro] *m.* *Paris subway*

mettre [mɛtr] to put, put on; **— fin à** to end, put an end to; **se —** to stand; **se — à** to begin to; **se — en colère** to get angry; **se — en route** to set off, start out

meuble [mœːbl] *m.* piece of furniture; *pl.* furniture

Mexique [mɛksik] *m.* Mexico

midi [midi] *m.* noon; **le Midi** the South *(of France)*

mieux [mj∅] better; **faire de son —** to do one's best

mil [mil] thousand *(for eleventh-century dates)*

milieu [milj∅] *m.* middle, midst

militaire [militɛːr] military

mille [mil] thousand

milliard [miljaːr] *m.* billion

millier [milje] about a thousand; **des —s** thousands

million [miljɔ̃] *m.* million

minuit [minɥi] *m.* midnight

minute [minyt]*f.* minute

modèle [mɔdɛl] *m.* model

moderne [mɔdern] modern

moindre [mwɛ̃dr] least

moins [mwɛ̃] minus, less, fewer; **à — que**

unless; **au —** at least; **de — en —** less and less; **le —** least; **— ... —** the less ... the less

mois [mwɑ] *m.* month

moitié [mwatje]*f.* half; **à — terminé** half-finished

moment [mɔmɑ̃] *m.* moment; **à ce —** at that moment; **en ce —** at the moment, now

monarque [mɔnark] *m.* monarch

monétaire [mɔnetɛɪr] monetary

monde [mɔ̃ːd] *m.* world; **beaucoup de —** a lot of people; **tout le —** everybody

monotone [mɔnɔtɔn] monotonous

monsieur [məsjø] *m.* Sir, mister, gentleman (*abbr.* **M.;** *pl.* **messieurs**)

monter [mɔ̃te] to go up

montre [mɔ̃ːtr]*f.* watch

montrer [mɔ̃tre] to show

monument [mɔnymɑ̃] *m.* monument

morceau [mɔrso] *m.* piece

mort [mɔɪr]*f.* death

mot [mo] *m.* word

moteur [mɔtœɪr] *m.* motor

mouchoir [muʃwaɪr] *m.* handkerchief

mourir [muriɪr] to die

mouvement [muvmɑ̃] *m.* movement

moyen [mwajɛ̃]: **le Moyen Age** Middle Ages

multiplié [myltiplie] multiplied

mur [myɪr] *m.* wall

musée [myze] *m.* museum

musique [myzik]*f.* music

nager [naʒe] to swim

naître [nɛɪtr] to be born

Napoléon [napɔleɔ̃] *m.* Napoleon

nappe [nap]*f.* tablecloth

nature [natyɪr]*f.* nature; **— morte** still life

naturel, –le [natyrɛl] natural

ne [nə] not; {**ne ... aucun(e)** not any, no ...; **ne ... guère** hardly, scarcely; **ne ... jamais** never; **ne ... ni ... ni** neither ... nor; **ne ... nul(le)** not any, no ...; **ne ... pas du tout** not at all; **ne ... personne** nobody; **ne ... plus** no more, no longer; **ne ... point** not a bit; **ne ... que** only, nothing but; **ne ... rien** nothing; **n'est-ce pas?** isn't it?

néanmoins [neɑ̃mwɛ̃] nevertheless

nécessaire [nesɛsɛɪr] necessary

nécessité [nesɛsite]*f.* necessity

négliger [negliʒe] to neglect

neiger [nɛʒe] to snow

néo-classique [neɔklasik] neo-classical

net, –te [nɛt] neat, clear

neuf [nœf] nine

neuf, neuve [nœf, nœɪv] new; **tout neuf** brand-new

New-York [njujɔrk] *m.* New York

nez [ne] *m.* nose

nièce [njɛs]*f.* niece

n'importe [nɛ̃pɔɪrt] no matter

noblesse [nɔblɛs]*f.* nobility

Noël [nɔɛl] *m.* Christmas

noir [nwaɪr] black

nom [nɔ̃] *m.* name, noun; **changer de —** to change one's name

nombre [nɔ̃ːbr] *m.* number

nommer [nɔme] to name

non [nɔ̃] no; **— pas** not; **— plus** neither

nord [nɔɪr] *m.* north

Normand [nɔrmɑ̃] *m.* Norman

Normandie [nɔrmɑ̃di]*f.* Normandy

nouveau, nouvel, nouvelle [nuvo, nuvɛl] new; **de nouveau, à nouveau** anew, again

Nouvelle-Orléans [nuvɛlɔrleɑ̃]*f.* New Orleans

novembre [nɔvɑ̃ːbr] *m.* November

nul, –le [nyl] no, not any

numéro [nymero] *m.* number

obélisque [ɔbelisk] *m.* obelisk

objet [ɔbʒɛ] *m.* object

observer [ɔpsɛrve] to observe

occidental [ɔksidɑ̃tal] western

occupé [ɔkype] busy

occuper [ɔkype]: **s' — de** to occupy oneself in, to take charge of

octobre [ɔktɔbr] *m.* October

œil [œɪj] *m.* eye

œuf [œf] *m.* egg
œuvre [œɪvr] *f.* work
officiel [ɔfisjɛl] official
officier [ɔfisje] *m.* officer
offrir [ɔfriːr] to offer
oiseau [wazo] *m.* bird
on [ɔ̃] one, they, people, you, we
oncle [ɔ̃ːkl] *m.* uncle
onze [ɔ̃ːz] eleven
opéra [ɔpera] *m.* opera
opinion [ɔpinjɔ̃] *f.* opinion
or [ɔːr] *m.* gold
ordinaire [ɔrdinɛːr] ordinary; **d'—** usually
ordonner [ɔrdɔne] to order
oreille [ɔrɛɪj] *f.* ear
organiser [ɔrganize] to organize
oriental [ɔrjɑ̃tal] eastern
originalité [ɔriʒinalite] *f.* originality
origine [ɔriʒin] *f.* origin
oser [oze] to dare
ôter [ote] to remove, take off
ou [u] or; **— bien** or else; **—...—** either ... or
où [u] where
oublier [ublie] to forget
ouest [wɛst] *m.* west
oui [wi] yes
ouvert [uvɛːr] open
ouvrir [uvriːr] to open; **s'— sur** to open on, look out on

page [paɪʒ] *f.* page
pain [pɛ̃] *m.* bread; **petit —** roll
paix [pɛ] *f.* peace
palais [palɛ] *m.* palace
panier [panje] *m.* basket
papa [papa] *m.* Dad
papier [papje] *m.* paper
paquebot [pakbo] *m.* boat, steamer
paquet [pakɛ] *m.* package
par [par] by, through
parce que [pars(ə)kə] because
parcourir [parkuriːr] to run through
pareil, -le [parɛɪj] similar
parents [parɑ̃] *m. pl.* parents, relatives
paresseux, paresseuse [parɛsø, parɛsøːz] lazy

parfaitement [parfɛtmɑ̃] exactly, precisely
parfois [parfwa] sometimes
parfum [parfœ̃] *m.* perfume
Parisien, -ne [parizjɛ̃, parizjɛn] Parisian (*person*)
parler [parle] to speak
parmi [parmi] among
parole [parɔl] *f.* word
participe [partisip] *m.* participle; **— passé** past participle; **— présent** present participle
participer [partisipe] to participate
particulier [partikylje] special
partie [parti] *f.* part
partir [partiːr] to leave
partout [partu] everywhere
pas [pɑ] not; **— mal de** quite a lot, quite a few
passant [pɑsɑ̃]: **en —** on the way
passé [pɑse] *m.* past; **— composé** past indefinite (*tense*) **— du subjonctif** past subjunctive
passer [pɑse] to pass, go through, spend; **se —** to happen, occur; **se — de** to do without, get along without; **— à côté de** to pass by
passion [pɑsjɔ̃]: **avoir la — de** to be crazy about
patience [pasjɑ̃ːs] *f.* patience
patrie [patri] *f.* homeland, native land
patron [patrɔ̃] *m.* boss
pauvre [poːvr] poor, unfortunate
payer [pɛje] to pay, pay for
pays [pei] *m.* country
Pays-Bas [peibɑ] *m. pl.* Netherlands
paysage [peizaɪʒ] *m.* landscape
peindre [pɛ̃ːdr] to paint
peine [pɛn] *f.* pain, trouble; **à —** scarcely, hardly
peintre [pɛ̃ːtr] *m.* painter
peinture [pɛ̃tyːr] *f.* painting
pelouse [pəluːz] *f.* lawn
pendant [pɑ̃dɑ̃] during; **— que** while
pendule [pɑ̃dyl] *f.* clock
pénétrer [penetre] to penetrate
pensée [pɑ̃se] *f.* thought

penser [pãse] to think; **Pensez donc!** Just think!

perdre [pɛrdr] to lose

père [pɛɪr] *m.* father

perfectionner [pɛrfɛksjɔne] to perfect, improve

période [perjɔd]*f.* period

permettre [pɛrmɛtr] to allow

personne [pɛrsɔn] *m.* nobody

personne [pɛrsɔn]*f.* person; **en —** in person

peser [pəze] to weigh

petit [pəti] small; **le —** the little one

petit-fils [pətifis] *m.* grandson

peu [pø] little, few; **un — de** a little; **— à —** little by little

peuple [pœpl] *m.* common people, masses

peut-être [pøtɛɪtr] perhaps

philosophe [filɔzɔf] *m.* philosopher

philosophie [filɔzɔfi]*f.* philosophy

photo [fɔto]*f.* photograph

photographie [fɔtografi]*f.* photography, photograph

phrase [frɑɪz]*f.* sentence

physique [fizik] physical

piano [pjano] *m.* piano

Picardie [pikardi]*f.* Picardy

pièce [pjɛs]*f.* room, play, piece

pied [pje] *m.* foot; **à —** on foot

pierre [pjɛɪr]*f.* stone

pire [piɪr] worse; **le —** worst

pistolet [pistɔlɛ] *m.* pistol

pittoresque [pitɔrɛsk] picturesque

placard [plakaɪr] *m.* cupboard

place [plas]*f.* place, seat, square (*of city*)

placer [plase] to place, put

plage [plaɪʒ]*f.* beach

plaindre [plɛ̃ɪdr] to pity

plaire [plɛɪr] to please; **s'il vous plaît** please

plaisanterie [plɛzɑ̃tri]*f.* joke

plaisir [plɛziɪr] *m.* pleasure; **avec —** gladly; **faire — à** to please

plan [plɑ̃] *m.* plan

planche [plɑ̃ɪʃ]*f.* board

plaque [plak]*f.* plate

plat [pla] *m.* dish

plein [plɛ̃] full; **— de monde** crowded

pleurer [plœre] to weep, cry

pleuvoir [plœvwaɪr] to rain

pluie [plɥi]*f.* rain

plupart [plypaɪr]: **la — de** most; **pour la —** for the most part

plus [ply] more; **le —** most; **— de** more than; **— ... —** the more ... the more; **— que** more than; **— tard** later; **de — en —** more and more

plus-que-parfait [plyskəparfɛ] *m.* pluperfect

plusieurs [plyzjœɪr] several; **— fois par semaine (jour)** several times a week (day)

plutôt [plyto] rather

poche [pɔʃ]*f.* pocket

poêle [pwal]*f.* frying pan

poème [pɔɛm] *m.* poem

poids [pwɑ] *m.* weight

point [pwɛ̃] *m.* point, period (*punct.*)

pointu [pwɛ̃ty] pointed

poisson [pwasɔ̃] *m.* fish

poivre [pwaɪvr] *m.* pepper

poli [pɔli] polite

pomme [pɔm]*f.* apple; **— de terre** potato; **—s frites** French-fried potatoes

pont [pɔ̃] *m.* bridge

port de mer [pɔɪr d mɛɪr] *m.* seaport

porte [pɔrt]*f.* door; **porte-fenêtre** French door

porter [pɔrte] to carry, wear; **— sur** to deal with

portrait [pɔrtrɛ] *m.* portrait

poser [pɔze] to put, ask

positif, positive [pɔzitif, pɔzitiɪv] positive

possible [pɔsibl] possible

poste [pɔst] *m.* job, position

poste [pɔst]*f.* post office

poule [puɪl]*f.* hen

pour [puɪr] for, to, in order to; **— que** so that, in order that

pourquoi [purkwa] why

poursuivre [pursɥiɪvr] to continue, pursue

pourtant [purtɑ̃] however, but

pouvoir [puvwaɪr] to be able to

pratique [pratik] practical

précieux, précieuse [presjø, presjøɪz] precious

précis [presi] exact, sharp; ... **heure(s) précise(s)** ... o'clock sharp

précisément [presizemɑ̃] exactly

préféré [prefere] favorite

préférer [prefere] to prefer

préhistorique [preistɔrik] prehistoric

premier, première [prəmje, prəmjɛɪr] first; **le — étage** second floor

prendre [prɑ̃ɪdr] to take, catch; **— au sérieux** to take seriously; **— un verre** to have a drink

préparation [preparasjɔ̃]*f.* preparation

préparer [prepare] to prepare

près [prɛ] near; **— de** near, nearly; **de —** from up close, closely

présent [prezɑ̃] *m.* present; **à —** right now, at the present time; **à — que** now that

présenter [prezɑ̃te] to present; **se —** to introduce oneself; **— ses respects** to give one's regards

président [prezidɑ̃] *m.* president

presque [prɛsk] nearly, almost

prêt [prɛ] ready

prêter [prɛte] to lend

preuve [prœɪv]: **faire — de** to show

prier [prie] to pray, beg, request; **je te (vous) prie** please

primitif, primitive [primitif, primitiɪv] primitive

principalement [prɛ̃sipalmɑ̃] principally

printemps [prɛ̃tɑ̃] *m.* spring; **au —** in the spring

prisonnier [prizɔnje] *m.* prisoner

prix [pri] *m.* prize, price

probable [prɔbabl] probable; **il est peu —** it is very unlikely

problème [prɔblɛm] *m.* problem

prochain [prɔʃɛ̃] next

production [prɔdyksjɔ̃]*f.* production, product

produire [prɔdɥiɪr] to produce

professeur [prɔfɛsœɪr] *m.* professor

profond [prɔfɔ̃] deep, profound

progrès [prɔgrɛ] *m.* progress; **faire des —** to improve, make progress

projection [prɔʒɛksjɔ̃]*f.* photographic slide

promenade [prɔmnad]*f.* walk; **faire une —** to take a walk (ride)

promener [prɔmne]: **se —** to take a walk, ride

promesse [prɔmɛs]*f.* promise

promettre [prɔmɛtr] to promise

prononciation [prɔnɔ̃sjasjɔ̃]*f.* pronunciation

propos [prɔpo]: **à —** by the way; **à — de** speaking of

propre [prɔpr] own

proprement dit [prɔprəmɑ̃ di] actual, properly so-called

propriétaire [prɔprietɛɪr] *m. or f.* owner, proprietor

protéger [prɔteʒe]: **se —** to protect oneself

prouver [pruve] to prove

province [prɔvɛ̃ɪs]*f.* province

provision [prɔvizjɔ̃]*f.* provision

prudent [prydɑ̃] careful

public, publique [pyblik] public

puis [pɥi] then, next

puis (*alt. form of* **peux**) [pɥi] (I) can

puisque [pɥisk(ə)] since, as

puissance [pɥisɑ̃ɪs]*f.* strength

puissant [pɥisɑ̃] powerful

puits [pɥi] *m.* well

quand [kɑ̃] when; **— même** even so

quant à [kɑ̃ta] as for, as to

quantité de [kɑ̃tite də] a lot of, lots of

quarantaine [karɑ̃tɛn]*f.* about forty

quarante [karɑ̃ɪt] forty

quart [kaɪr] *m.* quarter; **un — d'heure** quarter of an hour

quartier [kartje] *m.* section, quarter

quatorze [katɔrz] fourteen

quatre [katr] four

quatre-vingt-dix [katrəvɛ̃dis] ninety

quatre-vingts [katrəvɛ̃] eighty

que [kə] what, that, which; **Qu'il est...!** How ... it is! **Qu'est-ce que ...?** What ...? **Qu'est-ce que c'est? Qu'est-ce?**

What is it? **Qu'est-ce que c'est que ça?**
What is that?

Québec [kebɛk] *m.* Quebec

quel, quels, quelle, quelles [kɛl] what, which, who; **Quel dommage!** Too bad! **Quel jour sommes-nous?** What is the date? **Quel temps fait-il?** What's the weather? **Quelle heure est-il?** What time is it?

quelque [kɛlk(ə)] some; —s a few, some; — **chose** something; — **part** somewhere

quelquefois [kɛlkəfwa] sometimes, once in a while

quelqu'un [kɛlkœ̃] someone; **quelques-uns, quelques-unes** some

question [kɛstjɔ̃] *f.* question

questionnaire [kɛstjɔnɛɪr] *m.* questionnaire

queue [kø] *f.* tail, handle

qui [ki] who, which; **à —?** whose?

quinzaine [kɛ̃zɛn] *f.* two weeks, fortnight

quinze [kɛ̃ɪz] fifteen; — **jours** two weeks

quitter [kite] to leave

quoi [kwa] what; **A — sert-il?** What is it (used) for?

quoique [kwak(ə)] although

race [ras] *f.* race

raconter [rakɔ̃te] to tell, relate

radium [radjɔm] *m.* radium

rage [raɪʒ] *f.* rabies

raison [rɛzɔ̃] *f.* reason

ramasser [ramase] to pick up, collect, gather

rang [rɑ̃] *m.* row, rank

ranger [rɑ̃ʒe] to arrange, put away, store

rapide [rapid] fast

rappeler [raple] to remind; **se —** to remember, recall

rapport [rapɔɪr]: **par — à** in comparison to

rapporter [rapɔrte] to bring back

rare [raɪr] rare

rayonner [rɛjɔne] to shine out, spread out

réalité [realite]: **en —** in reality

récent [resɑ̃] recent

recevoir [rəsəvwaɪr] to receive

recherche [rəʃɛrʃ] *f.* search; —s research

récit [resi] *m.* narrative, recitation

réciter [resite] to recite

recommander [rəkɔmɑ̃de] to recommend

reconnaissance [rəkɔnɛsɑ̃ɪs] *f.* gratitude

reconnaître [rəkɔnɛɪtr] to recognize

reconstruire [rəkɔ̃strɥiɪr] to reconstruct, rebuild

réduire [redɥiɪr] to reduce

réellement [reɛlmɑ̃] actually

réfléchir [refleʃiɪr] to reflect, think

réflexion [reflɛksjɔ̃] *f.* reflection

refuser [rəfyze] to refuse

regarder [rəgarde] to look, watch

région [reʒjɔ̃] *f.* region

regret [rəgrɛ] *m.* regret

regrettable [rəgrɛtabl] regrettable

regretter [rəgrɛte] to regret

reine [rɛn] *f.* queen

rejeter [rəʒ(ə)te] to reject

rejoindre [rəʒwɛ̃ɪdr] to meet, join

religion [rəliʒjɔ̃] *f.* religion

relique [rəlik] *f.* relic

remarquable [rəmarkabl] remarkable

remarquer [rəmarke] to notice, note

remonter [rəmɔ̃te] to go up (*a river*)

remplacer [rɑ̃plase] to replace

remplir [rɑ̃pliɪr] to fill

remuer [rəmɥe] to move, stir

Renaissance [rənɛsɑ̃ɪs] *f.* Renaissance

renaître [rənɛɪtr] to revive

rencontrer [rɑ̃kɔ̃tre] to meet, encounter

rendez-vous [rɑ̃devu] *m.* appointment (*business or social*)

rendre [rɑ̃ɪdr] to give back, render, make; **se — compte de** to realize

renouveler [rənuvle] to renew

renseignement [rɑ̃sɛɲmɑ̃] *m.* piece of information; —s information; **se faire donner des —s** to get some information

rentrer [rɑ̃tre] to go back, come back

repas [rəpɑ] *m.* meal

répéter [repete] to repeat

répliquer [replike] to reply, retort

répondre [repɔ̃ɪdr] to reply, answer

réponse [repɔ̃ɪs] *f.* answer, reply

repos [rəpo] *m.* rest

repousser [rəpuse]: **se —** to repel each other

représenter [rəprezɑ̃te] to represent

reproduction [rəprɔdyksjɔ̃]*f.* reproduction

république [repyblik]*f.* republic

résister [reziste] to resist

respecter [rɛspɛkte] to respect

ressemblance [rəsɑ̃blɑ̃s]*f.* resemblance

restaurant [rɛstɔrɑ̃] *m.* restaurant

restaurer [rɛstɔre] to restore

reste [rɛst] *m.* relic; **—s** remains

rester [rɛste] to stay, remain; **il me reste . . .** I have . . . left

résultat [rezylta] *m.* result

résumer [rezyme] to sum up, summarize

résurrection [rezyrɛksjɔ̃]*f.* resurrection

retard [rətaɪr]: **en —** late

retenir [rətniɪr] to keep, retain

retour [rətuɪr] *m.* return; **de —** back

retourner [rəturne] to go back

réunion [reynjɔ̃]*f.* meeting

réussir [reysiɪr] to succeed

revanche [rəvɑ̃ːʃ]*f.* revenge

réveiller [revɛje] to awaken, wake

revenir [rəvniɪr] to come back

rêver [rɛve] to dream

révision [revizjɔ̃]*f.* review

revoir [rəvwaɪr] to see again; **au —** so long, good-bye

Révolution [revɔlysjɔ̃]*f.* (French) Revolution

revue [rəvy]*f.* magazine

rez-de-chaussée [redʃose] *m.* ground floor

Richard Cœur de Lion [riʃaɪr kœɪrdəljɔ̃] Richard the Lion-Hearted

riche [riʃ] rich

richesse [riʃes]*f.* wealth

rire [riɪr] to laugh

risque [risk] *m.* risk

risquer [riske]: **se —** to take a risk, venture

rival [rival] *m.* rival

rivaliser [rivalize]: **— avec** to rival

rivière [rivjɛɪr]*f.* river (tributary)

robe [rɔb]*f.* dress

roi [rwa] *m.* king

romain [rɔmɛ̃] Roman

Romain [rɔmɛ̃] *m.* Roman (*person*)

roman, –e [rɔmɑ̃, rɔman] Romance, Romanesque

roman [rɔmɑ̃] *m.* novel

rosbif [rɔsbif] *m.* roast beef

rose [roːz] pink

rose [roːz]*f.* rose

rouler [rule] to roll

route [rut]*f.* road, route

roux, rousse [ru, rus] red (*of hair*)

royaume [rwajoɪm] *m.* kingdom

rue [ry]*f.* street, road

ruine [rɥin]: **en —s** in ruins

Russie [rysi]*f.* Russia

sacré [sakre] sacred

sage [saɪʒ] wise

saignant [sɛɲɑ̃] rare (*of meat*)

saint [sɛ̃] holy; **Saint** Saint (*with a proper name*)

salade [salad]*f.* salad

sale [sal] dirty

salé [sale] salty, salted

salle [sal]*f.* room, hall; **— de classe** classroom; **— à manger** dining room; **— de bains** bathroom

salon [salɔ̃] *m.* living room

samedi [samdi] *m.* Saturday

sans [sɑ̃] without; **Sans blague!** No kidding!

sauf [sof] except

sauter [sote] to leap

sauvage [sovaɪʒ] wild

savant [savɑ̃] *m.* scientist, learned man

savoir [savwaɪr] to know, know how to

saxon [saksɔ̃] Saxon

scandinave [skɑ̃dinaɪv] Scandinavian

science [sjɑ̃ɪs]*f.* science

scientifique [sjɑ̃tifik] scientific

sculpteur [skyltœɪr] *m.* sculptor

sec, sèche [sɛk, sɛʃ] dry

second [səgɔ̃] second

secondaire [səgɔ̃dɛɪr] secondary

secrétaire [səkretɛɪr] *m. or f.* secretary

seize [sɛɪz] sixteen

séjour [seʒuɪr] *m.* stay

sel [sɛl] *m.* salt

selon [s(ə)lɔ̃] according to

semaine [s(ə)mɛn] *f.* week

semblant [sɑ̃blɑ̃]: **faire — de** to pretend to

sembler [sɑ̃ble] to seem, appear to be

sens [sɑ̃s] *m.* meaning, sense, direction; **bon —** common sense

sensible [sɑ̃sibl] sensitive

sentiment [sɑ̃timɑ̃] *m.* feeling

sentir [sɑ̃tiːr]: **se —** to feel

séparé [separe] separate

sept [sɛt] seven

septembre [sɛptɑ̃ːbr] *m.* September

sergent [sɛrʒɑ̃] *m.* sergeant

série [seri] *f.* series

serment [sɛrmɑ̃] *m.* oath

serpenter [sɛrpɑ̃te] to wind, twist

service [sɛrvis] *m.* favor

serviette [sɛrvjɛt] *f.* napkin

servir [sɛrviːr] to serve; **— de** to serve as; **se — de** to use

seul [sœl] only, single, sole, lonely

seulement [sœlmɑ̃] only

si [si] if, so, yes (*in contradiction of negative*)

siècle [sjɛkl] *m.* century

signifier [siɲifje] to mean, signify

simple [sɛ̃pl] simple

simplicité [sɛ̃plisite] *f.* simplicity

singulier [sɛ̃gylje] *m.* singular

sinon [sinɔ̃] if not, otherwise

situation [sitɥasjɔ̃] *f.* situation, location

situé [sitɥe] situated

six [sis, si, siːz] six

sœur [sœːr] *f.* sister

soie [swa] *f.* silk

soigner [swaɲe] to look after, care for

soigneusement [swaɲøzmɑ̃] carefully

soir [swaːr] *m.* evening; **le —** in the evening; **du —** P.M.

soirée [sware] *f.* party, evening

soixante [swasɑ̃ːt] sixty

soixante-dix [swasɑ̃tdis] seventy

soldat [sɔlda] *m.* soldier

soleil [sɔlɛj] *m.* sun

solide [sɔlid] solid

solidité [sɔlidite] *f.* solidity

sombre [sɔ̃ːbr] dark

sommeillant [sɔmɛjɑ̃] drowsy

sommet [sɔmɛ] *m.* summit

sonner [sɔne] to strike, sound, ring

sonnette [sɔnɛt] *f.* bell, buzzer

Sorbonne [sɔrbɔn] *f. college of University of Paris*

sorte [sɔrt] *f.* sort

sortir [sɔrtiːr] to go out

sou [su] *m. old piece of money*

souci [susi] *m.* anxiety, worry

souffrir [sufriːr] to suffer

soulier [sulje] *m.* shoe

source [surs] *f.* source

sous [su] under

souvenir [suvniːr]: **se — de** to remember

souvent [suvɑ̃] often

spectacle [spɛktakl] *m.* spectacle, show

splendide [splɑ̃did] splendid

statue [staty] *f.* statue

stupide [stypid] stupid

style [stil] *m.* style

stylo [stilo] *m.* pen

sud [syd] *m.* south

suffire [syfiːr] to suffice, be enough

Suisse [sɥis] *f.* Switzerland

suite [sɥit]: **et ainsi de —** and so on; **tout de —** immediately, right away

suivant [sɥivɑ̃] following, next; **— que** according to whether

suivre [sɥiːvr] to follow; **— un cours** to take a course

sujet [syʒɛ] *m.* subject; **au — de** about, concerning

supposer [sypoze] to suppose

sur [syr] on, upon

sûr [syːr] sure

surpris [syrpri] surprised

surtout [syrtu] especially

survenir [syrvəniːr] to arrive unexpectedly

survivre [syrviːvr] to survive

sympathie [sɛ̃pati] *f.* sympathy

système [sistɛm] *m.* system

table [tabl] *f.* table; **— à thé** tea table

tableau [tablo] *m.* picture, painting; **— noir** blackboard

tabouret [taburɛ] *m.* stool
tâche [tɑːʃ]*f.* task, job
talent [talɑ̃] *m.* talent
tandis que [tɑ̃di(s)kə] while
tant [tɑ̃] so much, so many; **Tant mieux!**
So much the better!
tante [tɑ̃ːt]*f.* aunt
tard [taːr] late
tarte [tart]*f.* pie, tart; — **aux fruits**
fruit pie
tas [tɑ] *m.* pile, heap
tasse [tɑːs]*f.* cup; — **à café** coffee cup;
— **de café** cup of coffee
taxi [taksi] *m.* taxi
technique [tɛknik]*f.* technique
tel, –le [tɛl] such; — **que** such as, as
téléphone [telefɔn] *m.* telephone
tellement [tɛlmɑ̃] so
témoin [temwɛ̃] *m.* evidence, witness
température [tɑ̃peratyːr]*f.* temperature
temple [tɑ̃ːpl] *m.* temple
temps [tɑ̃] *m.* tense, time, weather; **à —**
in time; **avec le —** in due time; **de**
— en — from time to time; **en même**
— at the same time; **— primitifs**
principal parts
tenir [təniːr] to hold; **— à** to be anxious
to
terme [tɛrm] *m.* term
terminer [tɛrmine] to end, finish
terre [tɛːr]*f.* ground, dirt, earth; **par —**
on the ground, on the floor; **Terre Sainte**
the Holy Land
tête [tɛːt]*f.* head
thé [te] *m.* tea
théâtre [teɑːtr] *m.* theater
théorie [teɔri]*f.* theory
thermomètre [tɛrmɔmɛtr] *m.* thermometer
Tiens, tiens! [tjɛ̃ tjɛ̃] Well, well! My, my!
tiers [tjɛːr] *m.* third
timide [timid] timid
tirer [tire] to pull, fire, shoot, gather, ex-
tract; **se — d'affaire** to get along, manage
tiroir [tirwaːr] *m.* drawer
tissu [tisy] *m.* fabric, tissue, cloth
titre [tiːtr] *m.* title

toit [twa] *m.* roof
tomate [tɔmat]*f.* tomato
tombeau [tɔ̃bo] *m.* tomb
tomber [tɔ̃be] to fall
ton [tɔ̃] *m.* tone; **d'un —** ... **in a** ...
tone
tôt [to] soon, early
toucher [tuʃe] to touch; **— à sa fin** to
be nearing its end
toujours [tuʒuːr] always, still
tour [tuːr]*f.* tower
tour [tuːr] *m.* turn, tour, trick; **à son —**
in one's turn
touriste [turist] *m.* tourist
tout, –e [tu, tut] (*pl.* **tous, toutes** [tu, tut])
all; **tout à coup** suddenly; **tout à fait**
entirely, absolutely; **tout ce qu'il faut**
voir all there is to see; **tout de même**
even so, just the same; **tout droit** directly, straight; **tout(e) ordinaire** quite
ordinary; **tout près d'ici** very near
here; **tous les deux** both, both of them;
tous les jours every day
tout [tu] *m.* everything; *pl.* **tous** [tus] all
toutefois [tutfwa] nevertheless
traditionnel, –le [tradisjɔnɛl] traditional
traduction [tradyksjɔ̃]*f.* translation
traduire [tradɥiːr] to translate
train [trɛ̃] *m.* train; **en — de** in the act
of, in the process of
traiter [trɛte] to treat
tranquille [trɑ̃kil] calm, peaceful
transformer [trɑ̃sfɔrme] to transform
travail [travaːj] *m.* work; (*pl.* **travaux**
[travo])
travailler [travaje] to work
traversée [travɛrse]*f.* crossing
traverser [travɛrse] to cross
treize [trɛːz] thirteen
trente [trɑ̃ːt] thirty
très [trɛ] very
tribu [triby]*f.* tribe
triomphe [triɔ̃ːf] *m.* triumph
triste [trist] sad
trois [trwa] three
tromper [trɔ̃pe] to deceive; **se —** to be
mistaken

trop [tro] too, too much, too many

trouver [truve] to find; **se —** to be found, be, be located

troyen, –ne [trwajɛ̃, trwajɛn] Trojan

tuer [tɥe] to kill

un, une [œ̃, yn] a, an, one; **les unes sur les autres** on top of each other

unir [yniːr]: **s'—** to unite, combine

université [yniversite] *f.* university

usage [yzaːʒ] *m.* use, usage

ustensile [ystɑ̃sil] *m.* utensil

utile [ytil] useful

utiliser [ytilize] to utilize, use

vacances [vakɑ̃s] *f. pl.* holidays

vaisselle [vɛsɛl] *f.* dishes, china

valeur [valœːr] *f.* value

valoir [valwaːr] to be worth; **— la peine** to be worthwhile, be worth the trouble; **il vaut mieux** it's better, one had better

varié [varje] varied, various

vaste [vast] vast

veille [vɛːj] *f.* eve, day (or night) before

vélo [velo] *m.* bike

vendre [vɑ̃ːdr] to sell

vendredi [vɑ̃drədi] *m.* Friday

venir [vəniːr] to come; **— de** to have just (*done something*)

vent [vɑ̃] *m.* wind

véranda [verɑ̃da] *f.* veranda

verbe [vɛrb] *m.* verb

véritable [veritabl] veritable, true

vérité [verite] *f.* truth

verre [vɛːr] *m.* glass

vers [vɛːr] toward

vert [vɛːr] green

vestibule [vɛstibyl] *m.* vestibule

vestiges [vɛstiːʒ] *m. pl.* vestiges, remains

viande [vjɑ̃ːd] *f.* meat

victoire [viktwaːr] *f.* victory

vide [vid] empty

vie [vi] *f.* life

vieillard [vjɛjaːr] *m.* old man

vieux, vieil, vieille [vjø, vjɛːj, vjɛːj] old; **mon vieux** old man, my lad

village [vilaːʒ] *m.* village

ville [vil] *f.* city, town; **en —** downtown

vin [vɛ̃] *m.* wine

vingt [vɛ̃, vɛ̃t] twenty

vingtaine [vɛ̃tɛn] *f.* about twenty, a score

virgule [virgyl] *f.* comma

visiter [vizite] to visit (*of places only*)

visiteur [vizitœːr] *m.* visitor

vite [vit] quickly, fast

vitrail [vitraːj] *m.* stained-glass window (*pl.* **vitraux**)

vitrine [vitrin] *f.* shop window

vivre [viːvr] to live; **Vive…!** Long live…!

vocabulaire [vɔkabylɛːr] *m.* vocabulary

voici [vwasi] here is, here are

voie [vwa] *f.* way, highway

voilà [vwala] there is, there are; **le —** there it (he) is

voir [vwaːr] to see; **faire —** to show

voisin, –e [vwazɛ̃, vwazin] (*m., f.*) neighbor

voiture [vwatyːr] *f.* car; **— à cheval** horse and carriage

voix [vwa] *f.* voice; **à haute —** aloud

voler [vɔle] to steal, fly

volontiers [vɔlɔ̃tje] gladly

vouloir [vulwaːr] to want; **— dire** to mean; **Veuillez…** Please…

voyage [vwajaːʒ] *m.* trip

voyager [vwajaʒe] to travel

vrai [vrɛ, vre] true; **à — dire** to tell the truth

vraiment [vrɛmɑ̃, vremɑ̃] really

vue [vy] *f.* view

y [i] there; **il y a** there is, there are; **il y a…** …ago

yeux [jø] *m. pl.* eyes (*sing.* œil)

zéro [zero] *m.* zero

English-French Vocabulary

a (an) un, une
able: be — pouvoir
about (*concerning*) de, au sujet de; (*approximately*) à peu près, environ; — thirty
une trentaine
according to selon, d'après
actor acteur *m.*
actress actrice *f.*
admit admettre
afraid: be — craindre, avoir peur
after après
afternoon après-midi *m. or f.*; —s l'après-midi
again encore, encore une fois, de nouveau, à nouveau
ago: ten days — il y a dix jours
agree être d'accord
agreeable agréable
all tout, –e (*pl.* tous, toutes); not at — pas du tout; after — après tout
almost presque; he — fell il a failli tomber
alone seul
along: get — se tirer d'affaire
aloud à haute voix
already déjà
also aussi
although quoique, bien que (*both require subj.*)
always toujours
A.M. du matin
America Amérique *f.*
American américain
amusing amusant
and et; — so aussi (*with inversion*)
angry fâché

announce annoncer
another un(e) autre, encore un(e)
answer réponse *f.*; (*verb*) répondre (à)
any aucun(e), de (*plus def. art.*)
anybody, anyone personne, quelqu'un; not — ne . . . personne
anything rien; — else rien d'autre, quelque chose d'autre
apologize s'excuser
apple pomme *f.*
April avril *m.*
arrive arriver
artiste artiste *m. or f.*
as comme, aussi; — . . . — aussi . . . que; — soon — aussitôt que; — for quant à; — much, — many autant
ask, ask for demander
asleep: fall — s'endormir
assignment devoir *m.*
astonish étonner; be —ed s'étonner
at à; — Delmonico's chez Delmonico; — last enfin; — once tout de suite; not — all pas du tout, ne . . . pas du tout, ne . . . point
attack attaquer
attend assister à
attic grenier *m.*
audience assistance *f.*
August août *m.*
autumn automne *m. or f.*
away: go — s'en aller, partir; right — tout de suite

bad mauvais
ball balle *f.*
basket panier *m.*

bathroom salle (*f.*) de bains
battle bataille *f.*
be être; (*weather*) faire; (*certain personal idioms*) avoir
bean haricot *m.*; **string —s** haricots verts
beard barbe *f.*
beat battre
beautiful beau (bel), belle
because parce que; **— of** à cause de
bed lit *m.*; **go to —** se coucher
bedroom chambre *f.*
beef bœuf *m.*; **roast —** rosbif *m.*; **—steak** bifteck *m.*
before avant; (*with inf.*) avant de; (*with clause*) avant que (+ *subjunctive*)
beg prier
begin (to) commencer (à), se mettre (à)
behind derrière
believe croire
bell (*buzzer type*) sonnette *f.*
belong to être à
beside à côté de
best meilleur, mieux; **do one's —** faire de son mieux
better meilleur, mieux
between entre
bicycle bicyclette *f.*, vélo *m.*
big grand
black noir; **—board** tableau (*m.*) noir
blue bleu
boat bateau *m.*
book livre *m.*
born: be — naître
borrow (from) emprunter (à)
both tous (toutes) les deux
bottle bouteille *f.*
box boîte *f.*
boy garçon *m.*
bread pain *m.*
break casser
bridge pont *m.*
bring apporter; **— back** rapporter
brother frère *m.*
brown brun
brush brosser, se brosser
build bâtir, construire

building bâtiment *m.*
but mais
buy acheter
by par, de; **— the way** à propos, au fait

cake gâteau *m.*
call appeler
calm tranquille
can boîte *f.*
can (*be able*) pouvoir
car auto *f.*, voiture *f.*; **in the —, by —** en auto
card carte *f.*
care: take — of s'occuper de
case cas *m.*; **in any —** en tout cas
castle château *m.*
cat chat *m.*
cathedral cathédrale *f.*
cellar cave *f.*
century siècle *m.*
chair chaise *f.*
chalk craie *f.*
change changer
chat causer
cheap bon marché (*invar.*)
cheese fromage *m.*
child enfant *m. or f.*
choose choisir
Christmas Noël *m.*; **— present** cadeau (*m.*) de Noël
church église *f.*
city ville *f.*; **old —** cité *f.*
class classe *f.*
classroom salle (*f.*) de classe
clean propre
clock pendule *f.*
close fermer
close: up — de près
coast côte *f.*
coffee café *m.*
cold froid
color couleur *f.*
come venir; **— back** revenir
comma virgule *f.*
complete complet, complète
concert concert *m.*

consequently par conséquent
construct construire
contrary: on the — au contraire
cool frais, fraîche; **it is —** il fait frais
correct corriger
cost coûter
count compter
country campagne *f.*; (*nation*) pays *m.*;
  in the — à la campagne
course cours *m.*; **of —** bien entendu
cover couverture *f.*; (*verb*) couvrir
crazy fou, folle
cross traverser
customer client *m.*, cliente *f.*
cut couper

dark sombre; **be —** faire sombre, faire
  nuit
day jour *m.*, journée *f.*; **the next —** le
  lendemain; **every —** tous les jours
dead mort
death mort *f.*
deceive tromper
December décembre *m.*
decide (to) décider (de)
delicious délicieux, –euse
describe décrire
desk bureau *m.*
dessert dessert *m.*
destroy détruire
dictation dictée *f.*
dictionary dictionnaire *m.*
difficult difficile
diligently diligemment
dine dîner
dining room salle (*f.*) à manger
dinner dîner *m.*
dirty sale
discover découvrir
disease maladie *f.*
divide diviser
do faire
dog chien *m.*
door porte *f.*
doubt: no — sans doute
downtown en ville
dozen douzaine *f.*

dress robe *f.*; (*verb*) habiller; **get —ed**
  s'habiller
drink boire
drive conduire; **— out** chasser
during pendant

early de bonne heure
easy facile
eat manger
eight huit
eighteen dix-huit
either: — . . . or ou . . . ou
eleven onze
else: or — ou bien; **anything —** autre
  chose
end fin *f.*, bout *m.*
enemy ennemi *m.*
England Angleterre *f.*
English anglais; (*language*) anglais *m.*
Englishman Anglais *m.*
enough assez
enter entrer (dans)
error erreur *f.*, faute *f.*
especially spécialement, surtout
even même; **— if** même si; **—
  though** quoique (*with subj.*); **— so**
  tout de même, quand même
evening soir *m.*, soirée *f.*; **—s, in the —**
  le soir
ever jamais
every tous, chaque, (toutes) les . . .
everybody tout le monde
everything tout *m.*
evidently évidemment
exactly exactement, précisément, parfaitement; **at — eleven o'clock** à onze
  heures précises
examine examiner
except sauf
expect attendre; **— to** s'attendre à,
  compter
expensive cher, chère
eye œil *m.* (*pl.* yeux)

face figure *f.*, visage *m.*
fact: in — en fait, en effet
fall tomber; **— asleep** s'endormir

family famille *f.*
famous illustre, fameux, célèbre
farm ferme *f.*
fast vite
father père *m.*
favorite favori, –te, préféré
fear craindre, avoir peur
February février *m.*
feel sentir, se sentir; — **like** avoir envie de
few peu de; **a —** quelques
field champ *m.*
fifteen quinze; **eleven —** onze heures et quart
fifty cinquante
fight se battre
film film *m.*
finally enfin
find trouver
finish finir, terminer
first premier, –ière; **the — of March** le premier mars; **(at) —** d'abord
fish poisson *m.*
five cinq
floor: ground — rez-de-chaussée *m.*; **second —** premier étage; **to the —** par terre
flower fleur *f.*
follow suivre
foot pied *m.*; **on —** à pied
for pour, pendant, depuis; (*introducing clause*) car
foreigner étranger *m.*
forget oublier
fork fourchette *f.*
former celui-là (celle-là, ceux-là, celles-là)
forth: and so — et ainsi de suite
fortnight quinzaine *f.*
forty quarante
fountain pen stylo *m.*
four quatre
franc franc *m.*
France France *f.*; **to —, in —** en France
French français; (*language*) français *m.*
Frenchman Français *m.*
Friday vendredi *m.*
friend ami *m.*, amie *f.*

from de; **— ... to ...** de ... en ...
front: in — of devant
fruit fruits *m. pl.*
furniture meubles *m. pl.*
furthermore d'ailleurs, de plus

garden jardin *m.*; **vegetable —** jardin potager
gentleman monsieur *m.* (*pl.* messieurs)
George Georges
German allemand; (*language*) allemand *m.*
Germany Allemagne *f.*
get: — dressed s'habiller; **— up** se lever
girl jeune fille *f.*; **French —** Française *f.*
give donner; **— back** rendre; **— up** céder
glad content
glass verre *m.*
go aller; **— away** s'en aller, partir; **— to bed** se coucher; **— out** sortir
goal but *m.*
good bon, bonne; **Good morning** Bonjour
government gouvernement *m.*
grain grain *m.*
grandfather grand-père *m.*
grandmother grand-mère *f.*
grandson petit-fils *m.*
gratitude reconnaissance *f.*
grave grave
gray gris
great grand; **a — deal** beaucoup
green vert
ground: — floor rez-de-chaussée *m.*; **on the —, to the —** par terre
guess deviner, croire

habit habitude *f.*
hair cheveux *m. pl.*
half demi; moitié *f.*
ham jambon *m.*
hand main *f.*; **in one's —** à la main
handkerchief mouchoir *m.*
handsome beau (bel)
happen arriver

happy heureux, heureuse
hard dur, difficile
hardly à peine, ne . . . guère
hat chapeau *m.*
have avoir; — **to** devoir; — **them see**
qu'ils voient; — **something made**
faire faire quelque chose
he il, lui
headache mal (*m.*) de tête; **have a —**
avoir mal à la tête
hear entendre
heavy lourd
hen poule *f.*
Henry Henri
her la, lui; (*poss.*) son, sa, ses; (*disj.*)
elle
here ici; — **is,** — **are** voici
hers le sien (la sienne, les siens, les siennes)
herself elle-même
hesitate hésiter
high haut
him le, lui; (*disj.*) lui
himself lui-même
his son, sa, ses; (*pron.*) le sien (la sienne,
les siens, les siennes)
hold tenir
holiday jour (*m.*) de fête
home: go — aller chez (+ *pers. pron.*)
homework devoir *m.*
hope espérer
horse cheval *m.*
hotel hôtel *m.*
hour heure *f.*
house maison *f.*
how comment; — **long** depuis quand
(*with pres. or imperf.*), combien de temps;
— **much** combien
however cependant
hungry: be — avoir faim
hurry se dépêcher
hurt faire mal à; — **oneself** se faire mal

I je, moi
idea idée *f.*
if si
ill malade
illustration illustration *f.*

illustrious illustre
immediately tout de suite
important important
in dans, à, en
inhabitant habitant *m.*
ink encre *f.*
inn auberge *f.*
instead of au lieu de
intelligent intelligent
interest intéresser; **be interested in**
s'intéresser à
interesting intéressant
into dans; — **town** en ville
invitation invitation *f.*
iron fer *m.*
it il, elle; le, la; ce (c')

jalopy guimbarde *f.*
James Jacques
Jane (Jean) Jeanne
January janvier *m.*
John Jean
judge juge *m.*
Julius Jules
July juillet *m.*
June juin *m.*
just: to have — (*done something*) venir de
+ *inf.*)

keep garder
kidding: No —! Sans blague!
king roi *m.*
kingdom royaume *m.*
knife couteau *m.*
know savoir, connaître; — **how to**
savoir; **well known** bien connu

lady dame *f.*; (*in direct address*) **ladies**
mesdames; **young ladies** mesde-
moiselles
land terre *f.*
landscape paysage *m.*
language langue *f.*
large grand
last dernier, –ière; — **year** l'année
passée; **at —** enfin; — **night** hier
soir
late tard, en retard

later plus tard
latter celui-ci (celle-ci, ceux-ci, celles-ci)
laugh rire
lawn pelouse *f.*
lead conduire, mener
learn apprendre
least moins, moindre
leave s'en aller, partir; (*go away from*) quitter
left gauche
left: I have only five days — Il ne me reste que cinq jours
leg jambe *f.*
lend prêter
less moins
lesson leçon *f.*
let laisser; —**'s go** allons
letter lettre *f.*
lettuce laitue *f.*
library bibliothèque *f.*
life vie *f.*
lift lever
light lumière *f.*
like aimer; **we would —** nous aimerions, nous voudrions
like: look — avoir l'air de
linen: table — linge (*m.*) de table
listen, listen to écouter
little petit, peu; **a —** un peu
live vivre; (*dwell*) habiter, demeurer; **— in** habiter
living room salon *m.*
locate: be located se trouver
lock fermer ... à clef
London Londres *m.*
long long, longue; **a — time** longtemps; **how —?** depuis quand? combien de temps?
longer: no — ne ... plus
look, look at regarder
look for chercher
lose perdre
lot: a — of beaucoup de, bien des; **lots of** bien des, quantité de
love aimer
low bas, –se
lunch déjeuner *m.*

machine machine *f.*
madam madame *f.*
magazine revue *f.*
mail courrier *m.*
make faire
man homme *m.*
many beaucoup de, bien des; **as —** autant; **so —** tant; **how —?** combien?
map carte *f.*
March mars *m.*
marry épouser
Mary Marie
matter: that doesn't — cela (ça) ne fait rien, n'importe; **no —** n'importe
May mai *m.*
me me, moi
meal repas *m.*
mean vouloir dire, signifier
meanwhile en attendant, cependant
meat viande *f.*
Mediterranean Méditerranée *f.*; **— Sea** Mer (*f.*) Méditerranée
meet rencontrer
Mexico Mexique *m.*
middle milieu *m.*
midnight minuit *m.*
million million *m.*; **a — men** un million d'hommes
mine le mien (la mienne, les miens, les miennes)
minute minute *f.*
Miss mademoiselle (*abbr.* Mlle)
mistake faute *f.*, erreur *f.*
Mona Lisa Joconde *f.*
Monday lundi *m.*
money argent *m.*
month mois *m.*
monument monument *m.*
more plus; **the — ... the —** plus ... plus
morning matin *m.*; **—s, in the —** le matin; **seven o'clock in the —** sept heures du matin
most la plupart des; (*with adj.*) le (la, les) plus
mother mère *f.*
movies cinéma *m.*

Mr. M. (*for* Monsieur)

Mrs. Mme (*for* Madame)

much beaucoup; **as —** autant (de *before noun*); **so —** tant

museum musée *m.*

must devoir, falloir; **you —** il faut; **you — not** il ne faut pas; **he — have forgotten** il a dû oublier

my mon, ma, mes

myself moi-même

name nom *m.*; **my — is** je m'appelle; **What is your —?** Comment vous appelez-vous? (*verb*) nommer, citer

napkin serviette *f.*

naughty méchant

near près de; **is —ing its end** touche à sa fin

nearly presque; **— do something** faillir faire quelque chose

necessary nécessaire; **it is —** il faut

need avoir besoin de

neighbor voisin, voisine

neither: — . . . nor ni . . . ni

never jamais, ne . . . jamais

new nouveau (nouvel), nouvelle

newspaper journal *m.*

next prochain; **— to** à côté de; **the — day** le lendemain

nice gentil, –le; (*weather*) beau

night nuit *f.*; **at —** la nuit; **last —** hier soir; **the — before** la veille

nine neuf

ninety quatre-vingt-dix

no non, aucun(e), nul(le); **— one** personne (ne *with verb*); **— doubt** sans doute

noise bruit *m.*

nor ni

Normandy Normandie *f.*

not pas, ne . . . pas, non pas

notebook cahier *m.*

nothing rien (ne *with verb*)

notice remarquer, apercevoir

November novembre *m.*

now maintenant, à présent, actuellement

o'clock heure(s)

October octobre *m.*

of de; **— course** bien entendu

off: take — ôter

offer offrir

office bureau *m.*, cabinet (*m.*) de travail

often souvent

old vieux (vieil), vieille, âgé

on sur; **— time** à l'heure

once: at — tout de suite

one un, une, on; **a small —** un(e) petit(e)

only seulement, ne . . . que

open ouvert; (*verb*) ouvrir; **— on** donner sur

opinion avis *m.*, opinion *f.*; **in my —** à mon avis

or ou; **— else** ou bien

order ordonner, commander

other autre

ought to (*cond. of* devoir)

our notre, nos

ours le nôtre (la nôtre, les nôtres)

ourselves nous-mêmes

out, outside dehors; **go —** sortir; **put — (*lights*)** éteindre

over au-dessus de; **— there** là-bas

package paquet *m.*, colis *m.*

paint peindre

painter peintre *m.*

painting peinture *f.*

palace palais *m.*

paper papier *m.*

parent parent *m.*

Parisian parisien, –ne; (*noun*) Parisien, –ne

part partie *f.*

pass passer

past passé; **a quarter — ten** dix heures et quart

pay, pay for payer

pen stylo *m.*

pencil crayon *m.*

people gens *m. pl.*; (*common people*) peuple *m.*

perfume parfum *m.*

perhaps peut-être (*with inversion*)

period point *m.*

person personne *f.*

pick up ramasser

picture image *f.*; tableau *m.*

pie tarte *f.*; **fruit —** tarte aux fruits

piece morceau *m.*

pity plaindre; **What a —!** Quel dommage!

place endroit *m.*, lieu *m.*; **take —** avoir lieu; (*verb*) mettre, placer

play jouer

please plaire (à); (**if you**) **—** s'il vous plaît, je vous prie

P.M. de l'après-midi, du soir

pocket poche *f.*

poem poème *m.*

poor pauvre

portrait portrait *m.*

position position *f.*; (*job*) poste *m.*

possible possible

post office poste *f.*

pound livre *f.*

practical pratique

prefer préférer

present (*gift*) cadeau *m.*; (*time*) présent *m.*; (*adj.*) présent

pretend (to) faire semblant (de)

pretty joli

prize prix *m.*

probably probablement

process: in the — of en train de

produce produire

professor professeur *m.*

progress: make — faire des progrès

promise promettre

proprietor propriétaire *m. or f.*

province province *f.*

pupil élève *m. or f.*

put, put on mettre; **put out** (*lights*) éteindre

quarter quart *m.*; **a — past ten** dix heures et quart

question question *f.*; **it is a — of** il s'agit de

quickly vite

quite (*rather*) assez; (*completely*) tout à fait

railing balustrade *f.*

rain pleuvoir; **it —s** il pleut

raise lever

rather assez

reach atteindre

read lire

reading lecture *f.*

ready prêt

really vraiment

reason raison *f.*

recall rappeler; (*to oneself*) se rappeler

receive recevoir

recent récent

recommend recommander

red rouge; (*of hair*) roux, rousse

remain rester

remember se rappeler, se souvenir de

reply réponse *f.*

report compte rendu *m.*

research recherches *f. pl.*

restaurant restaurant *m.*

return rentrer

rich riche

ride: take a — faire une promenade

right: — away tout de suite

ring sonner

river fleuve *m.*

road route *f.*, chemin *m.*

roast beef rosbif *m.*

roll petit pain *m.*

Roman romain; (*noun*) Romain *m.*

Romanic, Romanesque roman

room pièce *f.*; (*large*) salle *f.*; **bed—** chambre *f.*; **dining —** salle (*f.*) à manger

round rond

run courir

sad triste

salad salade *f.*

same même

Saturday samedi *m.*

say dire

scarcely à peine (*with inversion*); ne ... guère

school école *f.*

score vingtaine *f.*

sea mer *f.*
second second, deuxième; — **floor** premier étage
secondhand d'occasion
see voir
sell vendre
send envoyer
sentence phrase *f.*
Septembre septembre *m.*
serious sérieux, –euse; **take —ly**
prendre au sérieux
serve servir; — **as** servir de
set mettre; — **the table** mettre le couvert; — **out** se mettre en route
seven sept
seventeen dix-sept
several plusieurs
sharp: ten o'clock — dix heures précises
she elle
shine briller
shoe soulier *m.*
shop boutique *f.*
short court
should (*cond. of* devoir)
show montrer, faire voir
sickness maladie *f.*
side côté *m.*; **to his —** à ses côtés
signify signifier
silverware argenterie *f.*
sing chanter
sir monsieur
sister sœur *f.*
sit, sit down s'asseoir
situate situer
six six
sixteen seize
sixty soixante
size grandeur *f.*
skyscraper gratte-ciel *m.* (*invar.*)
sleep dormir; **go to —** s'endormir
sleepy: get — avoir sommeil
slide (*photographic*) projection *f.*
slowly lentement
small petit
smell sentir
smile sourire
snow neiger

so si; — **many,** — **much** tant; **and —**
aussi (*with inversion*)
soldier soldat *m.*
some de, de + *art.*; quelque(s); —
day un jour
someone, somebody quelqu'un(e)
something quelque chose
sometimes quelquefois, parfois
son fils *m.*
song chanson *f.*
soon bientôt; **as — as** aussitôt que, dès
que
sorry: be — regretter
Spain Espagne *f.*; **to —** en Espagne
speak parler
spend (*time*) passer
spoon cuiller *f.*, cuillère *f.*
spring printemps *m.*; **in the —** au
printemps
square carré; (*of city*) place *f.*
stairs, stairway escalier *m.*
stand se mettre
start commencer; — **out** se mettre en
route
stay rester
steak bifteck *m.*
step (*of stair*) marche *f.*
still toujours, encore
stone pierre *f.*
stop cesser, s'arrêter
store (*put away*) ranger
storm tempête *f.*
story histoire *f.*
straight droit, tout droit
street rue *f.*; **Racine Street** rue Racine
strike frapper
string beans haricots verts *m. pl.*
strong fort; — **enough** assez fort
student étudiant, étudiante; élève *m. or f.*
study (*office*) cabinet (*m.*) de travail;
(*verb*) étudier
subject sujet *m.*
succeed (**in**) réussir (à)
such tel, telle; —**things** de telles choses;
— **a** un tel, une telle
suddenly tout à coup
suffer souffrir

suit (*verb*) aller (*obj. is indirect*)
summer été *m.*
sun soleil *m.*
Sunday dimanche *m.*
suppose supposer; **be —d to** devoir
survive survivre
swear jurer
swim nager
Switzerland Suisse *f.*
system système *m.*

table table *f.*
take prendre; **— a trip** faire un voyage; **— place** avoir lieu; **— off** ôter
talk (about) parler (de)
tall grand, haut
tea thé *m.*; **—cup** tasse (*f.*) à thé
teach enseigner, apprendre
teacher professeur *m.*
tell dire (*pers. obj. is indirect*); raconter
ten dix
than que, de
that ce (cet), cette; ce (c'); cela (ça); que; **— one** celui-là (celle-là, ceux-là, celles-là)
the le, la, les
their leur, leurs
theirs le leur (la leur, les leurs)
them les, leur; (*disj.*) eux, elles
themselves eux-mêmes, elles-mêmes
then puis, alors, ensuite, donc
there là, y; **— is, — are** voilà, il y a
these (*adj.*) ces; (*pron.*) ceux-ci, celles-ci
they ils, elles; on; (*disj.*) eux, elles
thing chose *f.*
think penser; **—about** penser à; **— of** (*opinion*) penser de
thirteen treize
thirty trente; **ten —** dix heures et demie
this ce (cet), cette; ce (c'); ceci; **— one** celui-ci, celle-ci
thoroughly à fond
those (*adj.*) ces; (*pron.*) ceux-là, celles-là
thousand mille *invar.*), millier *m.*; **several —** plusieurs milliers (de)
three trois
throw jeter

Thursday jeudi *m.*
time temps *m.*; fois *f.*; (*of day*) heure *f.*; **on —** à l'heure; **in —** à temps; **the next —** la prochaine fois; **from — to —** de temps en temps; **What — is it?** Quelle heure est-il?
to à, en, chez, pour; **in order —** pour, afin de
today aujourd'hui
together ensemble (*invar.*)
tomato tomate *f.*
tomorrow demain; **day after —** après-demain; **two weeks from —** de demain en quinze
tonight ce soir
too trop; (*also*) aussi
tooth dent *f.*
tower tour *f.*; **Eiffel Tower** Tour Eiffel
town ville *f.*; **to (in, into) —** en ville
travel voyager
tree arbre *m.*
trip voyage *m.*; (*short*) excursion *f.*
trouble difficulté *f.*, peine *f.*
truth: to tell the — à vrai dire
try, try on essayer
Tuesday mardi *m.*
turn tour *m.*; **in his —** à son tour
twelve douze
twenty vingt
two deux
typewriter machine (*f.*) à écrire

uncle oncle *m.*
under sous
understand comprendre
United States États-Unis *m. pl.*
university université *f.*
until jusqu'à; (*with neg.*) avant
up: — close de près; **get —** se lever; **give —** céder
us nous
use employer, se servir de
useful utile
usually d'ordinaire, d'habitude
utensil ustensile *m.*

vegetable légume *m.*
verb verbe *m.*

very très, bien, fort
visit visiter
vocabulary vocabulaire *m.*
voice voix *f.*

wait, wait for attendre
waiter garçon *m.*
wake up se réveiller
walk marcher
wall mur *m.*; **on the —** au mur
want vouloir, désirer
war guerre *f.*
warm chaud; **it is —** il fait chaud
wash laver
watch montre *f.*; (*verb*) regarder
water eau *f.*
way: by the — à propos; **in the same — ** de la même façon
we nous
wear porter
weather temps *m.*; **What's the —?** Quel temps fait-il?
Wednesday mercredi *m.*
week semaine *f.*; **about a —** une huitaine
weigh peser
well bien
what que, quoi; ce qui, ce que; **What?** Que? Quoi? Qu'est-ce qui? Qu'est-ce que? **What!** Quoi! Comment!
when quand, lorsque
where où
whether si
which quel (quelle, quels, quelles); (*pron.*) lequel (laquelle, lesquels, lesquelles); qui, que
while pendant que, tandis que; en (*with present participle*)

white blanc, blanche
who qui, quel (quelle, quels, quelles)
whole tout; **the — class** toute la classe; **the — thing** le tout
whom (*rel.*) que; (*interr.*) qui?
whose (*rel.*) dont; (*interr.*) à qui?
why pourquoi
wide large
window fenêtre *f.*; **shop —** vitrine *f.*
wine vin *m.*
winter hiver *m.*; **in the —** en hiver
with avec
without sans; (*with clause*) sans que (+ *subjunctive*)
woman femme *f.*
wonder se demander
wood bois *m.*; **—s** bois *m. pl.*
word mot *m.*
work travail *m.*; (*verb*) travailler
world monde *m.*
worry inquiétude *f.*
worth: be — valoir; **it isn't — the trouble** cela ne vaut pas la peine
would (*cond. of verb*)
write écrire
wrong faux, fausse; **be —** avoir tort

year an *m.*, année *f.*
yes oui
yesterday hier
yet encore
you vous, tu, toi, on
young jeune; **— lady** demoiselle *f.*; (*in direct address*) mademoiselle
your votre, vos; ton, ta, tes
yours le vôtre (la vôtre, les vôtres), le tien (la tienne, les tiens, les tiennes)
yourself toi-même, vous-même

Index

moitié, 205
monter, compounded with **être,** 56
months, 28
mourir: compounded with **être,** 56; irregular tenses and forms, 56, 165

naître: compounded with **être,** 56; irregular tenses and forms, 56, 95, 165, 224
ne: ne . . . ni . . . ni, de and article omitted, with partitive, 111; **ne . . . pas,** 14–15, 56, 71*n.*; **ne . . . que,** 111, 112; omitted, 14; position of, 35, 111; with subjunctive clauses of negative implication, 146
negation: article omitted, with partitive, 77; in imperatives, 36, 37; **si** for **aussi** in, 91; **si** for **oui** in, 148*n.*; simple, 14–15
negatives, listed, 111
n'est-ce pas, 14
neuter pronouns, 68–69, 91
nouns: adjectives as, 47; gender, 2, 4*n.*, 47; partitive, 76–78, 111; of place and time, **où** with, 133; plural of, 3; in possession, 6; of quantity, 77
number; *see* plural
numbers: approximate, 206; cardinal, 26, 28, 176–77, 206; **de** for "than," 91; fractions, 205; as modifiers, 78; ordinal, 116*n.*, 178, 205

objective case, after **voici** and **voilà,** 4; *see also* direct objects, indirect objects, pronoun objects
offrir, irregular tenses and forms, 115, 224
on: for passive, 65, 174; **soi** with, 93; uses of, 65–66
où, relative pronoun, 133
"ought," 136
ouvrir, irregular tenses and forms, 115, 224

par: for **à,** 197; vs. **de,** in passive, 174
participles: compound, 189; past, 55–57, 70, 80*n.*, 102, 122, 124, 145, 173, 189, 207; present, 156–57, 189
partir: compounded with **être,** 56, 58; irregular tenses and forms, 58, 222
partitive nouns, 76–78, 111

partitive pronouns, 79–80
pas: omitted with **puis,** 70*n.*; position of, 15, 56
passé composé: to form, 55–56; vs. imperfect, 122–23; vs. *passé simple,* 164; with **pendant,** 167
passé simple, 164–65, 206
passer, compounded with **être** or **avoir,** 56
passive voice: to form, 173; infinitives with passive force, 197; **on** with active construction, for, 65, 174; reflexive construction, for, 174; substitutes for, 174
past indefinite; *see passé composé*
peine, inversion after **à peine,** 125
pendant, vs. **depuis,** 167
permettre: infinitive complement with, 195; irregular tenses and forms, 224
personne: agreement of, 111; position of, 112
peut-être, inversion after, 125
pire, irregular comparative, 90
plaire: indirect object with, 126; irregular tenses and forms, 126, 165, 224
pleuvoir, irregular tenses and forms, 70, 101, 165, 224
plupart: de not omitted with, 77; with plural complement, 77*n.*
pluperfect: with conditional perfect, 124; indicative, 122; with **pendant,** 167; subjunctive, 207
plural: of adjectives, 44, 46; of definite articles, 2; of indefinite articles, 2, 47*n.*; of nouns, 3; of possessive adjectives, 64
plus: beaucoup compared, 91; **davantage** for, 92; **de plus en plus,** 92; to form comparisons, 90, 91; **plus . . . plus,** 92
plusieurs, de omitted, 78
possession, 6, 64–65, 187
possessive adjectives, 64–65, 90
possessive pronouns, 187
pour, with future time, 167
pouvoir: irregular tenses and forms, 70, 101, 154, 165, 225; **puis-je,** 70*n.*
prendre, irregular tenses and forms, 95, 165, 225
prepositions: disjunctive pronoun with, 94; expressed in verb, 25; with geographical

tomber, compounded with **être,** 56

tout: with **aussi . . . que,** 91; with present participle, 157

tu: in familiar usage, 5, 32*n.*; omitted in imperatives, 35

valoir, irregular tenses and forms, 70, 101, 165, 226

venir: compounded with **être,** 56; irregular tenses and forms, 56, 81, 101, 165, 226; **venir de,** 125

verbs: auxiliary, 55–56, 102, 111, 122, 124, 145, 173, 189, 207; with both **être** and **avoir,** 56; "communication," 195–96; **e**-stems, 104, 144*n.*; false **e**-stems, 104; in **indre,** 188; of perception, 196*n.*; preposition expressed in, 25; reflexive, 36–37, 56, 57, 174, 219; regular, 23–24; spelling peculiarities, 23–24, 104, 144*n.*, 220; in **vrir** and **ffrir,** 114–15; in **yer,** 24, 144

Veuillez, infinitive after, 155

vivre, irregular tenses and forms, 49, 55, 165, 226

voici, 4

voilà: vs. **il y a,** 48; use of, 4, 7*n.*; **voilà . . . que,** for **depuis,** 166–67

voir: infinitive complement with, 196–97; irregular tenses and forms, 81, 101, 165, 226

vouloir, irregular tenses and forms, 70, 101, 154, 155, 165, 227

vous: number of, 59; omitted in imperatives, 35; in polite usage, 5

vowels, pronunciation of, xiii–xv

weather expressions, 16

"what," relative, 69

"which": as interrogative adjective, 113–14; as interrogative pronoun, 114

word order: declarative, 12; with **dont,** 132; interrogative, 13–14; in *passé composé,* 56; and pronoun objects, 33, 35, 36, 38*n.*; and reflexive objects, 37; *see also* inversion

y: vs. **là,** 80; uses of, 79–80